The Secrets *of* Eaton Square

The Secrets *of* Eaton Square

Sex, Scandal, and Infamy on the Road to Buckingham Palace

ALEXANDER LARMAN

ST. MARTIN'S PRESS
NEW YORK

First published in the United States by St. Martin's Press, an imprint of St. Martin's Publishing Group

EU Representative: Macmillan Publishers Ireland Ltd, 1st Floor, The Liffey Trust Centre, 117–126 Sheriff Street Upper, Dublin 1, D01 YC43

www.stmartins.com

The Library of Congress Cataloging-in-Publication Data is available upon request.

ISBN 978-1-250-38125-5 (hardcover)
ISBN 978-1-250-38126-2 (ebook)

First Edition: 2026

10 9 8 7 6 5 4 3 2 1

For Simon Renshaw, aka Boothby. “Down the hatch . . .”

CONTENTS

Here lies Augustus Percy Brown,
Who's shuffled off his care,
And when—his ghost comes up to town,
It stays in Eaton Square!

Bracey Vane, "Eaton Square"

I have not lived on a council estate, although I have lived in a terraced house since I was born.

Julian Amery MP, May 19, 1971

He neglected to mention that this "terraced house" was in Eaton Square.

The Secrets *of* Eaton Square

Prologue

The Balloon (Nearly) Goes Up: The Five Fields

Around half a century before Eaton Square ever came into existence, the area that would become the toast of the beau monde was a committed haunt of the demimonde instead. If, that is, the brigands, chancers, rapscallions, and downright rotters who lurked in the area even deserved such an appellation. Belgravia, as it was subsequently called, spent centuries existing not as its own highly desirable part of London high society but as a near-forgotten, semi-rural enclave that was most notable for buffering the journey between Westminster and Chelsea, and where market gardens were laid out to provide London's citizens with fresh food.

Had this been all it was known for, it would have been harmless enough—Covent Garden, before that district became London's largest fruit and flower market—but where there is proximity to wealth, there is the temptation to commit all manner of wickedness. The area on which Eaton Square itself was built was a large patch of marshland known as the Five Fields, which was synonymous with highwaymen, cutpurses, and opportunistic crime. It had acquired especial notoriety in 1728 for a murder that took place at the so-called Bloody Bridge, which crossed the Thames tributary the Westbourne, not far from present-day Sloane Square; it acquired its evocative name after a man's corpse was found with both its face and fingers removed.

Owned by Sir Thomas Grosvenor, who had acquired the "swampy meads" thanks to his marriage in 1677 to the then twelve-year-old Mary Davies, who brought it as part of her dowry—Grosvenor was twenty-one at the time—the Five Fields remained unexploited by Grosvenor and his descendants for more than a century. The acquisition of nearby Buckingham House in 1761 by George III as a private home for his wife, Queen Charlotte, and its subsequent informal renaming "the Queen's House," saw the once-unspeakable locale acquire, if not quite respectability, the attention of the emergent middle classes, as well as the more aspirant end of the aristocracy. After all, jockeying for social position was as much a sport—or a vocation—as any other activity that could be undertaken with one's clothes on in Georgian England. It would take an ambitious, intelligent man, who was smart enough to commission one of the leading master builders of his time, to capitalise on the opportunities that the area could offer.

Before then, however, the Five Fields exchanged one group of disreputable ne'er-do-wells for another. The footpads and outlaws slunk away to other, less visible parts of London, and they were replaced by brightly clad and seemingly shameless con artists who sought to elicit money from curious passers-by with displays of prowess and apparent skill, although competition from one's peers meant that such endeavours had to be ever more ambitious in nature. It was the right time for such bravado. London in the late eighteenth century was a riot of colour, novelty, and fashion, with the youthful George, Prince of Wales, simultaneously delighting and appalling society salons with his profligacy, high-profile mistresses, and frankly questionable aesthetic taste. Yet where the future king led, his future subjects, of varying levels of legality, sought to follow.

In the summer of 1784, the idea of ascending into the heavens in a hot air balloon had become the most talked-about venture in London. As with many things fashionable, the concept had originated in France. "Balloonmania," as it was called, had gripped the country from 1783, thanks to Joseph-Michel and Jacques-Étienne Montgolfier, two brothers who had, after numerous public displays and unmanned flights of varying degrees of success, managed to launch the first manned voyage of a hot air balloon on 21 November 1783. It led to an international aeronautical obsession but also tacitly suggested that it was only the French who had the chutzpah and technical skills to pull off such a daring feat. This meant, naturally, that when a man calling himself the Chevalier de Moret announced his intention to stage the first manned balloon flight in Britain from the future site of Eaton Square, it was greeted with an unusual amount of interest and enthusiasm, even from those who should have exhibited a healthy degree of scepticism.

One man who was more than usually equipped for such wariness was an Italian named Vincenzo "Vincent" Lunardi, who called himself the Daredevil Aeronaut. Along with his friend George Biggin, he planned to make the first manned flight from the Artillery Ground of the Honourable Artillery Company in Finsbury in the City of London on 15 September 1784. Lunardi was accordingly irked when Moret announced that he would make his own launch from the Five Fields a month earlier. He wrote to his guardian Gherardo Compagni to complain, "A Frenchman whose name is Moret; and who may possibly have assisted at some trials at Paris to launch Balloons in the manner of Montgolfier, advertised as it were in competition with me; and fixed on a day for ascending with his Balloon, previous to that, on which I had the permission of Sir George Howard to make my excursion from Chelsea-Hospital."

Lunardi knew that his own balloon was not yet ready for the contest but decided to gamble on his rival failing. "To hasten my own undertaking would have been entering into a ridiculous race with Moret; and if I had been inclined to such a measure, it was probable, that the day appointed for me would not have been changed, without a better reason than could have been assigned from the competition. I therefore waited, with as much patience as I could command, the event of Moret's experiment; imagining, however it would fail, from a view of the Balloon; but having no apprehension of such consequences as might involve my disappointment, or my ruin."[1]

When Moret arrived at the site of the launch on 10 August, his endeavour was greeted with all imaginable excitement and publicity, to say nothing of its lucrative potential, but also with understandable scepticism. An estimated—and probably exaggerated—fifty to sixty thousand people* came, after a bold advertisement offered "a Clear and Entertaining Description of that wonderful Invention, as it is to be launched and navigated." Lunardi, who was not present, commented, "The gardens and field around the place were crowded . . . not so much from economy, as incredulity and suspicion, of the undertaking. That was greatly owing to his manner of anticipating my design, which threw on him and me, undeservingly, the imputation of imposture."[2]

One anonymous bystander wrote of the event, "Yesterday the signals were given for the experiment of the aerostatic machine of Chevalier de Moret, in consequence of which an immense crowd of people, of all ranks, set off for Chelsea. They stationed themselves on all the heights and open grounds in the neighbourhood, and about one hundred of the most inquisitive and liberal paid their money to have admission to the garden, where the machine was preparing, from whom the Chevalier might receive in guineas, half-guineas, and crowns, about 50l."**

The balloon itself did not look like an airworthy contraption. The bystander observed, "The machine was constructed of very coarse canvas, porous and rotten, with a slight covering of paper. It had not substance to bear the weight of the air, if there really had been any serious intention to launch it into the atmosphere. It was elevated between two perpendicular poles, and filled with the smoke of straw. It presented a very beautiful spectacle when in this condition, but

* The population of London at the time was 750,000, suggesting that one in fifteen Londoners headed west that day if this was at all accurate.

** £50, or around £5000 in today's money.

it had no motive of ascension. The smoke filled it indeed, but there was no pressure, the cords were not in the smallest degree strained."

It soon became clear that Moret was ill-equipped for the magnitude of the task that he had professed himself capable of. "The poor Chevalier feeing this, was taken suddenly ill; the burning machine (and it was certainly warm work), had overcome him, and he threw himself on the grass panting for breath, and groaning in the spirit." Those who had paid money to see the spectacle were sanguine about their disappointment—"The company in the gardens had compassion on the misery of the adventurer"—but those around had less patience.[3]

Rumours spread that Moret was a fake—some suggested that he was nothing more than a mountebank doctor passing himself off as an aristocrat—and violence erupted.[4] "The circumstance being rumoured, the mob which were scrambling on the tops of the hedges and trees which surrounded the place, burst through the fences, and in three minutes the balloon was turned into a bonfire [*sic*], torn and scattered to all the winds of heaven; the wretched Chevalier himself would have fallen a victim to their rage, if he had not been rescued from their hands by the humanity of Sir Harry Englefield, and two or three other gentlemen."

Lunardi, perhaps relieved that his own endeavour was not threatened, saw events in a grimmer light. He observed, "when every effort was seen to fail, and the Balloon sunk into the fire which expanded it, the mob rushed in; tore it in a thousand pieces; robbed many of the company; levelled with the ground all the fences of the place and neighbourhood; and spread desolation and terror through the whole district." The event did little to make him believe that Londoners were a suitable audience for his aeronautical ambitions. "I saw into many of the consequences which would affect my own undertaking. Though the people of England are comparatively well informed and enlightened; yet the multitude in all nations is nearly alike. The misfortune of Moret was attributed to imposture; and suspicion of similar nature was extended to me. I felt all the immediate inconveniences of guilt . . . though nothing could be farther from my thoughts than any intention to be concerned in an imposition."[5]

Those around him took the matter less seriously, and the sport of the day was heightened by the disappointment. The anonymous bystander took the opportunity to indulge in some anti-French sentiment, observing that "the humorous spirit of John Bull turned the matter to a good account; and every person who had been fooled out of his money was made the subject of their pointed ridicule. Thus concluded the first boasted flight into the English air, and which, although it did not answer what was expected, by floating with the Chevalier beyond the clouds, and which perhaps was never intended, yet this celebrated Frenchman may boast of having made as many fools as any bubble that ever was attempted for the purpose of imposing on the credulity of poor John Bull, the famous Bottle Conjurer not excepted."

Moret scurried away, disappearing once again into obscurity, the fashionable crowd shrugged off their losses and dispersed, and Five Fields lay in anticipation of its greater purpose a few decades later. Lunardi, meanwhile, made a successful solo flight, without Biggin, on 15 September, in the presence of the Prince of Wales. George III even interrupted a cabinet meeting to allow his ministers to watch the ascent, saying, "We may resume our own deliberations at pleasure, but we may never see poor Lunardi again!"

The events of 10 August even had international reach. The botanist Joseph Banks suggested to his American friend Benjamin Franklin that the mob's rage was stagey at best, observing that "a most numerous assembly got together especially on the outside of the Enclosure it seemed however that the Chevr. knew by Previous experiment that his Machine was so ill Constructed & so heavy that it Could not raise even its own weight above 10 feet from the Ground . . . [The crowd] became quite outrageous & tore to pieces in a few minutes the whole apparatus."*[6]

* Franklin robustly (and perhaps humorously) responded, "I am glad to find that Experiments with the Balloons begin to be made in England. It is only by a Number

Eaton Square would never be the site of any further balloon launches. Its carefully manicured and preened gardens would have been wildly unsuitable for the spectacle; and, in any case, advances in aeronautics meant that by the time the square had attained its popularity and renown, such activities were almost commonplace. Yet Moret's actions at the square's former site would inadvertently anticipate much of what would happen there over the next two and a half centuries.

Eaton Square would be home, and play host, to some of London's finest men and women, as well as some of its most refined (and on occasion desperate) lowlives. Brigadiers would rub shoulders with actors, and Nazis would find themselves crossing the road next to former prime ministers. All would know the value of presenting themselves as plausibly and ostentatiously as possible, to obtain the preferment and success that they so desperately longed for, and to maintain their elevated standing in the square.

If only some of them had looked to Moret's example, trying desperately to make his gaudy and useless balloon ascend into the sky while increasingly restless people around him lost their tempers, they may have learnt something from the perils of such vanity of presentation, and acted in more modest and moderate fashion. This may have been wise. Yet if they had done, Eaton Square, and London, would have been wholly different and far less interesting places. Moret's balloon remained resolutely earthbound, but the trajectories of the square's inhabitants would often be stratospheric. Still, gravity has a habit of bringing even the most volitant of vessels down to earth, often with a bang.

---

of Trials that the Practice of Constructing, Filling, and Managing them can be perfected, so as to produce some Utility."

1

Thomas Cubitt and Robert Grosvenor: Eaton Square

"When we build let us think we build for ever."

If you walk out of the hideous noise and grimness of London's Victoria station, dodge the hopelessness of the nearby coach station, and take refuge in the altogether more salubrious surroundings of Elizabeth Street nearby—only a short walk from Eaton Square, in the heart of Belgravia—you will be faced with an extremely welcome contrast of environment and situation. One moment, the wary traveller is avoiding the siren screech of nail salons and burger restaurants, and the next they are strolling down what the tourist office proudly describes as "one of the prettiest and most Instagrammable streets in London . . . The flower-filled street merits exploration for its cosy restaurants and cafés, independent fashion boutiques and homeware shops."

There are plenty of places to take refreshment here, ranging from upmarket bakeries to a suitably high-end restaurant, The Elizabeth—but my preferred spot on Elizabeth Street has always been its local gastropub, the Thomas Cubitt. Named after the master builder who did more than anyone to give Belgravia in general and Eaton Square in particular its identity and integrity, the pub has carefully retained as much of the spirit and atmosphere of its Georgian building as possible, although I imagine that Cubitt, were he to return to London today, may find himself flummoxed by some of the items on the menu, and the prices.

He may have been pleased to see the presence of oysters, a common London foodstuff in the eighteenth and nineteenth centuries, but would have exclaimed heartily at the inflated price (£27.50 for half a dozen at the time of writing), just as I am sure that asking Cubitt to pay more than £40 for a steak, even a ribeye, would have been a step too far. And it's anyone's guess as to how he would have reacted to the presence of "Roast Cornish Cod with Artichoke Barigoule"—his for £32—or "Endives, Cacklebean Egg and Cured Pork salad," a snip at £16. He would have been on happier ground with the drinks menu—he is unlikely to have been a stranger to London Dry Gin—but with prices starting at £10.60 for a double of Hayman's, and rising to a considerable £16 for the (admittedly German) Monkey 47, Cubitt may have been forgiven for asking for a swift return to his eternal rest, rather than incur the fearful cost of a central London bar tab.

My own visits to the Thomas Cubitt have been fleeting, if always enjoyable. An impecunious author does not have the same spending power as the good-looking and energetic young people in their twenties and thirties who make up the clientele here; and I suspect, perhaps unfairly, that the name of Cubitt does not mean much to them. My most memorable lunch here occurred nearly twenty years ago, when I was working briefly on the magazine *The New Statesman*. My then-editor, Will, took me for lunch in what I swiftly realised was to be an end-of-term appraisal of my (admittedly modest) achievements in the office so far. Emboldened both by the entrepreneurial spirit of Cubitt and a half-pint of strong Belgian white beer, I launched into a passionate, albeit rather self-promoting, account of how I might develop my skills and strengths in the office, and that, if I was given the chance, I would become an asset to the magazine *sans pareil.*

I don't have a clue if Will bought any of it, but it was a good enough demonstration of intent and willing for my contract to be extended another month, and I was once again saved from the ravages of every freelance writer's worst nightmare: sitting in pyjamas and dressing gown, staring at the computer and hoping that someone will offer a deus ex machina, or, as we like to call it, paid work. This indolence would have been anathema to the ever-energetic Cubitt, a man who, like Willy Loman's brother Ben from *Death of a Salesman* might have said, "when I was seventeen I walked into the jungle, and when I was twenty-one I walked out. And by God I was rich."[1]

After a youth spent as the apprentice of his father, Jonathan Cubitt, a Norfolk carpenter, the ambitious Thomas—described by one descendant of his as "the penniless son of a Coltishall farmer"[2]—headed off to India, bound on a voyage as a captain's joiner. He returned having saved enough money to establish his own profession, which he pursued from around 1810, aged twenty-two. Upon his arrival in London, he worked as an independent carpenter labouring on grand municipal projects such as the Russell Institution on Great Coram Street in Bloomsbury, before taking the significant gamble of moving into independent practice.

This would offer him financial freedom, as well as the much sought-after status of "builder," but also ran the risk of getting him severely into debt, as he would have to pay the craftsmen working on his projects regardless of whether he himself was paid. It was far from uncommon for a dissatisfied patron simply to cancel the contract altogether, leaving his builder out of pocket and facing, at best, the humiliating return to being someone else's lackey or, at worst, bankruptcy, debt, and the ever-present spectre of the poorhouse.

Cubitt had had enough experience of poverty in his early life not to wish to repeat the experience. When he secured the lucrative contract to construct the London Institution in Moorfields—it was worth £20,000, or around £2.3 million today—he was presented with the stiff, even punitive, clause in the contract that he would forfeit his fees if the building was not completed on time, as well as being liable for the subcontractors' payment in any case. However,

Cubitt believed that he would get the work done more efficiently and swiftly if he employed his own men, and so asked for a clause stating that the workmen would be "on his own premises and subjected to the laws and system of the place."[3]

This proved to be revolutionary. Cubitt, by taking this step, not only established himself as that most distinguished of craftsmen—a "master builder"—but also broke the monopoly that unscrupulous or indolent labourers or their employers had on building projects if they refused to work. This even extended to architects, Cubitt deciding that "the best mode of proceeding with new buildings was to be independent of [them]."[4] It would save money and time, and reflected his own justified faith in his abilities as a draughtsman. If he, and a few trusted colleagues, could come up with the designs for buildings, it not only strengthened the level of control that he had over a project but increased his standing in a competitive and uncertain market.

From the outset of his career, Cubitt, who was aptly described in his obituary by *The Builder* as "a great builder and a good man,"[5] sought both to innovate and to make his uncertain and frequently unstable profession synonymous with integrity and achievement at the highest conceivable level. The London Institution was completed by the end of 1818 and opened in April 1819, establishing his reputation in the process. Cubitt therefore came to the attention of the Duke of Bedford, who commissioned him to build what would be known as the Bedford Estate in Bloomsbury in the early 1820s, but this was a less happy experience, owing to the relative obscurity of the area. Cubitt complained years later that "I have so many difficulties on the Bedford Estate that I do not know what is best to do. The fact is the place has become unfashionable. Everybody is running away to the west, and though my Houses may be classed with the best that have ever been built anywhere; and the situation is really good and airy, yet I cannot get rid of the Houses."[6]

Cubitt therefore needed two related things in order to turn his initial success into an assured reputation: a lucrative and high-profile project in West London that would not only make his name but keep him in the forefront of popular consciousness, and a patron who was prepared to offer him that project while acquiescing to Cubitt's wishes as regards design, execution, and personnel. It was an ambitious, even optimistic, desire, and had he been frustrated then his career may have foundered before it could prosper. Thankfully for Cubitt, and architectural history, he found both. The latter came in the form of Robert Grosvenor, 1st Marquess of Westminster, and the former in the shape of the once-unfashionable area where, half a century before, de Moret had tried and failed to launch himself into the air. Cubitt's work may have been more terrestrial, but his own ambition was equally soaring.

EVER SINCE SIR THOMAS GROSVENOR'S marriage to Mary Davies had established the plutocracy of the Grosvenor name, the family had been at the forefront of London society. Although the Grosvenors had been a well-known dynasty for centuries, their inevitable decision to fight on the side of Charles I during the Civil War had been financially punitive, and only Charles II's restoration in 1660 had seen their fortunes partially restored: a state of affairs that was compromised by the death of Sir Richard Grosvenor in 1665, leaving his eight-year-old grandson, Thomas, heir to the baronetcy. When, twelve years later, Thomas married Mary, he saw the family fortunes rebound, in large part because of the Grosvenors' coal and lead mines in Wales: a lucrative but unglamorous demonstration of the adage that where there is muck, there is brass.

Mary's "swampy meads" therefore represented the potential development of the Grosvenor fortunes in more urban fashion. Although the Grosvenor family continued to be bedevilled by controversy throughout the seventeenth and eighteenth centuries—Thomas was suspected of having Jacobite sympathies, in large part because Mary had converted to Catholicism shortly after her marriage, and his son Richard, who inherited the baronetcy in 1700, was accused of having similar leanings—they were able to rise above jealousy and factionalism by dint of their extraordinary wealth. By 1725, the *Daily Post* could write of how "the several new streets in Grosvenor Buildings in the Parish of St George, Hanover Square, and lying between Bond Street and Hyde Park were last week particularly named . . . In the centre of those new buildings there is now making a square called Grosvenor Square, which, for its largeness and beauty will far exceed any yet made in or about London."[7]

The family divided their time between the capital and their Cheshire estate, Eaton Hall, where the Grosvenors amused themselves by collecting art and racing horses. As the dynasty wore on, idealism and political astuteness were combined, with naturally the latter more to the fore. By the time that Robert's son Richard became Baron Grosvenor in April 1761, he was moving in grand enough society to be painted by Stubbs,* a dining companion of the prime minister George Grenville and a supporter of the future prime minister William Pitt. The writer and politician Horace Walpole acknowledged the family's elevation in society earlier that year when he wrote to his friend George Montagu to say "If you propose a fashionable assembly, you must send cards to Lord Spenser [and] Lord Grosvenor."[8]

Still, as would be the case with many of the later inhabitants of Eaton Square, apparent success and an elevated position in society inevitably led to scandal and gossip. Richard married Henrietta Vernon, daughter of Commissioner of Excise Henry Vernon, on 19 July 1764, but the marriage was soon tainted by scandal after she embarked upon an affair with George III's youngest brother, Henry, Duke of Cumberland. Walpole smirkingly referred to this in a letter to the Earl of Hertford in February 1765, alluding to "Lady Grosvenor, whose intrigue with the Duke of Cumberland made so much noise."[9] Grosvenor attempted to ignore the rumours and sniggering innuendo that he was faced with, but, when his wife and

* In his 1762 painting *The Grosvenor Hunt, Eaton.*

Cumberland, who pseudonymously styled himself Squire Morgan for his adulterous visits, were discovered in flagrante, he was unable to avoid the consequences any longer.

Accordingly, despite being mindful of Cumberland's royal connections, he "exhibited a libel against his wife for adultery," which he termed "criminal conversation" having taken place with Henrietta. Given the apparent one-sidedness of the affair, Grosvenor was awarded £10,000 as damages and costs of £3,000, or around £1.5 million today. Yet the obvious recourse of divorce was not available to him. Not only did he not want to drag his wife through a scandalous and mutually embarrassing process, but Grosvenor himself was no saintly figure, either. He undoubtedly was familiar with the authoritative guide to London's sex workers, *Harris's List of Covent Garden Ladies*, and was known to frequent low-grade brothels, even importuning streetwalkers by saying, "How do you do, my little wicked? Will you go and drink a glass of wine with me?" Many of the unfortunate young women took him at his word, and the consequences were predictably carnal, although he could be generous to his favourites, even helping one of them set up her own establishment.

Henrietta, mindful of her husband's proclivities and actions, decided that she would extract a form of revenge during the hearing for criminal conversation. Her and Cumberland's love letters were read out in court, causing deep embarrassment and hilarity alike, but she also prevailed upon many of the Covent Garden ladies who were known to Grosvenor to appear, testifying as to his brothel-creeping antics. The eventual outcome of the case was so embarrassing for all parties that the Lord Chamberlain forbade it to be discussed in any public venue: an early version of a D notice.* Perhaps surprisingly, given all the filthy linen so enthusiastically aired in court, the relationship between Grosvenor and Henrietta thereafter was not

* An official request not to publish specific, often embarrassing information.

without affection, and he settled an annual pension of £1,200 on her while they nominally remained married until his death in 1802.

His son, Robert, was too young to appreciate the scandal that his parents had been embroiled in, although its legacy hung over him for the rest of his life. Born in 1767, he had enjoyed a typical upper-class English education (Westminster; Harrow; Trinity College, Cambridge) before embarking upon his Grand Tour of Europe in 1786 in the company of the poet and critic William Gifford, who had served as his private tutor for much of the previous decade. Gifford was a self-made intellectual from a working-class background who had worked as a ship's boy and cobbler's apprentice before a wealthy patron had taken him up and paid for him to enter Exeter College, Oxford. He got on well with his charge, who he praised as "most amiable" and "accomplished," and Gifford, who would eventually go on to be one of London's most talked-about and biting satirists, instilled an aesthetic and intellectual sense in Robert that would persist throughout his life.

Robert led an existence as a young man wholly typical of the privileged aristocratic classes. He was painted by Thomas Gainsborough and served as a Tory MP, first for the Cornwall constituency of East Looe and then subsequently for the city of Chester. He married the Honourable Eleanor Egerton, daughter of the Earl of Wilton, in April 1794. Yet his time with Gifford had not been wasted. When he entered the House of Commons as an MP for the first time in 1788 and made his maiden speech, he quoted Demosthenes in Greek, which not only astonished his similarly classically educated fellow politicians but led the satirist John Wolcot, who wrote under the name Peter Pindar, to call him "the Lord of Greek." Robert spent around fourteen years in the Commons, until his father's death in 1802, when, at the age of thirty-five, he was elevated to the peerage and found the purpose and vigour that he had been searching for since he was a young man.

It would be erroneous to suggest that Robert Grosvenor, First Marquess of Westminster, was a renegade figure. He was the scion of one of Britain's grandest families, a fabulously wealthy and privileged man who took full pleasure in spending the money that he inherited and which his family holdings continued to provide for him, and someone who lived in luxury from the day of his birth until his death. He collected art on an enthusiastic and expensive scale—four canvases by Rubens cost him £10,000, a staggering sum even then, while Gainsborough's *The Blue Boy*, which he bought in 1809, was a bargain at £100—and was a considered aficionado of the turf, breeding and racing some of the best horses in the country. By 1819, he was reckoned to be one of the four wealthiest men in Britain.

At the same time, he defied expectations by embracing liberal politics and causes, going against his father's solidly, even reactionary, conservative instincts. Although Robert's personal friendship with Pitt the Younger saw him maintain his parliamentary seats for the Tories, when Pitt died on 23 January 1806, Robert crossed the floor to join the Whigs, in whose company he remained for the rest of his life.* It has been suggested that he did this "in consequence of being refused by Mr Pitt the first lordship of the Admiralty,"[10] but his lifelong liberal actions** suggest that, whatever personal grievances he may have had, he acted out of principle, not petulance.

As an MP, he had voted for abolition of the slave trade in 1796—his family's mercantile interests had never included slavery—and was a committed supporter of the reform of parliamentary representation, mindful of the knowledge that East Looe was a rotten borough. He was particularly outraged by the Peterloo Massacre that took place in Manchester on 16 August 1819, which was occasioned

* The other aristocratic Whig of note during this period was, of course, the "mad, bad and dangerous to know" Lord Byron.

** These were not always as expected. Both he and William Wilberforce, the great abolitionist, stood firmly against the introduction of Sunday newspapers, on the grounds that they would be "an additional weapon in the hands of infidelity." Had they known of the existence of the twentieth century's best-loved Sunday paper, the *News of the World*, aka "the News of the Screws," they might only have considered their intervention prescient.

by a gathering of people demanding the right to a free and fair democratic vote. He backed the main liberal causes of the day—the Reform Act, which was eventually passed in 1832; Catholic emancipation, which allowed Roman Catholics to sit in Parliament and vote, and which came into law in 1829; and the abolition of the Corn Laws, which were finally repealed in 1846 after a thirty-year struggle.

He also despised the decidedly Tory Duke of Wellington, although the two were on the same side when it came to Catholic emancipation. The reputation of the Iron Duke had plummeted since his victories at Waterloo; and when Wellington was to have been given the freedom of Chester in 1820, Robert vetoed the use of the town hall for the event, ensuring that the offer was quietly withdrawn.

Nor was the Marquess of Westminster a committed monarchist. Despite being, at various points, Lord of the Admiralty, Privy Councillor, and Knight of the Garter, Robert loathed George IV, who became king on 29 January 1820. The new monarch was an unpopular figure in the country, and his long regency had done little to endear him to his subjects, who correctly perceived him as indolent, lecherous, and ineffectual. His senior aides were even more scathing on account of observing him closely, with one writing, "A more contemptible, cowardly, selfish, unfeeling dog does not exist. . . . There have been good and wise kings but not many of them . . . and this I believe to be one of the worst."[11]

Robert shared these feelings, and had a particular distaste for George's treatment of his estranged wife, Queen Caroline, who he had unsuccessfully attempted to shame in a high-profile case brought in the House of Lords.* Like many in Britain, Robert believed that the king had behaved ungallantly and disreputably, and made a public display of his displeasure by throwing a Bible at the king's head. Had he been an ordinary citizen, he would have been arrested, even imprisoned, but such was his standing—and a feeling that he spoke

* This will be discussed in more depth in the next chapter.

for many in the country—that the incident was tactfully ignored, although it spelt the end of his political career.

With preferment in the country therefore denied to him, Robert decided to look to his own estate instead. That it was close to Buckingham Palace—where the king had decided to make his home, rather than nearby Carlton House—was something to be taken advantage of. At the beginning of 1824, the Five Fields remained largely undeveloped and unexploited, with its nineteen acres of prime land having seen one row of (admittedly considerable) houses built in Grosvenor Place, which survive to this day. Even this, however, had its controversies. The historian Lord Macaulay recounted the story of how "When Lord Hatherton changed his residence his servants gave him warning, as they could not, they said, go into such an unheard-of part of the world as Grosvenor Place. I can only say that I have never been in a finer house."[12]

However, the rest of the land was little more than open space, and, with much of central London now cramped and built-up, a peerless opportunity presented itself. Robert had first considered the idea of constructing various grand squares in the area in 1813, and had commissioned a plan from the visionary architect James Wyatt, who was responsible for such buildings as the Radcliffe Camera in Oxford, William Beckford's Fonthill Abbey in Wiltshire and the Royal Military College at Sandhurst.

Wyatt supplied a suitably expansive design, titled "Mr Wyatt's Plan," that would have created Belgravia, but in a rather different form to how we see it today. Rather than a series of garden squares, there would have been one main five-sided pentagonal "square" at the centre, and a series of expansive villas, with substantial private land, would have been constructed, each with its own access to a mews behind the property to allow ease of access. Eaton Square, as it became, would not have existed, and the entire development would instead have been one of the most ostentatious displays of wealth in London.

It is an intriguing what-if, but Wyatt's death in a carriage accident on 4 September 1813 forestalled his plans. Robert then turned to the brothers Alexander and Daniel Robertson, whose designs went similarly unconstructed, but their input was notable for having been the first architects to suggest the idea of Eaton Square as a square, with a larger number of less elaborate buildings constructed around it. After this came to nothing, the Grosvenor Estate turned to its new surveyor, Thomas Cundy, the elder, who had been appointed to the position in 1821. He may not have been as distinguished an architect as Wyatt, but he had nevertheless established a reputation for dealing with the often-challenging demands of the wealthy, rebuilding or constructing such estates as Sion House in West London and the now-demolished Northumberland House in the centre of London.

He was a man who others could work with, and so when Cubitt began negotiations with Robert in August 1824 for the development of the Five Fields, it was in the knowledge that he would be collaborating with Cundy. As far as the Grosvenors were concerned, Cubitt, who had already worked with them to design buildings in Berkeley Square, was trustworthy and ambitious, qualities that they respected, but this did not mean that he would be offered any special treatment or indulgence.

The terms that Cubitt was offered on 19 August were accordingly steep. He was to be offered the land for a total of 111 years, initially at a "grass rent" of £6 an acre for six years which would then rise to £50, £80, and—for the final ninety-nine years of the agreement—£150 per acre. He would also consent to undertake a substantial period of building at his own risk and expense, upon the conclusion of which he would be responsible for selling the houses and recouping his profits from the proceeds. The proposal put forward by the Grosvenor Estate was a demanding one. It stated: "Within the first six years, buildings were to be erected to the value of fifty thousand pounds; to be built agreeable to a design, to be planned by Mr Cundy, and approved by Lord Grosvenor."[13]

Cubitt asked for, and received, a slightly lower period of rent for the second period—£30 and £60 per acre, rather than £50 and £80—and an agreement was soon reached. Once he had worked with Cundy to come up with "a plan and elevation to be approved of by Lord Grosvenor," the minutiae of his task were outlined. "The Sewers to be made at Mr Cubitt's expense and the Area of Belgrave Square to be enclosed and planted at the expense of Lord Grosvenor within two years from Christmas next. Mr Cubitt will engage to secure £1,500 a year ground rent by the end of the first six years. The Footways to be paved with a Granite Curb and the streets made by Mr Cubitt."[14] He would be presented with a package of land between the south side of Belgrave Square and the King's Road—the rest having already been promised to the rival builder Seth Smith—and "Eaton Place," the first name for what would become Eaton Square and named after the Grosvenor family seat of Eaton Hall, would be its centrepiece.

Cubitt, who had also undertaken to work with the Duke of Bedford on his vast project at the same time, was making a significant step forward, both reputationally and financially. If the project came to fruition, it would make his name forever. If it failed, so would he.

OF THE THREE MEN WHO were involved in the development of the Grosvenor Estate at this time—Cubitt, Smith, and Cundy the younger—two suffered severe financial difficulties. Such an outcome was typical for surveyors and speculative builders in the period, as they were, in effect, gambling with their own—or their investors'—funds in the anticipation of great profits in the future from the sale of the properties that they had constructed. Robert, naturally, had little to lose, as he owned the land on which the houses were being built. Some might consider this principle unfair and antediluvian, but the basic tenets of leasehold—both in Eaton Square and properties around Britain—hold true at the time of writing, two centuries later. There is a distinct difference between the efforts of the three builders and architects, who engaged in a project of aesthetic and technical interest with both profit and urban interest in mind, and the mindset of their patron, who ultimately viewed the project as a low-risk form of greater enrichment.

Cubitt was the only one of the trio who not only remained solvent, but he became a legendary figure as a result of his work in Belgravia. His success came down to several different factors: a willingness to compromise when necessary but also to work alongside others who could supply expertise that he was lacking. There was an inevitable clash of cultures between the rough, uneducated Cubitt—a man who, not two decades before, had been working as a humble carpenter—and the wealthy aristocrat who he was dealing with. Yet when the foundation stone of what was intended to be Eaton Square's church was laid in September 1824, a month after the original contract was agreed and before any of the formal building commitments had been signed, Cubitt might have been forgiven for feeling a sense of achievement. Georgian London was not a place known for its meritocratic opportunities, but here he was, a master builder preparing to lay out and construct what had the potential to be the city's most notable and desirable area, capped off with its crowning glory of Eaton Square.

Throughout 1825, Cubitt's professional attentions were divided in several directions, and so he undertook an agreement with a financial syndicate, led by the City bankers William and George Haldimand, that was intended to provide him with security. This undertaking passed over financial responsibility for the Belgrave Square properties at a guaranteed rent of £739 17s, covering a quarter of the expense that Cubitt had undertaken to provide to the Grosvenor Estate and thereby considerably reducing his risk. The Haldimands were well-known figures in the City, and their investment gave Cubitt credibility; it also demonstrated that he had a clear knowledge of financial affairs and fiscal responsibility, being keen to underwrite his venture with the support of men from altogether different walks of life than the construction industry.

The grand project ran into difficulty at the end of 1825, with the death of Cundy on 28 December, but there was a ready-made solution that presented itself. His son Thomas Cundy, the younger, had worked with his father on many of his earlier projects and was himself a successful and talented architect in his own right. He therefore not only inherited his father's position as the Grosvenor Estate's surveyor but continued the collaboration with Cubitt as harmoniously as the builder had worked with his father. The first square to be laid out was Belgrave Square, which was planned in 1826 and had its first house constructed and ready for occupation by 1828. By then, Cubitt and Cundy had moved on to the considerably more challenging task of laying out and constructing Eaton Square.

It would have been a hugely expensive undertaking that would have tested Cubitt's financial abilities to their limit were it not for his typically sagacious decision to make the most of the opportunities that he was presented with. The Five Fields area lived up to its designation as "swampy meads," but Cubitt came up with the idea of removing the clay from the land that he would need to build on and turning it into bricks, thereby simultaneously making use of the natural resources that he was presented with and allowing him to build not on the shifting marshland but on the more solid gravel foundations underneath. This did, however, lead to the situation that, as the architectural historian E. Beresford Chancellor observed, "Belgravia is therefore, although lying so low that it has been proved that the attics in Eaton and Belgrave Squares are on the same level of the ground floors of Westbourne Terrace, viz. seventy feet above the Thames high-water mark, one of the healthiest spots in London."[15]

It is a further oddity of the square that, while the houses on it were being planned and built, the church, which would soon be christened St Peter's, was dealt with entirely separately. It was not designed by Cundy but by the architect Henry Hakewill, who was most notable for having been responsible for Rugby School's major buildings, including the chapel. He suggested a Gothic design, but was overruled. His compromise, a modern take on a Grecian church, was stymied by the requirement to fit a steeple onto it, thus making the building an uneasy marriage of two highly distinct architectural styles.

As one critic wrote at the time: "The addition of a steeple to a Grecian church forms a stumbling-block to our modern architects, forcing them to have recourse to many shifts to convert a Grecian temple into an English church, a forcible argument for the rejection of the classical styles altogether in this species of building."[16] The architectural commentator James Elmes was kinder, calling it "chaste and simple," but it was not to be an enduring design. It burnt down in 1836, attracting "vast crowds of all ranks and classes from every quarter of the metropolis." One journalist cattily observed that there were more nobility and gentry in their carriages than had been seen at any fire since the one in 1834 that destroyed the Houses of Parliament.*

Cubitt was less exercised about the construction of the church, remarking only that he would prefer the wooden hoardings outside to be protected by iron railings as "the property of the Builders is suffering considerably by the delay."[17] Nonetheless, it was not his direct responsibility, and when it was finished and consecrated in June 1827, it gave the new square a focal point and a purpose, even if its aesthetic qualities were lacking. It had been designed as a spillover for St George's, Hanover Square—another Grosvenor holding—and, as a "commissioners' church," had a large proportion of its cost paid for by the other institution.

For the rest of Eaton Square, however, there needed to be a careful plan in place, not least because the antiquary John Britton and the architect Augustus Charles Pugin were sufficiently impressed by the early design to include an image of the square in their 1828 collection *Illustrations of the Public Buildings of London*, thereby trusting that the finished result would live up to the considerable hopes placed upon it. Cubitt decided from the beginning that, rather than

* Vast, destructive conflagrations were clearly a common feature of the early Victorian era.

attempt to build the entirety of Eaton Square in one go, he would divide the work into three stages. The first would be the sixteen houses that would take up the north side of the square, which were designed as a series of wide, well-appointed buildings with white stucco pillars at the front and set over four or five floors, complete with classical-influenced Doric columns supporting the various porches that the properties boasted.

They were expensive to construct, but they were also aimed at the wealthy and discerning. Once Cubitt formally leased the first ten houses that he constructed from Robert, they were his to supply to various tenants at a profit. Some of the new residents bought the leasehold for an indefinite period, others preferred shorter leases of twelve or twenty-one years, and Robert himself took up residence on the square in number 100, which has remained one of the London family homes of the Grosvenors ever since. By 1830, the first occupants of Eaton Square were in situ.

They were an eclectic mixture of aristocracy—in the form of William IV's illegitimate son, Lord Frederick FitzClarence—and commerce. Hugh Richard Hoare, a scion of the Hoare's banking dynasty, took 118, the grandest and most expensive house, for a leasehold of £7,000, and Cubitt's friend the brewer and Whig politician William Whitbread took its neighbour, 117. Whitbread may have been educated at Eton and Trinity College, Cambridge, but was not so grand as to have forgotten his family's origins: His grandfather Samuel had come from a large Bedfordshire family and had made his fortune by producing and supplying large quantities of the ever-popular porter. Whitbread was particularly popular with Cubitt and the men who worked on the construction of Eaton Square because he ensured that they would be given comprehensive quantities of his company's beer, free of charge, so that the building work might pass particularly swiftly. Thirst is, after all, a terrible thing.

One of the earliest residents of the square was perhaps its most interesting occupant, who has subsequently been described as arguably the finest British architectural draughtsman of the nineteenth century. Cubitt may have looked with envy at the architect Charles R. Cockerell, who was almost exactly the same age as he but in a financial position to lease 87 Eaton Square, thanks to his successful practice—to say nothing of his equally successful and wealthy father, Samuel, proving that architecture was, like building and brewing, a trade inherited through families. Charles Cockerell had travelled on a Grand Tour to Greece, a protracted affair that lasted from 1810 to 1817, and upon his eventual return he used the knowledge and expertise that he had accrued to pursue what swiftly became a distinguished career.

It helped that Cockerell came back to London at a time when Hellenic architecture was in vogue, but the inspiration that he acquired on his travels formed the basis of a lifelong adherence to all things classical in form and execution.* He was, however, prepared to challenge lesser architects' thinking when it came to Greek revival architecture—including, perhaps tacitly, Hakewill's design of St Peter's—and wrote in his diary in 1821 that "since the rage for Greek has been amongst us all the rules which formerly protected us are now set aside & we are at sea without compass . . . We stick a slice of an anc[ien]t Greek Temple to a Barn which is called breadth & simplicity, than which nothing can be more absurd, as the Greek Houses were certainly of wood & brick & plaister [*sic*] painted & temporary things. I am sure that the grave & solemn arch[itectur]e of Temples were never adopted to Houses, but a much lighter style, as we may judge by the vases, the object being space & commodiousness."[18]

Robert, meanwhile, may have looked askance at his new neighbour, not because of any personal failings on his part, but because of his friendship with his nemesis the Duke of Wellington. Cockerell had at one point attempted to design a grand house for his patron that would rival Blenheim for size and stature, to be called

* Including, coincidentally, Oxford's Taylor Institution, where I am currently writing this chapter.

Wellington Palace, but nothing came of such an idea. In any case, Cockerell's time in Eaton Square was to be both personally and professionally fulfilling. Ten children would be born to him and his wife, Anna Rennie—daughter of the engineer John Rennie, the elder—and it was during this period that Cockerell designed buildings that included Cambridge University's old library; the London and Westminster Bank in the City; and the Church of Holy Trinity in Hotwells, Bristol. Yet after he left Eaton Square in 1838, he went on to yet greater success and renown. Following the resignation of Sir John Soane, he became surveyor and architect to the Bank of England, and masterminded many of the additions and changes to its building in the City of London, although increasing ill health from 1851 meant that his hugely distinguished practice all but came to an end before his death in 1863.

Once Cockerell's residence, and others, had been completed, Cubitt turned his attention to the second and more ambitious part of the project, which would make up the majority of Eaton Square and would allow for the two central rows of the square to be constructed to the specifications that the new tenants would expect. Such was Cubitt's increasing personal identification with the project that he was responsible for building the grand end house, 84 Eaton Square, himself. This would in due course be sold, rather than leased, to Robert King, Lord Lorton, a wealthy Anglo-Irish peer who is remembered today, if at all, for his strong support for Protestantism in Ireland and adherence to the anti-Catholic tendencies of the Orange Order: something that would have put him at odds with his neighbour Robert Grosvenor, the Marquess of Westminster, had it come up at one of the soirees that both men no doubt attended in the newly built grand houses on the square.

Unfortunately, Cubitt's great project was compromised by circumstances far beyond his control. Until Britain embraced free trade in 1840, it was caught between the economic consequences of waging the Napoleonic Wars, which had only ended in 1815, and the depression that had followed afterwards, not helped by a stock market crash, the Panic of 1825. This in turn meant that prices of everything from food to labour materials rose steeply, which affected building projects. Cubitt was driven to write of one of his Bloomsbury developments in 1855 that "it was my intention to have completed the street several years ago, but adverse circumstances from time to time have prevented it."[19]

Nothing so egregious befell the construction of Eaton Square, but it would not be finally finished until 1851. The greatest hiatus would come in the 1830s, when the central terrace's eastern end had to be paused from 1830 to 1837, during which time Cubitt attempted, with some success, to sell or lease at a profit the existing houses that he had constructed. Yet the first half of the decade was a near-calamitous time for Cubitt, as he faced the dual difficulty of finding the capital to pay for the houses he wished to construct and of finding tenants for the properties once they were built. It was a challenging period, but it was also a test of the builder in adversity.

To his credit, Cubitt never wavered; and through a mixture of holding his nerve and brinksmanship, he prospered. Several new tenants, including the MP George Byng, were prevailed upon to hand over deposits for their properties before they were finished, and all were happy to do so, in the knowledge that Cubitt was a respectable and trustworthy tradesman and that they were investing in London's most desirable new area. It was a mark of the standing that Eaton Square was held in, just over a decade since its construction had begun, that the government leased two of the houses, 88 and 89 Eaton Square, to serve as a temporary home for Charles Shaw-Lefevre, Speaker of the House of Commons. Shaw-Lefevre, a Whig, was a remarkably popular and diligent Speaker, who has the distinction of having held the post for the second-longest amount of time (just under eighteen years, compared with Arthur Onslow's thirty-three years the century before), and his presence in the square lent it political credibility.

Nonetheless, Cubitt had to make economies if he wished to complete Eaton Square in the style that he had promised Robert, and so the third section of the square, at the western end, was designed around 1840, with its construction beginning almost immediately afterwards. By now, Cubitt was working with the architect Charles James Freake rather than Cundy. Freake was another self-made man who must have enjoyed the incongruity of designing and building houses aimed at the extremely wealthy, although his own extraordinary energy and industry saw him leave an estate of nearly a million pounds when he died in 1884.

It would be disingenuous to describe the new properties on Eaton Square as being anything other than painstakingly constructed and designed, but they are undeniably more modest in scope and size than the grand mansions built in the previous decades, although "modest" is, of course, a relative term for their substantial dimensions. If the houses look slightly less grand than their neighbours, with bay windows rather than free-standing pillars, they are still impressive residences. By the time that Cubitt, in the final years of his life, built the last of its 104 houses between 1851 and 1853, completing a project that had taken him over a quarter of a century, he could look with a mixture of pride and, perhaps, faint bewilderment at what he had achieved. The square—in reality an elongated rectangle—measured 1,610 feet lengthways and 382 feet widthways, making it the largest and most prestigious garden square in the city.

Britain had changed enormously over the three decades that Eaton Square had been constructed. In the mid-1820s, Cubitt had begun work in an era in which the extravagance and general plenitude of George IV had dominated the country, and when he finished the square, it was two decades into the reign of Queen Victoria. She exemplified self-restraint, fidelity, and strict personal morality, all qualities that her uncle had so comprehensively lacked. After the economic downturn of the 1830s, the technological advances brought about by the Industrial Revolution and the rise of successful international trade meant that Britain was at the epicentre of the world, leading to what the historian G. M. Trevelyan categorised as the "mid-Victorian decades of quiet politics and roaring prosperity."[20]

Eaton Square, as the most fashionable address of the greatest city in the world, lay at the epicentre of this roaring prosperity. Although Robert Grosvenor had died in 1845 at Eaton Hall, at the age of seventy-seven, he had lived long enough to see that the project that he had allowed Cubitt to construct had been an unalloyed success. A statue of him was erected in 1998 in nearby Belgrave Square, designed by Jonathan Wylder. An apposite quotation of John Ruskin's was inscribed upon it: "When we build let us think we build for ever."

As for Cubitt, his final years were spent in a deserved state of semi-retirement, finishing off long-standing projects and taking on favours for friends. He was, however, still on hand to oversee his highest-profile commission, the building of the eastern front of Buckingham Palace, which began in the mid-1840s and continued until the state rooms there were finished and ready to be used in the spring of 1856. It was also typical of the man that, when he heard of the destruction of his Thameside workshop on 17 August 1854 by fire, causing around £30,000 worth of damage, his first, straightforward response to the disaster was to tell his men that they would be back at work within a week, and that he would offer £600 towards the cost of their new tools.

Cubitt was diagnosed with throat cancer in the summer of 1855 and dealt with his final illness in typically stoic and phlegmatic fashion, drawing up a suitably comprehensive will for his family in which he left behind the staggering sum of £120,000 to be divided between his children—£40,000 for the daughters and £80,000 for his sons—but also made sure that he provided for his employees, including his clerk, housekeeper, and coachman, granting them peppercorn leases* for the properties that they inhabited.

Cubitt was not a jovial man—one friend of his commented that "he looked as though he had taken the battle of life to heart very seriously indeed"[21]—but he was a conscientious and decent one. The

* This means a nominal or trifling sum.

"great builder and good man" may be remembered today by the pub that bears his name—the wider group is known as Cubitt House, in another nod to his legacy—but after he died on 20 December, the Norfolk carpenter's son may have been amused, and flattered, to know that Queen Victoria was sufficiently affected by his demise to write in her diary that "I am much grieved by the death of that excellent and worthy man, Mr Thomas Cubitt . . . In his sphere of life, with the immense business he had in hand, he is a real national loss. A better, kinder hearted or more simple, unassuming man never breathed."[22]

Would that the same could be said of many of the inhabitants of the square that he so painstakingly spent a good proportion of his life building.

2

William Arden, Ralph Bernal, Lord Truro, and Klemens von Metternich: 10, 44, 62, and 93 Eaton Square

"Affected religion and bastard morality"

Around a decade ago, I wrote what I hubristically termed an "anti-biography" of Lord Byron, *Byron's Women*. Unlike most lives of Byron, it did not solely revolve around the nefarious antics of the "mad, bad, and dangerous to know" peer, but was an examination of his relationships with the various, unfortunate women in his life, from his mother to his abandoned illegitimate daughter Medora Leigh, conceived with his half-sister Augusta. The book was received reasonably warmly, although it was published too early to coincide with the rise of the #MeToo and #TimesUp movements, which would have been a more appropriate time for my unvarnished presentation of the great poet and lover as a seedy sex addict, wife-beater, and pederast, whose treatment of men and women alike left a vast amount to be desired.

One regret that I have is that, in my eagerness to present the case against Byron as a man (and, at times, as a poet), I all but neglected to concentrate on the legacy that he left in Britain. When resident in London, Byron lived in the exclusive gentlemen's "sets" of the Albany in Piccadilly; the Five Fields area was not his natural habitat. Only a few months separated Byron's death from Cubitt beginning work on Eaton Square, and it is tempting to imagine that, had the wicked lord still remained resident in London, he may have become one of the square's first residents, should the perpetually impecunious poet have been able to afford it. Certainly, amidst the unimpeachably moral and upstanding likes of Cockerell and Robert Grosvenor, the first houses built there drew some rather more louche and questionable residents. Yet Cubitt had not established a model village along the lines of Bournville,* which prized churchgoing and forbade the consumption of alcohol, in Eaton Square. As long as tenants had enough money to afford the expensive leases, they were welcome, whatever their moral standing.

This was glad tidings as far as the inhabitant of 62 Eaton Square, Byron's friend William Arden, Lord Alvanley, was concerned. His father, Richard Pepper Arden, was a leading Whig politician who served as attorney general under Pitt the Younger and chief justice of the court of Common Pleas. *The Complete Peerage* wrote of him: "He was not a man of great oratorical powers, but possessed the qualities of intelligence, readiness and wit. . . . It would be vain to claim any great distinction for Lord Alvanley. He was a learned lawyer and a successful politician . . . The few productions that remain from his pen evince refinement, taste and facility of expression."[1] His son may have been expected to follow in his father's successful, if ultimately undistinguished, footsteps and pursue a career in the legal profession, but instead, after his father died in 1804 at the age of fifty-nine, he opted for another gentlemanly profession and joined the Coldstream Guards as an ensign, where he was promoted to captain in 1809.

He may then have gone on to lead a blameless life serving king and country, but when one's king-to-be was the sybaritic and self-indulgent prince regent, the more tempting option was not to follow

* A so-called "model village" founded by the Quaker Cadbury family for its factory employees.

the path of righteousness but instead to throw oneself headlong into the pleasures that Georgian London offered. Alvanley's friend Charles Greville caustically suggested that "He had rioted in all the dissipations of play and wine and women. . . . What [the philosopher Edward Burke] says with a sort of mock modesty of himself, was true of Alvanley—he had 'read the book of life for a long time, and other books a little!'"[2]

Alvanley's was an existence where the candle was not so much burnt at both ends as taken, lit, and then used for absurd purposes. Greville wrote, not without fondness, that "For the first years of his life he was too entirely plunged in dissipation and debauchery to repair in any way the deficiencies of a neglected education; later, he read a good deal in a desultory way, and acquired a good store of miscellaneous information."[3] He surrounded himself with a loose, louche circle of similarly wealthy and dissolute young men, which Byron—always ready to think the best of his fellow men, until he turned against them—affectionately termed "the Dandy Club" on the grounds that "I like the dandies, they were always very civil to me."[4]

Alvanley's boon companions were Sir Henry St-John Mildmay, a troubled man who eventually shot himself in 1848 when faced with mounting debts; Henry Pierrepont, the envoy to the Swedish court; the prince regent; and, most notoriously and fascinatingly of all, Beau Brummell, the self-proclaimed connoisseur of all things contemporary and modish. The five men were habitués of the fashionable but short-lived gentleman's club Watier's, which was set up in Piccadilly in 1807 only to be disbanded a dozen years later. It was named after the prince regent's personal chef, Jean-Baptiste Watier, but its primary interests and purpose were gambling rather than gourmet. The author and antiquary John Timbs observed that "In the old days, when gaming was in fashion, at Watier's Club both princes and nobles lost or gained fortunes between themselves."[5]

Byron held Alvanley in a mixture of affection and frustration, recognising both his intellectual skills and his willingness to play the buffoon to entertain those around him. He remarked to his friend the

Countess of Blessington that "Lord [Alvanley] is a delightful companion, . . . brilliant, witty, and playful; he can be irresistibly comic when he pleases, but what could he not be if he pleased? for he has talents to be any thing. I lose patience when I see such a man throw himself away; for there are plenty of men, who could be witty, brilliant, and comic, but who could be nothing else, while he is all these, but could be much more. How many men have made a figure in public life, without half his abilities! But indolence and the love of pleasure will be the bane of A—y, as it has been of many a man of talent before."[6]

Byron was not, however, present at the notorious masquerade ball of July 1813 which represented the dissolution of the short-lived Dandy Club. Alvanley, Pierrepont, Mildmay, and Brummell were hosting the event when the prince regent appeared, looking tired, sweaty, and out of sorts. The friendship between him and Brummell, in particular, had been in abeyance over the previous couple of years, since George became regent in February 1811. Like a rather superannuated Prince Hal, the future king had vowed to put away childish things, but it was he, rather than the ever-fashionable Brummell, who had expanded to suitably Falstaffian proportions through his gluttony and endless self-indulgence. When he arrived at the ball, he made a point of greeting Alvanley and Pierrepont but decided to make a further point of snubbing Mildmay and Brummell by looking at them without acknowledging them further: a rather childish means of demonstrating noblesse oblige. This led Brummell, never a man to shy away from an outrage, to turn to Alvanley and drawl, in words that became instantly notorious, "Alvanley, who's your fat friend?"

George was painfully sensitive about his considerable girth and the momentary satisfaction that Brummell gained from his snub was soon outweighed by the humiliation that he felt when he was cast out of royal favour and subsequently exiled from Britain. It was therefore left to Alvanley to keep the fire of conversation and wit alive, which he did with some panache. His fellow army officer and dandy Captain Rees Gronow noted in his reminisces that "To Lord

Alvanley was awarded the reputation, good or bad, of all the witticisms in the clubs after the abdication of the throne of dandyism by Brummell; who, before that time, was always quoted as the sayer of good things."[7] While, privately, Alvanley remained loyal to his old friend, at considerable expense, he adopted a more laissez-faire attitude in public, in order to keep his reputation as a wit alive; Gronow wrote approvingly that "Lord Alvanley had the talk of the day completely under his control, and was the arbiter of the school for scandal in St. James's."[8]

Nonetheless, by the time that Alvanley took up residence in Eaton Square, his youthful good looks had faded, due to his dissipated and expensive lifestyle. In order to maintain it, he had sold off most of his family estates, including Underbank Hall in Stockport and Arden Hall in Warwickshire. He was described by the social commentator Lady Elizabeth Spencer-Stanhope as "Short and somewhat stout, with a small nose and florid cheeks usually adorned with a lavish sprinkling of snuff, like his rival Lord Petersham, he cultivated a lisp which accentuated the humour of his utterances." She described him as "one of the wittiest men in Europe," but as he grew older, he became more eccentric in his habits and mannerisms. Alvanley had an especial penchant for a bizarre ritual when, reading before he went to sleep, he would either extinguish his candle by throwing a cushion at it, or if that failed, putting it under his pillow. Lady Elizabeth noted that "So well known, indeed, was this little habit of Lord Alvanley, that hostesses who were anxious not to have their houses set on fire at midnight would depute a servant to watch in a neighbouring apartment till his lordship composed himself to sleep."[9]

Eaton Square was a comedown of sorts for Alvanley, whose previous London home, in Park Street at St James's, was a byword for hospitality and largesse, not least because the delicacy of apricot tart was on offer all year round. His time spent living at number 62 until his death in 1849, by contrast, was largely uneventful. Alvanley was an almost anachronistic figure because, as Lady Elizabeth observed, "his reputation as a wit was well deserved, and at a date when both the dandies and the fine ladies prided themselves upon their undisguised insolence, Lord Alvanley remained a shining example of good-nature."[10] His friend the diarist Charles Greville talked fondly of "his marvellous wit and drollery, [which] made him the delight and ornament of society,"[11] and cited some lines from *Love's Labour's Lost* about the character of Berowne, or "Biron" as he was known in Greville's diary—the association brought about by the pun was wholly intentional—that he considered apt:

> . . . . A merrier man,
> Within the limit of becoming mirth,
> I never spent an hour's talk withal:
> His eye begets occasion for his wit,
> For every object that the one does catch
> The other turns to a mirth-moving jest,
> Which his fair tongue (conceit's expositor)
> Delivers in such apt and gracious words,
> That aged ears play truant at his tales,
> And younger hearings are quite ravished;
> So sweet and voluble is his discourse.

The major occasion on which Alvanley disturbed his "mirth-moving jests" and "sweet and voluble discourse" was to fight a duel with the Irish soldier and politician Morgan O'Connell on 4 May 1835 at Chalk Farm in North London. The circumstances under which this particular encounter was engaged were, as usual with Alvanley, mock-heroic and therefore comic in nature. Daniel O'Connell, the so-called Liberator of Ireland, was the prime mover behind Catholic emancipation in the first half of the nineteenth century, as well as being one of the leading abolitionists of his time, and saw himself as a principled, moral man. He was therefore unlikely to be well disposed towards Englishmen who he saw as dilettantes and fops, and so when he encountered Alvanley in the House of Lords, he angrily denounced him as a "bloated buffoon."[12]

It was obligatory, given the public and heinous nature of the insult, for Alvanley to demand satisfaction from the then fifty-nine-year-old politician, but O'Connell refused to fight, having participated in a fatal duel on 1 February 1815 against the Protestant John d'Esterre. He had forsworn duelling thereafter, calling it "a practice inconsistent with common sense, and a violation of the divine law." Nevertheless, honour had to be satisfied, and in one of the more bizarre cases of primogeniture of the time, he offered his son Morgan in his stead.

The thirty-year-old former soldier presented Alvanley with a far greater challenge, and as the wronged party trudged towards his destiny, he encountered, as luck would have it, a Methodist parson, who exhorted him to give up the sinful and probably fatal course on which he was bound. "Pray, sir, go and mind your own affairs, for I have enough to do now to think of mine," Alvanley snapped at the man of God, who replied "Think of your soul!" Even in such circumstances, Alvanley was ready with his much-prized wit. "Yes, but my body is now in the greatest danger."[13]

En route to the duel, Alvanley was able to summon up his usual bravado. Accompanied by his friends Damer Dawson and Thomas Slingsby Duncombe, Alvanley slipped and fell before he reached the planned site. Never one to miss an opportunity for a jest, he exclaimed, gesticulating at his considerable frame, "My Lord, you get me down well enough, but should I fall, I do not know how the devil you will ever get me up again."[14] Yet for all the trepidation and potential danger, the encounter was almost comically anticlimactic. Both men fired two shots and missed entirely, before a third shot was accidentally fired by O'Connell, again to no effect.

Greville summed up the aftermath pithily: "Damer seems to have been a very bad second, and probably lost his head; he ought not to have consented to the third shots upon any account. Alvanley says he execrated him in his heart when he found he had consented to it. [Colonel Hodges, the referee of the duel] acted like a ruffian, and had anything happened he would have been hanged. It is impossible to know whether the first shot was fired by mistake or not. The impression on the minds of Alvanley's friends is that it was not, but it is difficult to believe that any man would endeavour to take such an advantage. However, no shot ought to have been fired after that. The affair made an amazing noise. As O'Connell had threatened to mention it in the House of Commons, Damer went to [Sir Robert Peel, the then prime minister] to put him in possession of all the circumstances, but he said that he was sure O'Connell would not venture to stir the matter there."[15]

That proved the conclusion of Alvanley's duelling days, and his final years were spent wracked with ill health in Eaton Square, before he eventually died on 16 November 1849. Greville wrote a tribute to him in which he noted his withdrawal from public life, regretfully observing that "If I had not been too lazy to write about anybody or anything, I should not have suffered the death of Lord Alvanley to pass without some notice. The world, however, has no time to think of people who are out of its sight, and a long illness which had confined him entirely, and limited his society to a few old friends, caused him to be forgotten, and his departure out of life to be almost unobserved."[16]

His old friend was clear-sighted about his charms and faults alike. He noted that "[Alvanley] was naturally of a kind and affectionate disposition, good-natured, obliging, and inclined to be generous; but he was to the last degree reckless and profligate about money; he cared not what debts he incurred, and he made nothing of violating every sort of pecuniary engagement or obligation. He left the friends who assisted him in the lurch without remorse, and such was the bonhomie of his character, and the irresistible attraction of his society, that they invariably forgave him, and after exhausting their indignation in complaints and reproaches, they became more intimate with him than before."[17]

Alvanley's death—of which Greville wrote admiringly that "For the last four years of his life he was afflicted with painful diseases, and his sufferings were incessant and intense. He bore them all with a fortitude and a cheerfulness which never failed him, and which excited universal sympathy and admiration"—concluded the life of one of the most entertaining characters of the Georgian era, who seemed diminished and out of place in Victorian times. His presence in Eaton Square was an anachronism, so redolent of another era was he.

Greville's final judgement on the infuriating but ultimately hugely likeable figure was a generous one. "He was so gay, so natural, so irresistibly comical, he diffused such cheerfulness around him, he was never ill-natured; if he quizzed anybody and bantered them, he made them neither angry nor unhappy; he had an even and constant flow of spirits, and till his health became impaired you were *sure* of him in society. He was vain, but it was a harmless and amusing vanity, which those who knew him well understood and laughed at."[18] And fittingly he had the final laugh. When asked by one friend what his epitaph should be, the inveterate gambler quipped, "Here lies Alvanley, awaiting the last trump."[19]

ANOTHER INHABITANT OF EATON SQUARE who was regarded as a wit, although not in the same league as Alvanley, was Ralph Bernal, a Whig politician and art collector. He lived at number 93, after initially moving to 74 Eaton Square shortly after its construction. He was born the son of Sephardic Jews of Spanish descent, but was not brought up in his parents' faith. Instead, he was eventually baptised a Christian at St Olave's church in Hart Street in 1805, while still a student at Christ's College, Cambridge, perhaps in the knowledge that Jews were barred from many areas of public life, including entering the House of Commons.* After a brief attempt at a legal career, which he abandoned in 1811 after the death of his father, Bernal embraced politics instead and served as the Whig MP for variously Lincoln, Rochester, and Weymouth. Before he had committed to

* As they would be until 1858.

the law and the Commons, he had toyed with becoming an actor, and had attracted acclaim for public performances of Shakespeare. His deep, rich voice lent similar credibility to his time in Parliament and at the bar.

Bernal is unlikely to have been remembered by posterity were it not for two, distinct but related, aspects of his life. The first, and more benevolent, was the sheer enthusiasm with which he approached his art collecting, of which he was the most distinguished individual practitioner since Horace Walpole the previous century. Bernal's Eaton Square home was decorated with the finest antiques and objets d'art imaginable, and he kept more than four thousand items in his house, which he zealously guarded and showed to only a few select friends and acquaintances, as well, of course, to fellow politicians and aristocrats whom he wished to impress.

He specialised in the acquisition of what he called "curious objects," which included rare glass, ceramics, plate, and miniatures, but his tastes were eclectic. They began in the medieval period and encompassed suits of armour and stained glass as well as contemporary chinoiserie. The author Humphry Ward declared in 1897 that "No one of his contemporaries in England . . . knew so much as he about old armour or mediaeval goldsmiths' work, or of Sèvres, or about majolica, or Chinese porcelain."

Bernal may have been discreet about his collection, but he also attracted mockery for it, some of it from an antisemitic perspective. The satirical publication *Punch* guyed him as "Mr Issachar Aarons," "an exemplary member of the Hebrew persuasion" and ridiculed his fine antiquities as little more than aged bric-a-brac, sneering that it included "a set of cupping-glasses, supposed to have been in Shakespeare's mind's eye when he exclaimed 'Cup us till the world goes round.'"[20]* Yet for every letter writer to *The Times* who sighed that Bernal's objets were "sufficiently interesting but of no peculiar rarity

---

*The allusion is to *Antony and Cleopatra,* rather than—as might have been anticipated—to *The Merchant of Venice.*

or value," many others craved an invitation to Eaton Square to view the wonders that lay behind its doors.

Enough men and women of influence were thus admitted for Bernal to be elected president of the British Archaeological Association (BAA) in 1853: a hugely prestigious organisation, founded in 1843 by the antiquarians Charles Roach Smith, Thomas Wright, and Thomas Joseph "Mummy" Pettigrew,* that tried to move away from the perceived stuffiness and aristocratic, urban bias of the Society of Antiquaries of London. The two groups would be rivals—"association," with its overtones of fraternity and equality, was a deeply loaded term—and when Bernal came to make his inaugural address as president to its Rochester Congress in October 1853, it was an occasion that would not only require his rhetorical prowess and statesman's oratory but would also politicise the association irrevocably.

It was a challenge that Bernal proved equal to. His address began with the usual modest plea for his audience's attention—"I do hope that you will not find me wanting, either in a warm attachment to archaeological pursuits, and in the energy (health permitting) indispensable in following them up, or in that sincerity and feeling which, when reciprocated with a kindred spirit, cements the bonds of any association"[21]—and then he spoke with vigour and conviction. He praised archaeology as "the faithful and diligent auxiliary of history and ethnology"[22] and declared that the "great and prosperous"[23] Britain was now desperately in need of a specific, dedicated museum devoted to the study and collection of antiquities that would rival collections in the Louvre in Paris and beyond.

There was a dig at the Society of Antiquaries and its snobbery—"Let us hope that all these various associations may work efficiently, in the genuine spirit of harmony, and in no other feeling of rivalry but that of evincing a generous courtesy and good-will to each other"[24]—before Bernal then spent a considerable amount of his

* So named after his interest in Egyptology, rather than any Oedipal leanings.

speech demonstrating his bona fides when it came to his former parliamentary seat. He concluded with a stirring, patriotic peroration that could not have failed to cheer and stir his no doubt partisan audience. Before he denounced the evils of "chilling apathy, barbarous destruction, or mischievous ignorance,"[25] he talked with passion and feeling of what the BAA's true mission should be:

> We must all look with anxiety and interest on the efforts and progress of those of our fellow-subjects who, emigrating from the country of their fathers, carry with them the energy and resolution of their race to distant and unpopulated regions. It is their lot to become the pioneers of civilization and the founders, we may hope, of new and flourishing societies. But there will always exist in the human breast a lingering fondness for old haunts and old associations. There is a chord in its inmost recesses which, jarred or untuned as it may be by the rude collisions and vicissitudes of life, will ever sound in responsive harmony to the impulse of ancient recollections. We have the happiness to inhabit a land rich in historical and sacred monuments, and teeming with exciting and memorable associations of past events. The hallowed temples of the worship of our ancestors,—the noble castles which, menacing or protecting by turns the freedom dear to Englishmen, always bore testimony to their perseverance and courage,—the sites of the domestic hearths of our forefathers—the graves which sheltered their last repose,—the venerable groves, scenes of their sports and pastimes, whose leafy arches and lofty trunks were the fit models from which the pious architect of early ages formed his sculptured curves and solid columns, devoutly remembering that God made the country, and man made the town,—all, all are entitled to claim our direct and enthusiastic attention and admiration.[26]

It would undoubtedly have won Bernal a round of ecstatic applause. He may have been a Whig, but the decidedly conservative message of his address was one of British exceptionalism and of delight in his country's fine and noble heritage. It was unfortunate that he managed to serve as president for only a few months as, on 26 August 1854, he died of a sudden attack of fever at 93 Eaton Square, leaving one of the greatest private collections of antiquities in the country. He was widely mourned, both as a politician and a keen aficionado of antiques. His rival James Robinson Planché, a fellow of the Society of Antiquaries, saluted him as "distinguished among English Antiquarians by the perfection of his taste, as well as the extent of his knowledge,"[27] and his obituary in *The Times* suggested that "in matters of art and taste Mr Bernal's judgment was justly esteemed as one of the best in England."[28]

Upon Bernal's death, the question of what would be done with his collection became pressing. Many might have hoped for a similar outcome as that of Sir John Soane's art collection and home upon his death seventeen years previously. Estranged from his son, Soane had ensured that his collection would be donated to the nation and kept intact in his house as a public museum, as they have remained ever since. Unfortunately, although John Charles Robinson, curator of the Society of Arts, attempted to persuade the government to buy Bernal's collection en masse in order to keep it together, with a view to its forming the nucleus of the recently founded South Kensington Museum*—public funds could not be found and so the entire collection was sold off the following year in a grand sale that consisted of four thousand lots, lasted for thirty-two days and realised the impressive total of £70,000, or around £12 million today.

If this was all that Bernal was known for, he would be fondly remembered as a patron of arts and antiquities long before such things were commonplace. However, there was another, darker side to the acquisition of his wealth and possessions. Bernal's father, Jacob Israel Bernal, was a successful and prolific merchant who had made

* Now better known as the Victoria and Albert Museum, or V & A. In the end, some of Bernal's possessions did end up there, and can be viewed by the curious today.

his money trading with the West Indies. He was also a slave trader. When he died in 1811, his will left his son "all . . . my Plantations, Negroes, Mountains, Penns, Woods and Estates in the . . . Island of Jamaica." This was made up of three estates, given the incongruously bucolic names of Cherry Garden, Richmond, and Edinburgh Castle, and meant that overnight Bernal became the absentee owner of 545 men, women, and children.

Had he inherited such a grim legacy a century before, Bernal might have thought nothing of it. After all, much of the British Empire's pre-Victorian prestige and wealth had been built on the sufferings and sorrows that slavery had engendered, and many of the country's greatest cities and monuments had been built with money that came as a direct result of the slave trade. Yet throughout the eighteenth century, there had been growing unease that the "respectable trade" as it was first sincerely, then ironically, known was both inhumane and bad for business from a mercantile perspective.

Abolitionists led by the politician and evangelist William Wilberforce eventually spearheaded the Slave Trade Act of 1807, after eighteen years of wrangling and politicking, which prohibited the practice. The text of the act sternly held that it should "take effectual Measures for the Abolition of the African Slave Trade in such Manner, and at such Period as might be deemed advisable. And whereas it is fit upon all and each of the Grounds mentioned in the said Resolutions, that the same should be forthwith abolished and prohibited, and declared to be unlawful." Many other European countries followed suit, and, by the time of Jacob Bernal's death, the slave trade was beginning to be outlawed after centuries of its practice.

Bernal, however, was not willing to accept the end of his family's lucrative profession, and so established himself at the forefront of a group that became known as "the West Indian politicians." These MPs, who were Whigs and Tories alike, all had commercial interests in the West Indies and beyond, which were threatened by the abolition of slavery, and so they vigorously fought the Slavery Abolition Act until its final ratification in 1833. Bernal made a series of speeches and interventions in the Commons in defence of slavery and the interests of slave traders; and on 19 May 1826, he made a particularly widely circulated statement in which he argued that public feeling had been "unfairly and unkindly directed against West Indian proprietors" and that "the question of property should never be lost in these discussions."

"Property," of course, referred to the humans who were trafficked across the world for profit. Bernal, for all his love of exotic objects, proved to be rather less invested in the men, women, and children from other cultures whose ancestors had made his treasures. He suggested that, if abolition had to be undertaken, it should not be pursued with "indiscreet haste" but instead followed "with a due regard to the capability of the negroes for receiving those advantages which it might be proposed to confer on them." He also argued that he and his fellow slave traders were pursuing a course of action that "had been long recognised and sanctioned by Great Britain," and that as a result, they were "entitled to the strong, determined, and undisguised protection of Parliament" of their financial rights.

He went even further in another speech in November 1830, when he announced, "Affected religion and bastard morality had been called in . . . to destroy the sacred and recognised rights of property in the West-Indies." He attended well over a hundred meetings of the Society of West India Planters and Merchants, a powerful and well-funded group designed to promote the interests of its members in Parliament; and he argued that, should abolition take place, it would cause more harm than benefit. A contemporary report of one speech he made on 24 July 1833 suggested: "His negroes, he believed, would have but little advantage in the change. They were now happy and comfortable—nothing proper was refused them—and in sickness they were taken care of."

Bernal, an intelligent and cultured man, was anything but a fool, so his wilful ignorance of the appalling conditions that his slaves were being kept in—certainly anything other than "happy and comfortable"—can never be excused or justified. Like other owners of slave plantations, he would never have seen the misery caused by slavery in person,* but it was convenient for him to turn human suffering into numbers on a balance sheet, and the tears and blood shed by strangers thousands of miles away would doubtless end up paying for some charming piece of chinoiserie.

Abolishing slavery took a great deal of time and money. It now seems incredible that slave traders had to be compensated, and handsomely, but Bernal and others insisted on their rights as property owners and successfully argued that they must be paid. In consequence, the Slavery Abolition Act's less celebrated cousin, the Slave Compensation Act, was brought into existence in 1837. A total of £20 million—or the almost unimaginable sum of £3,247,363,057.47 today—was allotted for the likes of Bernal. He himself received £11,450 for the emancipation of the 564 slaves that he owned; 21 more than he had inherited two and a half decades before. So vast was the total money allotted, and so complex the financial machinations involved, that the British government was paying some merchants' descendants reparations until 2015, via interest-bearing annuities. The slaves, of course, received nothing.

Ralph Bernal was not a deliberately evil person, or at least he would not have recognised such a description of himself. His own Jewish heritage was something that gave him a taste of what it was like to be discriminated against and to occupy the margins of society, although his wealthy upper-middle-class existence meant that such privations as he underwent were fleeting and soon forgotten when he returned to his prizes in his Eaton Square mansion.

Yet the acquisitive side of his nature, keen to spot an overlooked bargain or some finely crafted object, cannot be divorced from the cold, practical man of business, fiercely defending his and his fellow merchants' interests against the march of progress—or, as he might have viewed it, attempts to deprive him of his "most extraordinary

* The Quakers Joseph Sturge and Thomas Harvey did, in 1837, when they visited Bernal's Jamaica estate to research their book *The West Indies in 1837*. They painted a predictably grim picture in which, if the slaves were not actively abused, they were treated without compassion: twelve-hour days, brief breaks for breakfast and dinner, "no half Fridays, no payment for extra labour . . . Invalids get no food, nor old people any support from the estate."

and unrivalled collection." He referred to his gathering of majolica earthenware, but he could equally have alluded to the hundreds of unfortunate, hopeless slaves, working and dying in despair while, thousands of miles away, their unconscious and unconcerned patron slumbered soundly in Eaton Square.

IF BERNAL'S REPUTATION HAS SUFFERED precipitously since his death, then most of the men (and it was, until the twentieth century, an almost exclusively male-dominated enclave) who lived on Eaton Square in its early decades were neither as louche as Alvanley or as controversial as the celebrated art collector. Politicians, lawyers, and the military made up many of its residents.

The square was home to such figures as the former lord chancellor Lord Truro, who died at 83 Eaton Square on 11 November 1855 after a distinguished career that involved being both solicitor general and attorney general in the administration of Lord Melbourne and becoming the grandiose-sounding chief justice of the court of Common Pleas, a position that he held between 1846 and 1850. However, had he encountered Robert Grosvenor, he may have endeared himself to the landowner by dint of a service that he had performed rather earlier in his career in 1820.

Although he had been called to the bar in 1817, at the age of just thirty-five, after having undertaken a quasi-apprenticeship as a freelance practitioner, or "special pleader," he was asked to serve in the defence of Queen Caroline in 1820 in the Pains and Penalties Bill of that year, which was government legislation introduced in the House of Lords at the behest of George IV to remove the title of queen from her and to dissolve the marriage, thus allowing him the freedom that he craved. However, the only grounds on which a divorce could be obtained were those of infidelity. She was therefore accused of having committed adultery with an Italian man, Bartolomeo Pergami. Once George III died on 29 January 1820, his son pursued the case with a zeal born of both frustration and wounded pride.

Truro, then known as Thomas Wilde, may have been relatively untested. Both the queen and the politicians responsible for the case—as well as the king—could well have believed that he would be a pushover, allowing the queen to be publicly damned with only the most token defence put forward for her. The entire affair smacked of a kangaroo court and brought shame on the much-vaunted ideas of "British justice." Caroline was not allowed to speak in her own defence, and the entirety of the House of Lords was required to be present, to pile further humiliation on the wretched queen. Wilde, meanwhile, was no silken-voiced Demosthenes. The barrister and author James McMullen Rigg said of him, "Wilde had none of the personal advantages which heighten the effect of oratory. He was thick-set and of no great stature; his features were irregular, his voice was unmusical, his delivery monotonous. He had even an impediment of speech, which he evaded rather than overcame by the use of synonyms."[29]

It was therefore to everyone's surprise—and, in many cases, chagrin—that the thirty-eight-year-old Wilde, acting in what was widely presumed to be a hopeless case, instead proved himself to be, as his fellow lawyer and radical politician Lord Brougham described it, "extremely able and acute" when it came to cross-examination. Rigg had acknowledged that Wilde "had no lack of nervous English; and his mastery of the technicalities of pleading, his connection and experience, joined to great natural talent and equal industry, rendered his success only a question of time."[30] In the Lords, Wilde and Brougham were able to dismantle the case against Caroline with a mixture of skill and careful cross-examination. Not only did it become clear that many of the witnesses who were all too willing to testify to the intimacy that the queen had enjoyed with Pergami had been bribed to appear, but a letter of April 1796 was produced that made it clear that George, himself a flagrant and committed adulterer, had given his wife permission to lead her life as she saw fit.

The outcome of the case was wildly humiliating, both for the king and for those who had brought it. Although the bill was theoretically passed, its majority was reduced to nine on the third reading, and the prime minister Robert Banks Jenkinson, 2nd Earl of Liverpool gravely announced that he "could not be ignorant of the state of public feeling with regard to this measure." Caroline became a public heroine, George a laughing stock (the historian E. P. Thompson wrote, of the endless cartoons and satirical pamphlets that circulated of him, "No British monarch has ever been portrayed in more ridiculous postures nor in more odious terms than George IV during the Queen Caroline agitation"),[31] and Wilde established a successful practice off the back of his triumph, which he maintained until even greater public recognition came his way as solicitor general in 1839, the year before he was knighted.

During his time in Eaton Square, Truro almost certainly encountered the Codrington family, who lived at number 10. They were said to have been descended from John Codrington, who acted as Henry V's standard-bearer at Agincourt, and served their country with a similar degree of distinction and acclaim. Sir Edward Codrington was an admiral who fought with Nelson at Trafalgar and then commanded a combined British, Russian, and French force against the Ottoman Empire in the Greek War of Independence, winning the decisive Battle of Navarino on 20 October 1827 by dint of his superior firepower and tactical skill. Byron, a noted supporter of Greek independence, who had died three years previously, would undoubtedly have been pleased by the outcome of the battle, which proved to be the final time in history that a major conflict was decided by seagoing vessels.

It meant that Codrington came to be regarded as a national hero in both Greece and Britain, and everything from roads in Greece to a pub in Chelsea* are named after him. His son Sir William became an army officer who served with distinction in the Crimean

* The Admiral Codrington, as it's called, was once famous for serving the best cheeseburgers in London. Its chef Fred Smith left the pub to become head chef at none other than the Byron chain of burger restaurants; another bizarre but amusing piece of synchronicity between two wildly different men.

War—one of the few to have done so, and a deserved recipient of the Knight Commander of the Order of the Bath in consequence—and one of his other sons, Sir Henry, followed in his father's nautical footsteps and served under him at Navarino as a junior officer. He was eventually appointed to the position of Admiral of the Fleet in 1877, a few months before he died at the family home in Eaton Square.

The Codringtons were, in other words, the exemplars of what Victorian values were held up to be: public service, distinguished military prowess, and an adherence to family loyalty at all times. That such values would result in the acquisition of considerable wealth was a happy by-product. Yet military service, even at the highest level, was not enough to make a family wealthy enough to enjoy a lavish existence in Eaton Square. In 1797, Codrington, along with his siblings William and Caroline, inherited Sir William Codrington's slave plantations in Antigua, from which they continued to draw an income until the abolition of slavery in 1833.

Two years later, Sir Edward was awarded £2,588 6s 6d by the government in compensation for the 190 slaves who had been freed from his plantation, thereby joining the considerable ranks of those who had profited from the misery of others. His elder brother Christopher Bethell Codrington had gone further. Like Bernal, he had fought vigorously against the abolition of the slave trade, claiming once again that his own slaves were well looked after and happy, and that to set them free would be a gross injustice. His anger may have been performative, and designed to raise the price of the compensation that he inevitably received: He would eventually be awarded over £30,000 for his claims. In any case, the Codrington name, which once proudly adorned the library of All Souls College in Oxford, has become increasingly tarnished through its associations, and, in 2020, a plaque to Sir Edward at his former home in Brighton was taken down.

* * *

Not everyone who spent time in Eaton Square did so as a permanent resident. Some of the highest-profile people to have been associated with it in its first decades were merely relative passers-by, coming and staying for a few weeks or, at most, a handful of months. First among equals in this regard was none other than His Most Serene Highness Klemens von Metternich. During Metternich's period as chancellor of the Austrian Empire, which lasted from 1821 until his resignation in 1848, he was not only the most powerful man in Austria, implementing the political and diplomatic system that bore his name, but had a good claim to be the most consequential figure in Europe after the defeat of Napoleon at Waterloo in 1815. Appropriately enough, it was shortly after Napoleon's downfall that the Congress of Vienna, which Metternich had masterminded, resolved a series of territorial initiatives that were designed to safeguard Europe from another cataclysmic war. He had done his job thoroughly and conscientiously enough—albeit with a committed eye to his own self-interest—to ensure that no such large-scale conflict would ensue for another century.

The machinations and triumphs of Metternich are, alas, outside of the scope of this book to discuss in the detail that they merit, but just as Napoleon found himself falling from the heights of emperor of the French to a miserable exile in Saint Helena, so Metternich fell out of favour with the new regime in Austria and was compelled to deliver his resignation on 13 March 1848. Described by one diplomat as having "shrunk to a shadow of his former self," he was advised by Archduke Ludwig that, if he remained in his home country, his and his family's safety was uncertain, and so he complained that "I am no longer anybody. . . . I have nothing more to do, nothing to discuss."[32]

By the time that Metternich and his family arrived in London on 20 April, after a torrid and unsettling journey through a Europe that seemed in thrall to revolutionary excitements, it was a welcome relief to find that British life was a more stable one. He leased 44 Eaton Square for four months over the summer of 1848, and, like the rather more impoverished Karl Marx the following year, threw himself into London's intellectual and social life. The seventy-five-year-old statesman was befriended by the young politician Benjamin Disraeli, then two decades away from his first period as prime minister and eager to learn from the advice—and guile—of a man who had been all-powerful just a few years earlier, but now was an aged and diminished figure who was happy to share his experiences with an admirer.

The most consequential figure with whom Metternich associated during his time at Eaton Square was another veteran of the Congress of Vienna, in the form of the now seventy-nine-year-old Duke of Wellington. Although Wellington, who daily visited his old friend and occasional sparring partner, was effusive in his hospitality, and did what he could to integrate Metternich into London society, the former Chancellor noted the absence of any invitation to Buckingham Palace from Queen Victoria. He knew that he was no longer a consequential figure worth associating with, but instead an anachronistic representation of an ancien régime. In his own way, he was every bit as irrelevant as his neighbour Alvanley, then in the final stages of his declining health.

Metternich enjoyed aspects of his exile, which included visits to everywhere from the British Museum to breweries, and the opportunity to spend long hours at his desk writing carefully thought-out letters to friends and colleagues, which were received with a mixture of embarrassment and occasional consternation in Austria. He remained certain of his actions and his own brilliance, declaring to his friend Francois Guizot that "error has never come into my mind."[33] Yet he could never forget that he was only passing through London, rather than making any headway in the city. After a few months he and his family left the capital and Eaton Square for the more raffish charms of Brighton, the town that had so enraptured the then prince regent that he had had the Royal Pavilion constructed as his seaside residence. Metternich, however, had to make do with the rather less grandiose settings of 42 Brunswick Terrace for his next staging post on his humble Grand Tour.

Chancellors, dandies, slave owners, attorneys general: Eaton Square had, in the decades since Robert Grosvenor and Thomas Cubitt agreed to its construction, defined itself as one of the most consequential and important addresses in London. The square would not change a huge amount in the second half of the nineteenth century; those who were living there at the dawn of 1900 were not so very different to most of the first residents. But as British society stood on the edge of evolution and irrevocable change, even Eaton Square could not remain impervious to the shift forever.

3

George Grey, George Peabody, Matthew James Higgins, and Hugh Grosvenor: 14 Eaton Place, 71 and 80 Eaton Square

"The richest individual who ever died"

After I wrote my first two books, *Blazing Star* and *Restoration*, I came up with a can't-miss idea for the third. I had always been interested in Oscar Wilde and the fin de siècle movement but felt that there had been so many biographies of Wilde and his circle (some excellent, some dismal) that I had no useful or original insight into the well-trodden path that that unfortunate, brilliant man took over his brief and glittering career. Then I thought more closely about the street on which he lived, Tite Street in Chelsea. It was not only home to Wilde and his family but also to the likes of James McNeill Whistler, John Singer Sargent, and subsequently Radclyffe Hall, *Goldfinger* screenwriter Paul Dehn, and Augustus John. It was, in Wilde's evocative description, truly "the street of wondrous possibilities."

I was excited by the idea and, most important, my publisher was excited, too. A contract was prepared, a generous advance discussed, and preliminary research begun. And just before I started writing the book, I opened the review pages of the paper one evening to find, to my horror and incredulity, that a young American writer, Devon Cox, had beaten me to it, with a well-received group biography centred around Tite Street, called, inevitably, *The Street of Wonderful Possibilities.*

Duplicate ideas for books can, and do, happen, especially in anniversary years or if there has been some seismic event that leads authors—and publishers—to believe that readers are going to be flocking to bookshops to read new titles about it. (See, or rather don't, the explosion in Covid-themed novels shortly after the pandemic.) Yet it seemed extraordinary that my idea—arrived at, it must be owned, after a suggestion from my wife, Nancy—had found its echo in another's research and that there had been no public announcement of the book. Seeing no possibilities, wondrous or otherwise, I scrapped the project altogether, moved on to *Byron's Women*, and continued to think about ways in which I might explore the social and scandalous history of an iconic area of London.

Thankfully, the book that you are now reading has shown me that Eaton Square has an even richer and more complex history than Tite Street. Yet there are fascinating parallels between the two areas, located less than a mile from each other. At first glance, both are wealthy, exclusive enclaves of south-west London, home to some of the city's most distinguished residents, and with enviable historical stories to tell. Both attracted a specific kind of inhabitant in their earliest days—writers and artists for Tite Street, and politicians, soldiers, and lawyers for Eaton Square—and both remain iconic landmarks, where the mere mention of their names connotes an entire style and means of life. As we shall see shortly, music hall comic songs of the late nineteenth century would mention Eaton Square to elicit a laugh, and novelists would use it as a location for their disparate literary purposes.

Still, what was undeniably true was that Tite Street—laid out more than half a century after Eaton Square, with construction beginning in 1877 courtesy of the Metropolitan Board of Works—was as much a product of mid-Victorian idealism and enterprise as Eaton Square represented the values and ambitions of Thomas Cubitt and Robert Grosvenor and, to a wider extent, the end of the

Georgian era. Although built in the nineteenth century, and indeed completed a considerable period into Queen Victoria's reign, Eaton Square exemplified nothing so much as the architectural and social culmination of the long eighteenth century. The likes of Alvanley, Cockerell, and Sir Edward Codrington were Georgians both by birth and temperament, whereas Wilde and Whistler were thoroughly Victorian in both regards, even if their actions and behaviour would have made Victoria herself distinctly unamused.

One nearby resident who the queen would have wished to associate herself with, however, was Sir George Grey, whose home on 14 Eaton Place was located immediately by the western side of Eaton Square. Grey was the antithesis of the foppish artistic types who lived on Tite Street, being an active and forward-looking colonial administrator who served in a series of prestigious posts in the heyday of the British Empire, including as governor of South Australia; governor of Cape Colony; and both governor and premier of New Zealand, where he took office between 1861 and 1868, and then between 1877 and 1879. Liberal by both politics and disposition, after graduating from Sandhurst and spending his early military service with the 83rd Regiment of Foot in Ireland, he sympathised with its downtrodden inhabitants and came to consider British incursions there unnecessary and brutal.

He began his career in the empire at the age of twenty-eight and swiftly rose to high office, thanks to his diligence, compassion for the natives—and nations—that he oversaw and a genuine interest in the work that he undertook. He was in many regards the anti-Bernal, someone who paid lip service to the cultures whose work he so diligently collected but had no genuine interest in their customs or values, save as a means of financial gain. Grey, however, was so deeply interested in the peoples that he encountered in his travels—some of which were spent on HMS *Beagle*, shortly after Charles Darwin had travelled half a decade as its passenger—that he taught himself how to speak the Māori language in order to better understand the people of New Zealand.

Upon his return to England in 1859, Grey spent much of his time at Eaton Place, working on a translation of traditional stories and myths, which was published with the concise title *Polynesian Mythology, and Ancient Traditional History of the New Zealand Race, as Furnished by Their Priests and Chiefs*. In the preface to the first edition, he wrote, "I soon perceived that I could neither successfully govern, nor hope to conciliate, a numerous and turbulent people, with whose language, manners, customs, religion, and modes of thought I was quite unacquainted,"[1] and "[I felt it] to be my duty to make myself acquainted, with the least possible delay, with the language of the New Zealanders, as also with their manners, customs, and prejudices."[2]

After what Grey termed "a far more difficult matter"[3] was accomplished, there was then the question of his feelings about the "numerous and turbulent people."[4] He concluded his preface with what was, for 1855, a compassionate and open-minded approach, but the legacy of the then-emergent discipline of "muscular Christianity"—the belief that contemporary Christian faith should be accompanied by diligent work, athletic prowess, and the evangelical extolling of the glories of God—was pervasive in his thought.

He wrote: "It must further be borne in mind, that the native races, who believed in these traditions or superstitions, are in no way deficient in intellect, and in no respect incapable of receiving the truths of Christianity; on the contrary, they readily embrace its doctrines and submit to its rules; in our schools they stand a fair comparison with Europeans, and, when instructed in Christian truths, blush at their own former ignorance and superstitions, and look back with shame and loathing upon their previous state of wickedness and credulity; and yet for a great part of their lives have they, and, for thousands of years before they were born, have their forefathers, implicitly submitted themselves to those awful superstitions, and followed those cruel and barbarous rites."[5]

That these "native races" might have considered a religion in which the central symbol was that of a man suffering upon an instrument of torture no less "cruel and barbarous" was not something that Grey considered, or wished to dwell on. Even for someone sympathetic and intellectually aware, as he undoubtedly was, the question of equivalence between colonial subjects and a true-born Englishman was an impossibility.

Grey, who rejoiced in the nicknames of "the Great Proconsul" from his admirers and "Grey the Inscrutable" from his detractors, spent a considerable amount of his life abroad, but he always believed that he acted scrupulously and honourably on behalf of his sovereign and the empire alike. While many colonial administrators of the era are now reviled, Grey continues to be a respected figure,* and when a statue of him was erected in Cape Colony—today better known as Cape Town—in his lifetime, the citation called him: "a governor who by his high character as a Christian, a statesman, and a gentleman, had endeared himself to all classes of the community, and who by his zealous devotion to the best interests of South Africa, and his able and just administration, has secured the approbation and gratitude of all Her Majesty's subjects in this part of her dominions."[6]

If Grey exemplified the best values of the outward-looking Victorian era as an administrator and explorer, then it would be another resident of Eaton Square—himself an immigrant from the former colony of America—who represented different but equally desirable ideals, in his case those of philanthropy. George Peabody was born into poverty in South Danvers, Massachusetts, on 18 February 1795, one of seven children; when his father died, the teenaged Peabody worked in a shop in order to sustain his family. He later commented, "I have never forgotten and never can forget the great privations of my early years."[7] His straitened upbringing—less humble, more

* Although not one wholly spared criticism; a statue of him erected in New Zealand had its head broken off in anti-British demonstrations on Waitangi Day (6 February) 1987.

desperate—imbued in him a drive to succeed but also to aid others in similarly impecunious circumstances.

At the age of twenty-one, he headed for Baltimore, where he met Elisha Riggs, a merchant, who offered him a partnership in the sale of dry goods. Peabody may not have come from money, but he was sagacious and energetic, and the company Riggs, Peabody & Co. became a conspicuous success. By the time Peabody was thirty-two, he decided that it was time to head to England on a number of business ventures, including the sale of American cotton and bonds. He travelled between Britain and America consistently for the next decade until, in 1837, Peabody believed that his energies and industry were better spent in the Old World than the New and became a permanent resident of London.

He had moved to the city in an eventful time. Not only was Victoria newly on the throne but the poor were facing destitution on a hitherto unsuspected scale, thanks to the introduction of the Poor Law Amendment Act of 1834. Passed by a Whig—rather than Tory—government, this draconian edict meant that the impoverished would no longer be eligible for any state relief unless they presented themselves to workhouses, which were intentionally grim and Spartan institutions that gave their inmates the bare sufficiency of life and nothing more, separating children from their parents on the grounds that, by entering a workhouse, those desirous of help had forfeited the usual privileges and pleasures of family life.

Even at the time, this attracted outrage; and so, without any state mechanism in existence to provide help and succour to the disadvantaged, it fell to individual philanthropists to do what they could to improve the lot of their fellow man. Peabody, who had begun a successful banking business shortly after his arrival in London, swiftly became a man of means, transforming his company into the most successful American bank in the city with the aid of his partner J. S. Morgan* and making himself a glittering figure on the London

* Father of John Pierpont Morgan Sr., better known as "America's greatest banker" J. P. Morgan.

social scene. Any American who visited Peabody at his office could expect a letter of introduction; favourable credit terms; and, if he so wished, a seat in Peabody's private box at the opera. In return, the financier saw that he and his company, Peabody, Morgan & Co., became the default option for any well-heeled expatriate.

This prudence made Peabody hugely wealthy, with a personal fortune that ranked in the millions. Mindful of his origins, he did not overindulge himself* and never married—he was believed to have a mistress in Brighton who he was more generous towards, although she was left nothing in his will—but he was more interested in offering his money and skills alike to making his adopted hometown. The first idea he had was to establish a series of clean, cholera-free drinking fountains throughout London, and, advised that this would probably be both hugely expensive and, given the level of water pollution, impossible to accomplish effectively, then turned his attention to problems with education. He came into contact with Lord Shaftesbury, the social reformer, whose "ragged schools," a series of free educational establishments aimed at the impoverished in society, had done much to change the fortunes of children who would otherwise have been abandoned by conventional schools.

Shaftesbury was impressed by Peabody's energy and enthusiasm, but suggested that, rather than concentrate his funds on one section of society, Peabody should instead deal with attempting to reform London's grim and inadequate housing supply. Even as the rapid growth of the railway system meant that the solvent working classes were now accommodated in small, cheaply built brick terraced houses—a far cry from the lavish mansions of Eaton Square—the poor were either condemned to a living death in the workhouse or packed into insanitary, frowsy slums, where conditions were grim and life expectancy was short.

* Unprepossessing in appearance—his biographer Ron Chernow describes him as possessing "a rumpled face, with a knobby chin, bulbous nose, side whiskers, and heavy-lidded eyes"—Peabody was nevertheless self-conscious (or vain) enough to dye his dark hair with "African balm" shortly after he moved to London.

Peabody, seeing the reflection of his own insalubrious origins, acted decisively and generously. He initially believed that a donation of £150,000 would be adequate to establish the Peabody Donation Fund, which had as its object the creation and maintenance of public housing, but before long he realised that, in order to make a substantial and lasting difference, an offering of more than three times that amount—no less than £500,000—would be necessary. When he announced his gift in a letter to *The Times* on 26 March 1862, with the launch of the Trust, he stated that his purpose was to "ameliorate the condition of the poor and needy of this great metropolis, and to promote their comfort and happiness." The newspaper called his establishment of the trust "an act of more than princely munificence" and declared: "We have today to announce an act of beneficence unexampled in its largeness and in the time and manner of the gift."[8]

The first result of Peabody's largesse was a development in Commercial Street, Spitalfields in the east of London, which was designed by the architect H. A. Darbishire and opened on 29 February 1864 for the "artisans and labouring poor of London." It was utilitarian, basic, and devoid of any fripperies. Peabody's stern moral code was to be found in edicts laid down by the trust for its first residents: Tenants were to be solvent, sober, keep respectable hours, pursue professions that Peabody himself might have approved of, and pay rent on time. Its founder may have been a philanthropist, but he was no soft touch.

Certainly, the blocks, which proliferated in deprived areas of London and exist as social housing even today, were preferable to the slums that they had replaced, but they were still grim. Built in dark red brick, with steep stairs and forbidding-looking iron railings, they seemed determined to remind their residents how fortunate they were to have a home, and their stock has not endured over the past century. The architectural historian Nikolaus Pevsner—admittedly, no great admirer of social housing—called the buildings "familiar but nonetheless detestable."[9]

Whatever the aesthetic limitations of the Peabody Donation

Fund's accomplishments, it improved the lives of a huge number of London residents. By the beginning of the 1880s, nearly fifteen thousand people lived in a Peabody dwelling, which numbered around five thousand individual units. His adopted country wanted to honour him. So not only was he made a Freeman of the City of London* in 1862, but he was awarded an honorary doctorate of civil law by the University of Oxford. And London wanted to immortalise him and his achievements: A statue was commissioned in 1869, by the sculptor William Wetmore Story, to be erected outside the Royal Exchange in the City, where it can still be seen today.

It was unveiled by the Prince of Wales—the future Edward VII—on 23 July 1869, but Peabody's health was failing. He had been unable to keep a planned appointment with Queen Victoria the previous month, departing instead on a final business trip to America, and it was noted: "The Queen is very sorry that Mr Peabody's sudden departure has made it impossible for her to see him before he left England, and she is concerned to hear that he has gone in ill health. She now writes him a line to express her hope that he may return to this country quite recovered, and that she may have the opportunity of which she has now been deprived, of seeing him and offering him her personal thanks for all he has done for the people."[10]

Peabody did indeed return to 80 Eaton Square for one final time at the end of the year, but he did not recover from his weakened health and died on 4 November 1869, aged seventy-four. His greatest legacy, in addition to the vast sums that he bequeathed to both British and American institutions—as much as $8 million by some estimates—was that he became the living embodiment of the savvy, socially engaged Victorian philanthropist. Like a post-redemption Ebenezer Scrooge, Peabody used the skills that he had accumulated during his time as a financier to ensure that every penny that he gave away counted; and, rather than driving a hard bargain when it came

* One of two Americans to receive this honour, the other being Dwight Eisenhower.

to the repayment of interest, he ensured that his money was directed towards those who were in desperate need, rather than in frivolities and self-indulgence.

The company that he founded still thrives today, boasting that it helps 220,000 residents, 26,275 of them predominantly elderly people in need of personal care and support, in a total of 108,000 homes. It is unlikely that most of them know a great deal about the history and circumstances of the man behind the company that has provided them with a place to live, but Peabody's gruff but sincere decency ensured that, at a time when London was becoming an ever more difficult and crowded place to live, some of its residents could retain an element of dignity.

OTHER THAN THE GROSVENOR FAMILY, Peabody may well have been the wealthiest man to live in Eaton Square in the nineteenth century. Still, most of the other residents were hardly impecunious, and the elevated professions represented there were a cross-section of wealthy London in the second half of the century. Which is why it is deeply surprising to find a journalist living on the square in this period, although he was hardly a conventional writer. Matthew James Higgins, aka "Jacob Omnium," was resident at 71 Eaton Square, where he lived between his marriage in 2 July 1850 and his death on 14 August 1868. Higgins was a series of strange and apparently contradictory things: an Old Etonian, a close friend of the author Thackeray, a clubman, a fervent and angry correspondent decrying society's many ills, extraordinarily tall (at six foot eight), and a plantation owner. Like many Eaton Square residents, these contradictions made the man.

His pseudonym was taken from the first article that he published, "Jacob Omnium, the Merchant Prince," which appeared in the August 1845 issue of the *New Monthly Magazine.* By that stage of his life, Higgins had studied at Eton and Oxford—he never graduated from the latter, having misspent his studies in the pleasures of the turf and the tavern*—and, after the sudden death of his father (also named Matthew Higgins), had been brought up by his mother, Janette. He may have expected to go into the military, but his great height made such a career impossible, and so he embraced a literary life instead.

The son's inheritance was a complex one, both financially and morally. His father had derived his wealth from a notable plantation, the Alliance estate, located in British Guiana—better known today as the independent South American nation of Guyana. It was then, as the name suggested, a British colony, as it had been since the Dutch ceded it in 1815, and its economy was primarily derived from the harvesting and sale of sugar cane. The labour, of course, provided by slaves.

There was no question of Higgins not making use of his father's legacy. Although he came of age shortly before the Slavery Abolition Act was implemented in 1833, he headed off on a Grand Tour financed by the proceeds from the Alliance, before deciding, unlike most slave owners, that he would visit British Guiana himself, to see what conditions were like there and to acquire a deeper understanding of the industry that his family had grown wealthy from. When his mother died in 1838, and he inherited the estate, he travelled there for a lengthy visit, not returning to Britain until the following year. He was sufficiently interested in the Alliance to repeat the trip in 1846, but rather than his journey inspiring any particular sense of compassion in him, it convinced him to publish a series of pamphlets, of which the best known is the 1847 publication *The Real Bearings of the West India Question*, subtitled *As Expounded by the most Intelligent and Independent Free-Trader of the Day.*

Higgins argued that, rather than taking the enlightened view that slavery must end immediately as an inhumane and barbaric practice, it needed to continue for the time being as an economic necessity, and that the British government should offer plantation owners

* He was also Catholic, which may have made graduation impossible.

financial assistance in order that they could support the transition from the status quo to the new era that legislation had brought in. He also suggested that businessmen like himself faced an unfair disadvantage when compared with countries that had not outlawed slavery and therefore had considerably cheaper costs in the execution of their labour.

Viewed today, and in light of Higgins's other publications and letters, the pamphlet seems an almost Swiftian work of satire, a *Modest Proposal* for the Victorian era. Rather than giving any credence or interest to the miserable conditions that the slaves were suffering—and which he had seen repeatedly for himself—it was a demonstration of self-interest on a grand scale. Yet Higgins was also writing at a time when the acquisition of large sums in compensation meant the difference between families retaining their wealth and facing severe financial difficulty. His marriage to the heiress Emily Blanche Tichborne may have been a love match, but it was also born of economic necessity. If the family's income was no longer assured by the Alliance plantation, then journalism alone was unlikely to keep Higgins in the considerable style that he decided he belonged in.

Still, he was a committed and prolific writer. After the first appearance of Jacob Omnium in print, he kept it as his main pseudonym but also dabbled with a range of others, which included John Barleycorn, Paterfamilias, Mother of Six, Civilian and—appropriately enough, for an Eaton Square resident—West Londoner. He did not write for money, *pace* Samuel Johnson, but instead used his literary skills and anger at social injustices (which naturally did not include the slavery question, unless it was the lack of money directed towards their owners) in a range of publications that included the *Edinburgh Review*; the Peel-backing *Morning Chronicle*; and, most significantly for his literary career and subsequent standing, *The Times* and the *Cornhill Magazine*.

It was when he began writing for *The Times* that he came into contact with the journalist and novelist William Makepeace

Thackeray. He, unlike Higgins, did not have the comfortable—if morally questionable—safety net of money inherited from the slave trade and therefore had to embrace the destiny of so many men and women before and after him and, as he put it, "[write] for his life." Thackeray was a keen observer of social mores, which he chronicled under a range of pseudonyms that rivalled Higgins's for creativity. Anyone reading *Punch* or *Fraser's Magazine* who had enjoyed the work of Ikey Solomons, Fitz-Boodle, or the Fat Controller would have been familiar with the work of the author of *The Luck of Barry Lyndon*, to say nothing of his future masterpiece, *Vanity Fair*.

Thackeray and Higgins met at a party thrown by the *New Monthly Magazine*, to which both had contributed, and they gravely enquired as to each other's real names. Sharing a similar sense of humour and crusading sensibility, they swiftly became friends. When Higgins's correspondence with *The Times* led to a significant piece of legislation that scrapped the secretive Palace Court in 1849—a court that existed under the sovereign's imprimatur, rather than the usual law of the land—Thackeray wrote a ballad "Jacob Omnium's Hoss" under the pseudonym "Pleaceman X" that celebrated Higgins's achievement.

Higgins once flirted with the idea of taking his social activism into the House of Commons, but after being unsuccessful in contesting the constituency of Westbury in 1847—he stood on a Peelite platform as a Tory and was defeated by the businessman James Wilson, who was elected as a Whig—he spent a contented life post-advantageous marriage writing correspondence from his study in Eaton Square and devoting the rest of his days to long-extinct members' clubs such as the Philobiblon (devoted to bibliophilia and book collecting) and the Cosmopolitan Club, a highly exclusive establishment with a membership list capped at sixty that included the Prince of Wales, William Gladstone, and Anthony Trollope, and claimed to be "largely renowned for conversation."

He joined the staff of the evening newspaper *Pall Mall Gazette* in 1863, thus switching from correspondent to commentator, but it was hardly a demanding role. In any case, his death in 1868, after he became ill while bathing in the polluted water of the Thames, meant that he was unable to establish himself as the crusading journalist he might have become had he lived longer.

One strange incident that Higgins did become involved with towards the end of his life, which occupied him both personally and professionally, was one of the Victorian era's most celebrated legal cases: that of the Tichborne claimant. As the rules the period prioritised primogeniture, there was no question that Emily Tichborne could ever have inherited the family's baronetcy, despite being the eldest surviving child of Sir Henry, and so the Tichborne title passed to his nephew Roger, who was born in 1829. Twenty-five years later, after he fell in love with his cousin Katherine, he headed on a long voyage to South America and Mexico, after this piece of consanguinity was frowned upon by the Tichborne families. Unfortunately, in 1854, he set out for Jamaica from Rio de Janeiro on the ship the *Bella*, which promptly sank, apparently with all lives lost. The baronetcy duly passed to his younger brother Alfred, a wastrel, in June 1862 and the family's tragedy appeared to be complete.

This might have been the conclusion of the story, but Lady Henriette Tichborne—Emily's aunt and Roger's mother—refused to believe that her son had died. After hearing rumours that he might have made his way to Australia rather than returning to Britain, she continually advertised in Australian newspapers for information about Roger's whereabouts and offered "a most liberal reward" if the news was to be good. Lady Tichborne would eventually get her wish. In October 1865, a local butcher, Thomas Castro, announced that he was Roger Tichborne, and that he had assumed the pseudonym of Castro after arriving in Australia, having survived the shipwreck. He headed to Europe, and met Lady Tichborne in Paris in January 1867. She, understandably enough, was desperate to believe that this unprepossessing and stout figure was her long-lost son, and publicly announced that she recognised him as soon as she saw him, despite the scepticism of those around her who remembered Roger—or, as he was known, "the Claimant"—as being wholly different from the figure who she extolled as his substantial embodiment.

Higgins, ever the self-appointed crusader for all things righteous, decided that he would bring the matter into the public domain with a letter to the *Pall Mall Gazette*. On 28 May 1867, he wrote that he had suggested to the Claimant's lawyer John Holmes that he bring Tichborne's former commanding officer in the 6th Dragoon Guards, General Richmond Jones, face-to-face with the presumed Roger Tichborne, suavely noting that "should your client be disposed to receive General Jones's visits, all questions as to his identity will probably be disposed of one way or the other." The Claimant sent word via Holmes that he was not, in fact, disposed to see General Jones, on the grounds that the positive identification offered by Lady Tichborne should be proof enough for all sceptical parties. An unconvinced Higgins ended his letter in the most scathing of terms: "I may as well add that up to the present moment no steps have been taken by Mr Holmes to assert his client's alleged rights legally."[11]

Two months later, with debate as to the truthfulness or otherwise of the Claimant's occupying people throughout Britain, an unsigned article appeared in the *Gazette* under the headline "Tichborne vs Tichborne." It purported to be a dispassionate and objective look at the facts of what it called "this extraordinary case," but the writing style is unmistakably Higgins's, with every line oozing disbelief. "Now here comes the strangest part of the story. The claimant, on landing in England, did not present himself to any member of his numerous family, from all of whom he had parted on excellent terms in 1854"—this was not wholly accurate—"nor did he present himself to any of the officers of his regiment, in whose society he had passed the last four years of his sojourn in England, and who are of course the most competent persons to establish his identity." The snub of General Jones had not been forgotten.

Although the article allows Lady Tichborne her perspective—"her ladyship declares that [the Claimant's] features, disposition and voice are unmistakable, and must, in her judgement, be recognised by any impartial and unprejudiced persons who knew him before he left England, and that his memory as to everything which occurred up to the time of his leaving England is perfect"—the dismissal of the thirty-four witnesses who signed affidavits as to the veracity of the Claimant's identity as "obviously absurd, false and worthless" has a satirist's venom to it, and a journalist's eye for detail. "One is made by a blind man who once heard Mr Roger Tichborne speak before he left England, in 1853, and having heard the claimant speak in 1867, is convinced of his identity, because he has 'a Tichborne voice.'" Higgins concluded with a mixture of weariness and threat that "as, according to the Dowager Lady Tichborne's affidavit, the claimant's person and manner is [*sic*] little changed, and as his memory is perfect, there can be little doubt that as the case comes on to be tried, the claimant will readily obtain justice."[12]

Higgins's death the following year meant that he was unable to follow the case to its conclusion or to direct further cutting remarks about those involved in the Claimant's interests. Lady Tichborne had already died by the time that the case came to court in May 1871. She may have gone to her grave believing that she had been reunited with her son, but her death meant that the rest of the family immediately cut off the allowance of £1,000 a year that she had settled on him at their reunion. Nonetheless, the Claimant's case had attracted a wide degree of popular support, and he was able to live on an increased income of £1,400 a year, although many around him, such as his solicitor Holmes, grew disillusioned and withdrew their backing. They were vindicated during the civil case, which collapsed when it became clear that the Claimant was none other than a butcher's son named Arthur Orton, and a sensational criminal trial followed in 1874, which resulted in Orton being sentenced to fourteen years for perjury and his defence barrister, Edward Kenealy, being disbarred from practice after concocting a fantastical defence of his client that suggested that he was the victim of a conspiracy involving the Catholic Church, the government, and the legal profession itself. It can only be imagined how Higgins would have guyed Kenealy, but the former lawyer had his revenge of sorts: He succeeded in being elected as "the People's Candidate" for Stoke-on-Trent in 1875, thus managing to enter the only exclusive club that Higgins had found himself barred from.

If Sir Roger Tichborne would have found himself perfectly at home amongst the salons and private gardens of Eaton Square—and the Claimant would have been turned away before he could get anywhere near the servants' entrance, let alone the front door—then it was a reflection of the exclusive and upper-class milieu that had been created for, and by, its residents. After Robert Grosvenor's death in 1845, his son Richard inherited the title and continued to build up his by now hugely considerable wealth, not least by marriage to Lady Elizabeth Leveson-Gower, younger daughter of the Duke of Sutherland, one of the few men who was even wealthier than the Grosvenors. Greville described Sutherland as "a Leviathan of wealth; I believe the richest individual who ever died."[13]

The second Marquess of Westminster led a blameless and largely uneventful life. He was friendly with Queen Victoria, being one of the first to dine with her after her accession in 1837, and lived at Grosvenor House rather than in Eaton Square itself. He and Lady Elizabeth entertained on the grandest of scales there, with hundreds of distinguished and often royal guests for balls and dinner parties, yet he was personally modest and a committed philanthropist, giving away large sums to charity in both London and the family's rural seat in Chester. When he died in 1869, at the age of seventy-four, *The Times* saluted him, saying, "he administered his vast estate with a combination of intelligence and generosity not often witnessed."[14] He was, in other words, the very model of a Victorian man of means.

His son Hugh Lupus Grosvenor, who inherited the title at the age of forty-four, was a rather different character. It is stretching the facts to describe him as being more suited to life in Tite Street than Eaton Square, but he was certainly more interested in the pursuit of pleasure for its own sake than his father ever was, something that drew a stern rebuke from the second marquess in 1851: "Your habits are expensive and you live in expensive society . . . With only a life interest in this strictly curtailed property, I am sorry I cannot aid you, and, as I warned you the other day, I have not a sixpence in the funds."[15]

One of the reasons for Hugh's expensive lifestyle was his choice of bride. Lady Constance Leveson-Gower was the daughter of the 2nd Duke of Sutherland and, more significantly, of Harriet Howard, who served as Mistress of the Robes and therefore was a particular favourite of Queen Victoria. She was also his cousin, at a time when consanguinity was hardly frowned upon. Constance was an intimate of royalty from an early age, but she was also a society hostess who enjoyed the company of wits and writers, rather than just aristocrats. Oscar Wilde, then a student at Magdalen College, Oxford, was invited to meet her by his friend Frank Miles in 1877, and came away smitten. He declared that Constance—who, coincidentally, bore the same Christian name as his precautionary wife—"is the most fascinating, Circe-like, brilliant woman I have ever met in England: something too charming."[16] Those who attended her balls at Grosvenor House spoke equally warmly of her, with Lord Esher observing that "if you were early, you would be greeted by the ample welcome of Constance, and a gracious salutation from the grave seigneur who was her husband."

It is possible, even likely, that had Constance lived, she would have proved the conduit between the grand lords and ladies of Grosvenor House and Eaton Square and the artistic demimonde of Tite Street. Unfortunately, it was not to be. She contracted Bright's disease in 1875, at the age of forty-six, and had Wilde known that the Circe-like woman who entertained him to tea two years earlier was suffering from an illness that would eventually kill her in 1880, he would have been even more impressed by her radiance and forbearance. In the event, she died at fifty, and Queen Victoria recorded her death in her journal: "Had a telegram from the Duke of Westminster saying it was all over. Too sad."[17] Her eldest son attended the burial, along with Gladstone.

Hugh Grosvenor allowed a decent enough interval of two years between Constance's death and his second marriage, but his choice of new bride may have raised eyebrows in even the most open-minded of households. Katherine Cavendish was twenty-four, and the sister of his son-in-law, as well as being the daughter of the late Lord Chesham. Hugh had attended Chesham's funeral in July 1882, and had been entranced by Katie, as she liked to be known.

Although the age difference of thirty-four years was considerable, and some of the duke's children with Constance were older than she was, Katie proved to be as charming and warm a hostess as her predecessor had been, turning her London and Cheshire homes into convivial havens for her and her husband's four children. Their youngest daughter, Helen, was born on 5 February 1888, just under a year after Hugh's son Henry married William IV's great-granddaughter Dora Erskine-Wemyss, suggesting that the Grosvenor family—like some of the very poorest in the Peabody housing estates—was one that spanned a wide range of ages and situations, albeit tied together by almost inconceivable amounts of wealth and privilege. The ground rents on the Eaton Square properties continued to rise, and the Grosvenor family wealth was sustained by them and other properties throughout Belgravia and Mayfair.

Hugh may have got into trouble when he was younger for his enjoyment of racing, and speculation thereon, but in later life, he devoted himself to two activities: charitable endeavours and breeding horses. In the former capacity, he took over Peabody's lead and funded hospitals, paying for nurses and doctors, as well as taking an interest in the preservation of Hampstead Heath, where he found a faintly unlikely comrade-in-arms in Octavia Hill, the social reformer and founder of the National Trust. The two worked together to found the Hampstead Heath Protection Society, which exists to this day, under the revised name the Heath & Hampstead Society. In the latter capacity, he established a successful stud farm in Cheshire and spent a considerable amount of money on prize horses, of which the most renowned was Bend'Or, which won the Epsom Derby in 1880 and was considered by his jockey Fred Archer to have been the greatest horse he had ever ridden. It was in recognition of this, and many other achievements, that Hugh was awarded the distinction of master of the horse by Queen Victoria, a post that he held from May 1880 for five years.

Unlike his near-saintly father, Hugh Grosvenor could be intractable and irascible on occasion. He had a tempestuous relationship with Gladstone, who was prime minister for the period that Hugh served as master of the horse, and the two eventually fell out over the question of Home Rule to the Irish. In words that would have displeased Eaton Square's former tenant Higgins, but would probably have pleased Alvanley, Hugh dismissed Irish politicians as "miserable men whose bloody hands had brought ruin and murder to their country."[18] Such was his anger that Hugh disposed of a portrait of Gladstone that Millais had painted and that had hung at Eaton—ever conscious of the value of such possessions, he ensured it was sold,* rather than thrown away—but he soon restored correct relations with the prime minister, writing to him shortly afterwards on his birthday to send him every wish for his health and happiness, even as he punctiliously noted their differences in Irish politics. Nonetheless, Hugh may have been quietly relieved that, although the 1893 Government of Ireland Bill passed the Commons at its second reading, it was defeated in the Lords and never became law.

Gladstone, the grand old man of Victorian politics, died on 18 May 1898, and Hugh commemorated his neighbour and friend by serving as chairman of his memorial committee. Yet he was ailing himself and eventually died on 22 December 1899, seeing out the century that he and his forbears had done so much to define in their own images.** Many thought him kind and decent, and he had

* It can today be found in London's National Portrait Gallery.

** It was typical of him, however, that he spent the final year of his life shooting, attending his granddaughter's wedding—at a time when his youngest child was only the esteem and respect of Queen Victoria until the end. She sent a wreath of immortelles to the funeral, to be placed on the coffin, with the note "A mark of sincere respect and regard and esteem from Victoria R.I."

His death, and hers two years later, spelt the end of an era for Eaton Square and its residents: a very different fin de siècle to what was occurring nearby in Tite Street. Yet it might have either angered or amused Hugh to know that, less than a decade after his death, Eaton Square was to have a new resident who had made his name and considerable wealth out of burlesquing the likes of him and his friends, to the wider joy of the nation.

---

eleven—and putting forward the Seats for Shop Assistants Bill in the Lords, which he called "a step in the right direction of the prevention of cruelty to women."

4

W. S. Gilbert: 90 Eaton Square

"A magnificent ruin, no doubt, but still a ruin"

Eaton Square has been home to people from all walks of life—the moneyed walks, in any case—but it has seldom been a natural haunt for impecunious writers.* To generalise unsentimentally about our profession, most of us are closer to George Orwell's vision of the book reviewer** than we are to the Adonises (and, it must be said, wealthy Calibans) who made their homes in the square. The exclusivity of the area has appealed to some in the creative fields, mainly actors and musicians, but the more impecunious likes of poets and biographers find themselves in the unfortunate position of having their noses figuratively pressed to the glass outside. Our fate is to gaze, often enviously and sometimes in horror, at the exploits of those wealthier, if not always more glamorous, than those who make their living by their pen. And then to chronicle them as accurately and unsentimentally as we can.

This sense of fascination and, at times, contempt for the denizens

* Although of course, there have been exceptions here, too—see chapter 8.

** Orwell famously wrote of them/us that "He is a man of 35, but looks 50. He is bald, has varicose veins and wears spectacles, or would wear them if his only pair were not chronically lost. If things are normal with him he will be suffering from malnutrition, but if he has recently had a lucky streak he will be suffering from a hangover." George Orwell, "Confessions of a Book Reviewer," *Tribune*, 3 May 1946.

of Eaton Square has translated into numerous works of fiction and drama. There are some writers who might be expected to feature the square who do not—Wilde and Dickens, for instance—but others have seen it as a fitting residence for their characters, as well as using it as shorthand for power and privilege. During my research for this book, it has been a pleasure to root through the various allusions to it in the literature of the nineteenth and twentieth centuries, and so, for my own edification, I have sought to discover the first mention of it in a novel.

My first thought was its brief cameo in Trollope's satirical masterpiece *The Way We Live Now*, published in 1875, in which the square gets a passing, derisory reference ("When Lady Pomona, instigated by some friend of high rank but questionable taste, had once suggested a change to Eaton Square, Mr Longestaffe had at once snubbed his wife. If Bruton Street wasn't good enough for her and the girls then they might remain at Caversham")[1] but in fact Trollope had already given Eaton Square a more significant role nearly two decades before, in his 1859 novel *The Bertrams*.

The book—which is not, in truth, one of its author's most celebrated today—revolves around two men, George Bertram and Arthur Wilkinson, and their friendship-cum-rivalry as both manage the vicissitudes of life in mid-nineteenth-century London. References to the square come initially through the character of Sir Henry Harcourt, the highly successful twenty-eight-year-old MP and solicitor general. After approving allusions to Harcourt's "fine new house in Eaton Square" and "expensive house in Eaton Square," Trollope writes, with tongue only faintly in cheek, about the advantages that Harcourt's preferment has brought him:

> But for our friend Sir Henry every joy was present. Youth and wealth and love were all his, and his all together. He was but eight-and-twenty, was a member of Parliament, solicitor-general, owner of a house in Eaton Square, and possessor of as much well-trained beauty as was to be found at that time within the magic circle of

> any circumambient crinoline within the bills of mortality. Was it not sweet for him to wander through the rye? Had he not fallen upon an Elysium, a very paradise of earthly joys? Was not his spring-tide at the full flood?[2]

Well might one ask. Harcourt's Elysian paradise is, however, complicated by Bertram's continued love for Harcourt's wife, Caroline. Matters worsen for Harcourt, and his dreams crumble. Trollope's repetitive, mocking reminder of "the fine house in Eaton Square" is laden with the most bitter dramatic irony imaginable, as the author writes: "His reign had been sweet, but it had been very short. Prosperity he had known how to enjoy, but adversity had been too much for him."[3] The house, and square, become associated both with happiness—Bertram and Caroline acknowledge their mutual love there—and sorrow. Harcourt, tiring of his ill fortune, shoots himself in his home at the climax of the novel, with the chapter appropriately enough titled "Eaton Square."

Henry James took an equally clear-sighted look at life in the square in his final novel, *The Golden Bowl*, in which the hugely wealthy Adam Verver and his younger wife, Charlotte, live there. Their relationship is complicated by the appearance of the Italian nobleman Prince Amerigo, who is about to marry Verver's daughter, Maggie, but who has, in quintessential Jamesian manner, been involved with Charlotte in the past. James writes of Amerigo's not altogether wholesome intentions: "To haunt Eaton Square, in fine, would be to show that he had not, like his brilliant associate, a sufficiency of work in the world. It was just his having that sufficiency, it was just their having it together, that, so strangely and so blessedly, made, as they put it to each other, everything possible."[4]*

Whenever Eaton Square is mentioned in the novel, in fact, it is

* Reading this typically tortuous, quintessentially Jamesian offering, a writer friend reminded me of Rebecca West's adage that he wrote "sentences which sprawl over the pages with such an effect of rank vegetable growth that one feels that if one took cuttings of them one could raise a library in the garden."

without relish. The reader is told that it is "a dim desert," "monotonous," and somewhere redolent of "duskier days." The reader may do well to remember that James himself spent his later years in the Georgian splendour of Lamb House in the Sussex town of Rye, after abandoning London and his home in De Vere Gardens in Kensington: The grandiosity and wealth of the square was not his natural habitat, hence his jaded and detached authorial tone.

JAMES AND TROLLOPE WERE NOT alone in taking an ironic view of Eaton Square and its inhabitants. By the late Victorian era, music hall comedians and ballad singers vied with one another to produce satirical songs about well-known people and places that would entertain their well-liquored audience, whose tolerance for delicate Jamesian irony may have been somewhat reduced when they were several glasses of gin in.

One of these numbers, 1883's "The Belle of Eaton Square, or, I bought Her a Carriage & Pair," was billed as "A. G. Vance's Great Song"*—its performer was Alfred G. Vance, a well-known London music hall artiste who was a favourite of the Prince of Wales—and concerned love across the class divide, in the shape of a "false deceitful woman" who has lured the singer on, and compelled him to part with vast sums of money in buying her "a carriage and pair / To drive out in the morning." She then jilts him at the altar to marry "a man with padded legs," namely the carriage's well-furnished coachman, and announces their intention to join "the skeleton army,"[5] an anti-temperance movement that specialised in rowdily disrupting the work of the more respectable Salvation Army.

No doubt the song—which comes complete with lengthy spoken-word interludes that allowed Vance an opportunity to improvise and interact with the audience—was warmly received, but other than its

* The less heralded composer and lyricist was Joseph Tabrar, who is now best remembered for his nauseating 1892 novelty song "Daddy Wouldn't Buy Me a Bow Wow."

title—which, of course, may well be ironic—it has nothing to say about Eaton Square or its inhabitants. Another similarly rowdy and class-conscious comic number, written and sung by the performer Bracey Vane in 1885, was titled simply "Eaton Square" and took a rather more direct approach to the subject:

Now I'm a swell just coming forth,
To cut a dash in town,
I've made a fortune in the North,
Where I was known as Brown.
Though pickled onions was my line,
I give myself an air,
I don't know your address; but mine
Is ninety Eaton Square!

The song continues in a similar vein for several more verses, as the northern arriviste boasts of his newly acquired wealth and standing, and the chorus, tweaked every time, suggests that Mr Brown is thoroughly enraptured by his new home:

Oh! Piccadilly's all very well,
If you want salubrious air
But if you incline to come the swell,
Why—hang out in Eaton Square!

There are also unexpected parallels between the James and Trollope novels, with their sense that a home in Eaton Square spells automatic social advancement and the narrator's gloating belief that the impoverished aristocracy will be only too keen to get into bed, figuratively and literally speaking, with a horny-handed son of toil who has, as it were, the onions:

Now as I'm getting bored of life,
I mean to settle down,

And take a Duchess for my wife,
And make her Mrs Brown.
And though at first she won't say "Yes"
Pretend that she don't care—
She'll marry me—and my address—
At ninety Eaton Square!

To modern sensibilities, the song's satire may seem broad and obvious, as well as missing a great deal by being seen on the page rather than in performance. Even written down, however, there is still an appealingly dark wit in the final verse:

When I am dead and buried,
My tastes will not grow worse,
For on the stone above my head
I'll make them put this verse—
"Here lies Augustus Percy Brown
Who's shuffled off his care,
And when—his ghost comes up to town,
It stays in Eaton Square!"[6]

Whether or not there was a real-life antecedent for Mr Brown,* the expense and exclusivity of Eaton Square meant that both Alfred Vance and Bracey Vane had to reside in other rather less upmarket areas of London. Yet the square would be a home for actors and other entertainers throughout the twentieth century, and it was unsurprising that one of the great writers of his age would reside there towards the end of his life. That this writer was someone who had made his considerable fame and fortune lampooning the attitudes

* It is conceivable, although not definite, that this might have been a piece of satire aimed at Queen Victoria, whose relationship with her loyal servant and friend John Brown saw her labelled "Mrs Brown." Certainly, when he died in 1881, she wrote: "The comfort of my daily life is gone—the void is terrible—the loss is irreparable!"

and aspects of the Victorian era—including several of the types of inhabitant of Eaton Square—meant that there is an amusing irony that the dramatist, librettist, and satirist William Schwenck Gilbert chose to spend his final years amongst his targets.

THE FIRST (AND INDEED SOLE) reference to Eaton Square in Gilbert's work is a passing one, at the end of his 1868 poem "Trial by Jury." This brief squib, written for inclusion in the magazine *Fun*, predated his collaboration with Arthur Sullivan by three years. The two were introduced to each other in 1870; and their first work together, the light comic opera *Thespis*, was produced at the end of 1871 as a Christmas entertainment. *Trial by Jury*, in its original form, was little more than a jeu d'esprit, an amusing one-page satire on the legal profession in which the venerable judge, presiding over a case of breach of promise, declares that:

> In the course of my career
> As a Judex, sitting here,
> Never, never, I declare,
> Have I seen a maid so fair![7]

Improbably, unprofessionally, and inevitably, the judge decides, "Place your briefs upon the shelf / I will marry her myself!" As the assembled company half hail, half castigate him for being a "sly dog," His Honour invites everyone to join him to celebrate his nuptials, suggesting to all of them: "Come all of you—the breakfast I'll prepare / Five hundred and eleven, Eaton Square!" Had anyone suggested to the then thirty-year-old Gilbert that not only would he come to be regarded as the premier satirist of the late Victorian era, whose work is frequently revived and much lauded today, but that four decades later he would become a resident of Eaton Square himself—albeit at number 90, rather than the fictitious 511—he may have regarded it as an utterly absurd outcome, or simply taken it in his stride as yet another topsy-turvy reversal of fortune of the kind that he spent his entire professional life writing about.

Gilbert moved into 90 Eaton Square in January 1906, largely because of his declining health. He stayed there for the coldest winter months, until the milder spring meant that he could leave London. He had spent much of the previous year suffering from arthritis and rheumatism, and quipped: "I had gout all my life till 1900, when rheumatoid arthritis came along. They eloped together—the only scandal I ever had in the family."[8] Gilbert was no longer the dashing young man who caused laughter and uproar in equal measure in grand society, but a stately figure who described himself as "a crumbling ruin—a magnificent ruin, no doubt, but still a ruin—and, like all ruins, I look best by moonlight."[9] Shortly before he moved to Eaton Square, he walked from his country estate of Grim's Dyke in Harrow Weald into the centre of London, and although he proudly said, "Not bad for a crumbling old josser of 69," he also complained that "I think this will be my last year on earth."[10]

He was wrong about this, although not by very much. Gilbert's own death, which came to him aged seventy-four in the year 1911, was of a piece with any other absurdism—and black humour—as anything else in his life. While he and his wife, Lucy, lived at Grim's Dyke, they often invited local residents to come and swim in their ornamental lake, which Gilbert had extended. After a recent return from Eaton Square, Gilbert was conducting a swimming lesson for two comely local girls, Winifred Emery and Ruby Preece on 29 May 1911. When Preece was in the middle of the lake, not realising how deep it was, she panicked and shouted, "Oh, Miss Emery, I am drowning!" Gilbert, without any hesitation, called out to Preece not to be afraid and that he was coming, before swimming out to the centre of the lake. His last words to Preece were, "Put your hands on my shoulder and don't struggle."

Unfortunately, in so doing, Gilbert suffered a massive and fatal heart attack, and his body had to be recovered from the lake, even after Preece and Emery left it safely. Giving evidence to the inquest, Preece recalled: "I put my hand on his shoulder and I felt him suddenly sink. I thought he would come up again. My feet were on the mud then. Miss Emery called for help and the gardeners came with the boat." Emery later informed Gilbert's biographers Sidney Dark and Rowland Grey that "it seemed a long time before they recovered the body." The image that it summons up is a blackly comic one, that of the grand old man of Victorian lyrics being prodded with boat hooks by the gardeners. Had Gilbert been able to witness it from whatever celestial perch he found himself in, he would, one hopes, have found it all rather amusing.

Yet before this tragicomic end, Gilbert's career was one of the most successful and eventful of any literary figure of his era. While he remains best known for his work with Sullivan, his was a life marinaded in the written word from birth. His father, another William Gilbert, wrote novels with titles such as *Memoirs of a Cynic*, and gave his son the nickname "Bab," which explained the later name *The Bab Ballads* for W. S. Gilbert's early work. After Gilbert failed to join the army ("the war came to a rather abrupt and unexpected end, and no more officers being required, the examination was indefinitely postponed"), he spent "four uncomfortable years" as an assistant clerk in the education department of the Privy Council Office. It was not time wholly wasted, however. It gave Gilbert first-hand experience of the dunderheaded clumsiness of official jargon, and after he "[emancipated] myself from the detestable thraldom of this baleful office,"[11] he became a barrister, having laid out £300 on furnishing chambers and obtaining a pupillage with a senior lawyer.

Gilbert's time at the bar was not a success. He was a nervous and awkward public speaker, and his inexperience meant that he was seldom the advocate that his clients required. On one occasion, he had failed so completely to defend one woman that she bent down, undid her boot, and threw it at his head, "accompanying the assault with a torrent of invective against my abilities as a counsel, and my line of defence."[12] The boot missed, struck a reporter, and saw to it that Gilbert's reputation as a lawyer would sink into the doldrums. However, the law's loss was journalism's gain. He began contributing articles to a new magazine, *Fun*, from 1861, and eventually became its drama critic. It was poorly paid, at £1 a column, but he was able to subsidise his humorous writing with his stabs at the law. This strange co-existence went on until he met Sullivan in 1870, by which time he had also built up a modest reputation as a playwright and librettist.

Sullivan, meanwhile—six years Gilbert's junior—was establishing his own name as a composer, writing oratorios and concert pieces that included the enduring *Overture di Ballo*. He wrote it the same year that he met Gilbert, and it became his most popular non–Gilbert and Sullivan work. Had the two men carried on their separate paths, he would still have been a distinguished, if perhaps now obscure, figure in British music. Yet by the time that they worked together on *Thespis; or, The Gods Grown Old*, "an entirely original Grotesque Opera in Two Acts," the roots of an enduring collaboration had formed.

Although *Thespis* was not a particular success, and the two continued to work on their own separate projects, they also collaborated on songs together, with words by Gilbert and music by Sullivan. Eventually, Gilbert decided to expand his earlier piece for *Fun* and took the libretto of *Trial by Jury* to Sullivan to see if there was anything that might be done. He later recalled that "[Gilbert] read it through, and it seemed to me, in a perturbed sort of way, with a gradual crescendo of indignation, in the manner of a man considerably disappointed with what he had written. As soon as he had come to the last word he closed up the manuscript violently, apparently unconscious of the fact that he had achieved his purpose so far as I was concerned, inasmuch as I was screaming with laughter the whole time."[13]

When their first true collaboration, of the style that we define today as "Gilbert and Sullivan," opened at the Royalty Theatre in Dean Street on 25 March 1875, *Trial by Jury* was an immediate success.

The critic of the *Daily News* wrote that "it would be as difficult to conceive the existence of Mr. Gilbert's verses without Mr. Sullivan's music, as of Mr. Sullivan's music without Mr. Gilbert's verses. Each gives each a double charm."[14] A quintessentially English double act was therefore born, and then finessed when both met the impresario Richard D'Oyly Carte, who wished to create a dedicated company for English comic opera. It would not be long until the combination of librettist, composer, and manager ensured that there would be a steady stream of successful operettas being produced throughout the late 1870s and 1880s.

Looked at now, Gilbert and Sullivan's collaboration during this period was not only astonishingly prolific but wildly eclectic in their satirical aims and targets. *Patience*, for instance, took pot-shots at Oscar Wilde and the aesthetic movement in general, and *H.M.S. Pinafore*, their breakthrough hit in 1878, focused on the British obsession with naval exceptionalism and the meaningless rise of untalented people who happened to be in the right place at the right time. Little has changed in the intervening century and a half. Gilbert had been perfecting his mixture of wit and venom—but never quite viciousness—for a considerable time, and "Sir Joseph Porter's Song" took aim at the likes of Sir Edward Codrington and other grand inhabitants of Eaton Square, naval giants whose careers may have owed more than a little to preferment and endearing themselves to their betters:

When I was a lad I served a term
As office boy to an Attorney's firm.
I cleaned the windows and I swept the floor,
And I polished up the handle of the big front door.
(He polished up the handle of the big front door.)
I polished up that handle so carefullee
That now I am the Ruler of the Queen's Navee!
(He polished up that handle so carefullee,
That now he is the ruler of the Queen's Navee!)

Gilbert excelled at writing witty, memorable lyrics that were brought to life by Sullivan's tuneful and accessible music. Their shows were hugely popular and attracted wealthy, discerning audiences who may have enjoyed seeing fun being poked at their rivals and enemies—as long, of course, as the barbs never came too close for comfort. Certainly, given Eaton Square's long association with politics, some of his lyrics from "Sir Joseph Porter's Song," may have struck a chord with its residents:

> I grew so rich that I was sent
> By pocket borough into Parliament.
> I always voted at my party's call,
> And I never thought of thinking for myself at all.
> I thought so little, they rewarded me
> By making me the Ruler of the Queen's Navee!

This was, however, relatively small beer compared with Gilbert's single finest achievement, the Major-General's song, a patter song from 1879's *The Pirates of Penzance.* Tongue-twisting and fiendishly dextrous in the demands that it makes of its performer, it combines wit, social satire, and a hefty helping of self-referentiality ("[I] whistle all the airs from that infernal nonsense *Pinafore*"), and has been adapted by countless lesser comedians and writers to sometimes amusing, sometimes irritating effect. Yet nobody can seriously hope to compete with Gilbert for ingenuity and invention, all of which is buoyed enormously by Sullivan's music:

> I am the very model of a modern Major-General,
> I've information vegetable, animal, and mineral,
> I know the kings of England, and I quote the fights historical
> From Marathon to Waterloo, in order categorical;
> I'm very well acquainted, too, with matters mathematical,
> I understand equations, both the simple and quadratical,
> About binomial theorem I'm teeming with a lot o' news,

With many cheerful facts about the square of the hypotenuse.
I'm very good at integral and differential calculus;
I know the scientific names of beings animalculous:
In short, in matters vegetable, animal, and mineral,
I am the very model of a modern Major-General.

GILBERT AND SULLIVAN HAD A warm but businesslike relationship. The surviving letters between the two are brisk, factual—"Dear Sullivan," "Dear Gilbert," and the like—and as concerned with financial matters as they are with artistic ones, as has been the case for writers and musicians before and since. As the partnership continued, however, they formed a closer friendship, and by 1889, after *The Gondoliers* opened in December, they wrote to each other in almost passionate terms. Gilbert declared: "I must thank you again for the magnificent work you have put into the piece. It gives one the chance of shining right through the twentieth century with a reflected light."

Not to be outdone, Sullivan responded: "Don't talk of reflected light. In such a perfect book as *The Gondoliers* you shine with an individual brilliancy which no other writer can hope to attain. If any thanks are due anywhere, they should be from me to you for the patience, willingness, and unfailing good nature with which you have received my suggestions, and your readiness to help me according to them."[15] There were inevitably ructions. Gilbert exclaimed in March that year that a letter from Sullivan, complaining (rightly) that his work as composer had been subsidiary to Gilbert's as lyricist, "filled me with amazement and regret" and that "you are an adept in your profession, and I am an adept in mine. If we meet, it must be as master and master—not as master and servant."[16] The argument was soon resolved, and another masterpiece embarked on.

Yet the beginning of the end between the two of them began when Carte, puffed up with the success of his endeavour, opened the Savoy Theatre in 1881. It was a groundbreaking place, the first theatre in the world to be lit entirely by electricity rather than gas, and also hugely expensive. As Gilbert and Sullivan received an income based on the theatre's profits, they took a keen interest in Carte's perceived extravagances, and as early as 1882, Gilbert was complaining that the nightly costs of running the theatre, at £130, were absurd and desperately in need of reduction. (It would be around £20,000 a night today: a considerable sum.)

Sullivan was more blasé about what he perceived as necessary, if irksome, expenses, but Gilbert was incandescent with anger at what he saw as Carte's fripperies, which included charging two-thirds of the costs of the carpet at the Savoy Theatre to the duo rather than covering it himself. He wrote to his partner on 22 April 1890 from his home in South Kensington in fury at "*£500 for new carpets for the front of the house*" (his italics) and suggested that he had had a conversation with Carte in which, after being asked if he was dissatisfied with the current management of the theatre, and Gilbert replying that he was, the impresario said, "Very well, then; you write no more for the Savoy—that's understood."[17] Sullivan sided with Carte, feeling that Gilbert had overreacted. So, on 5 May, Gilbert decided that matters had reached a logical conclusion. "The time for putting an end to our collaboration has at last arrived . . . I am writing a letter to Carte (of which I enclose a copy) giving him notice that he is not to produce or perform any of my libretti after Christmas 1890. In point of fact, after the withdrawal of *The Gondoliers*, our united work will be heard in public no more."[18]

It was not long after this that Gilbert left Kensington for Grim's Dyke, both figuratively and literally removing himself from London and the milieu that he had done so much to satirise. Sullivan and he tried to mend their quarrel over the carpets and Carte's financial (mis)management of their affairs, but there was too much bad blood between the two for the earlier, happier days of their collaboration to be recaptured with any degree of true feeling. As Sullivan sighed in a letter to his former friend, "I have not yet got over the shock of seeing our names coupled in hostile antagonism over a few miserable pounds."[19]

They reunited briefly to work on two final operettas together, 1893's *Utopia Limited* and 1896's *The Grand Duke*. Yet Gilbert was as difficult to work with as before—a typical letter, from November 1892, saw him announce that "Having regard to the tone and purport of your last letter I must assume that it was written with the definite object of putting an end to the possibility of a collaboration"[20]—with his ill humour worsened by painful attacks of gout. He commented in 1893 that "I have not been able to do anything but swear for the last eighteen days," and those around him soon tired of what they saw as his belligerence.

The theatre owner and publisher Henry Labouchère said of Gilbert that "he was exceedingly touchy and prone to take offence about trifles. This I have remarked is very frequently the case with wits. Whilst they never spare others, they particularly dislike being laughed at themselves." This was untrue and unfair, but it was true that Gilbert would first explode with anger, and then laugh at the absurdity once the initial fury had abated. A calm, mild man could not have written the lyrics and plays that he did, and a truly incandescent one would not have found the humour and absurdity that Gilbert so ably and consistently discerned throughout his career.

After *The Grand Duke* failed—it lasted a comparatively brief 123 performances at the Savoy Theatre—the relationship between Gilbert and Sullivan ended. They were not on bad terms per se, but never exchanged a direct word after 1896, although they briefly shared a stage for applause at the first night of a revival of *The Sorcerer* in 1898. Gilbert attempted to broker a peace by suggesting that they unite for a revival of *Patience* in November 1900, and Sullivan expressed theoretical interest, but he was suffering from the bronchitis that would eventually lead to heart failure on 22 November 1900, aged fifty-eight.

Gilbert, who had himself been unwell, had headed to Egypt in an attempt to recover his health, and so was not able to attend his friend's funeral. He wrote a letter to Sullivan's nephew Herbert in which he expressed guilt and regret over their lack of a face-to-face reconciliation, saying, "I wish I had been in England, so that I might have had an opportunity of joining the mourners at his funeral." He wrote of his "personal sorrow" and sympathy at Sullivan's "terribly sudden death" and took comfort from knowing "that I was impelled, shortly before his death, to write to him to propose to shake hands over [our] recent differences & even a greater satisfaction to learn, through you that my offer of reconciliation was cordially accepted."[21] Sullivan remembered his old collaborator in his will, and left him his original score to *Ruddigore*.

The following year, Richard D'Oyly Carte died of dropsy and heart disease, aged fifty-six, and with him ended the grand age of Gilbert and Sullivan, and also of cost-be-damned munificence. Once again, it fell upon Gilbert to rise above the tensions and difficulties of previous fraught relations and business practices and write a fitting letter of condolence to Carte's widow, Helen. He stated: "The sad news of your husband's death—which only reached me on landing here half an hour ago—has touched me profoundly. Believe me, I sympathize with you in your bereavement & I sincerely wish I could have been in England to pay the last token of respect to his memory— . . . I am deeply sorry for you—deeply sorry for the grief that has overtaken a lady for whom, in all the vicissitudes of our business relations, I have always felt a sincere admiration &, I hope I may add, affection."[22]

THOUGHTS OF HIS OWN MORTALITY were ever-present, but he dealt with them in typically wry fashion. A newspaper article mistakenly referred to him as "the late W. S. Gilbert," and rather than simply imitate Mark Twain, he wrote to say, "There is a line in your issue of yesterday that must have sent a thrill of joy through many a worthy home. . . . I am always sorry to spoil sport, but common candour compels me to admit (reluctantly) that I am still alive."[23]

In 1904, just a couple of years before the move to Eaton Square,

Gilbert announced in a letter to *The Times* that he would no longer be writing comic operas. He declared that "Savoy opera was snuffed out by the deplorable death of my distinguished collaborator, Sir Arthur Sullivan. When that event occurred, I saw no one with whom I felt that I could work with satisfaction and success, and so I discontinued to write *libretti*."[24] Although he wrote one unsuccessful play, *The Fortune Hunter*, in 1904, Gilbert now regarded himself as largely retired, and amused himself, as many wealthy and famous men did, by activities in his substantial country house.

Even here, however, there were oddities. Unlike most of his peers, Gilbert detested blood sports and hunting, and once observed, "I have a constitutional objection to taking life in any form. I don't think I ever wittingly killed a black-beetle. It is not humanity on my part. I am perfectly willing that other people should kill things for my comfort and advantage. But the mechanism of life is so wonderful that I shrink from stopping its action. To tread on a black-beetle would be to me like crushing a watch of complex and exquisite workmanship."[25] His Grim's Dyke home was a sanctuary for animals of all kinds and sizes, ranging from Persian cats and Pekinese dogs to lemurs and fawns. In many regards, he seemed to prefer animals to humans; they could not, after all, answer him back.

It was also an amusing, if perhaps inevitable, result both of Gilbert's legal training and his high standing in society that the man who had had such boisterous sport satirising judges and arbiters of all kinds should himself become a justice of the peace in 1893, and served as a magistrate for the rest of his life. It was typical of him that, when the high sheriff appointing him to the position asked, "You have, I believe, studied the law as a barrister and have a sound knowledge of it?" Gilbert replied, "That is so, but I hope you will not consider it an impediment."

On at least one occasion, he privately paid the fine of a man who had been convicted of assault, so as to spare him an inhumane and degrading prison sentence, writing, "I can't bear to think of that poor devil going to prison for a month on *nulla bona*,* so I enclose a cheque for the amount owing by him." Usually, he dealt with malefactors with a mixture of understanding and typical dark humour. When he was punishing a would-be suicide,** who he bound over, he warned him, "If you attempt suicide again, you will be brought before us and punished for both offences, but if you succeed, you will be beyond our jurisdiction."

He could be caustic, too. When one arrogant young man was put before him for a driving offence, he fined him five pounds for reckless driving, but added the cutting rejoinder "Had you been a gentleman I should have fined you ten."[26] His wit, however, was seldom far away. When he saw a squabbling elderly couple, and the woman said, "he's a nasty old man, he beats me, and he's got an abscess in his back," Gilbert, impromptu, muttered, "Not a case of 'abscess makes the heart grow fonder.'"[27]

By the time that he moved to Eaton Square in 1906, Gilbert had made his peace with the waning of his creative fire. He wrote the play *The Fairy's Dilemma* in 1904, but it was criticised for being old-fashioned and old hat; Max Beerbohm, who saw it at the beginning of its ninety performances, first praised Gilbert lavishly for his *Bab Ballads* and called him "enshrined amongst my minor gods," but then went on to say that his latest production was redolent of the 1870s, not the new Edwardian age. In any case, Gilbert's major income was drawn from continuing performances of his and Sullivan's work, overseen by Helen Carte: The cost of 90 Eaton Square, at £351 for three months a year, could easily be met from his considerable earnings.

When he lived at Eaton Square, Gilbert, the grand old man of Victorian musical theatre, settled into a routine similar to any of his neighbours. He liked to spend his days at one of his clubs, whether the Junior Carlton or the Beefsteak, and shortly after his arrival at

* A legal term meaning literally "no property."
** To attempt to kill oneself was illegal in Britain until 1961.

the square, he was honoured with membership of the actors' and lawyers' club, The Garrick. He had been accidentally blackballed from it nearly four decades previously, but, in a nod to his considerable prestige, he was informed that, if one of his friends would propose him, he would be elected immediately, and so Gilbert joined the ranks of his fellows.

He was not a modest man. As his biographer Hesketh Pearson wrote, "But when he was feeling up to the mark he would explain that he was the most beautiful person in the world, that his forty-eight inch waist was exactly right for a man in his sixties, that his weight was that of Apollo (not in marble), that his life had been faultless as clear crystal, and that he was the greatest genius of his age."[28] Gilbert liked the idea of being a roué, and although there is no evidence that he was ever unfaithful to Lucy, he was ever-present with a quip or jest. While he suggested that "one feels *so* safe and (involuntarily) good" when it came to other women, he played up to a non-existent reputation, once suggesting, when asked if he had seen much of a leading actress, "not much; only her face and hands."[29]

His attitude towards his best-known work was protective, and this could tip over into being proprietorial. He upbraided Helen for casting a revival of *The Yeomen of the Guard* without his explicit personal approval in late 1906, complaining, "If Sullivan had been alive, you would no more have thought of casting one of the operas without obtaining his approval of every minute detail of the cast than you would have thought of setting the Savoy on fire."[30]

He may have attended the first night, bowing and waving at his admirers, but believed that his legacy was being besmirched by incomprehension, informing Helen, "The production, as a whole, is discreditable to the memory of Sullivan, to me, & to the magnificent reputation which he & I built up for the Savoy Theatre. The piece has received a blow from which it will never recover—& I presume that a similar blow is to be struck at the other pieces you propose to produce. I can only hope that your astounding change of attitude towards me is due to the influence of [the producer Stanley Boulter].

It is horrible to me to think that it is the outcome of your own volition."[31]

Another revival was soon planned, this time of *The Gondoliers*, and Gilbert publicly disassociated himself from this, writing to *The Times* on 22 January 1907 that "It is the practice of the Savoy management to announce that the operas with which I am associated are produced 'under the personal direction of the author.' As this expression is usually held to comprehend a much wider range of duties than those which, under existing circumstances, fall to my share, I shall feel obliged if you will allow me to explain that in the present series of revivals my responsibility is confined exclusively to the ordinary duties of a stage manager."[32]

As he chose to make the schism between himself and Carte so public, it could not pass by without comment, and in an otherwise laudatory review of the production, the *Times* reviewer wrote that they trusted that Gilbert's comments did not signify "the beginning of another breach between [Gilbert] and the management. As the surviving member of the famous triumvirate, he has an authority to which no one else can possibly pretend; and everything should of course be done to obey his wishes in every detail."[33] That obeying Gilbert's wishes might prove to be onerous, at best, and downright impossible at worst was not remarked upon by the tactful critic.

The year 1907 soon brought happier news for Gilbert. He may have occasionally felt himself déclassé when compared with some of the other residents of Eaton Square, being a mere entertainer and humourist. Therefore, when he was nominated for a knighthood in early June, he could not have accepted with greater alacrity or pleasure, even if he joked that "my first impulse was to decline it" and called it "a tin-pot, twopenny-halfpenny sort of distinction." He liked to pretend that it was "a mere triviality . . . from any but a professional point of view, an unmeaning scrap of tinsel," but his truer feelings could be discerned by his statement that "it has a somewhat special significance in my eyes, as I am the only dramatic author upon whom . . . it has ever been conferred."[34]

He was correct. While other playwrights, such as John Vanbrugh, had previously been knighted, they had received the awards for other services to their country. Gilbert would be the first playwright to receive the distinction solely for his writing, and although his contemporary Arthur Wing Pinero was also knighted in 1909, no other dramatist would be so honoured until Noël Coward in 1970.* He may have quipped that "This indiscriminate flinging about of knighthoods is making me very nervous; it's quite possible they may give one to my butler. He's a very good fellow and I'm afraid it will upset him," but he was pleased by it, although it would have hung heavy on him to acquire airs and graces. When a female friend asked him timorously, "What must I call you now? Sir William?" he was swift to respond "Call me 'Bill.'"[35]

Another pleasant facet of Gilbert's later years was that he formed an abiding and warm friendship with Arthur Sullivan's nephew Herbert, who liked to be known as "Bertie." Armchair psychologists might speculate that one reason why Gilbert was so keen on maintaining a friendship was guilt at the way that he treated Bertie's uncle towards the end of the partnership and a feeling of sorrow that Sullivan died before the two had had a chance to reconcile, although his robust treatment of Carte's widow suggested that there was a clear limit to the way in which Gilbert allowed personal sentiment to intervene with business.

Nonetheless, the correspondence between the two during this period shows Gilbert's jollier side. He good-naturedly thanked Bertie for a gift of oysters—"we are all prepared to die in excruciating agonies on the altar of friendship"[36]—and Bertie's response to his knighthood was a masterpiece of brevity that would have done the recipient proud. "Sincerest congratulations only it ought to have been a Dukedom."[37]

After Gilbert received his accolade from Edward VII on 15

* Terence Rattigan's KBE in 1971 meant that, of the first four playwrights to be knighted, two of them were or had been residents of Eaton Square.

July—he celebrated with lunch at the Savoy Grill and a swim at Grim's Dyke, and it is hard to know which gave him greater pleasure—he settled down to a contented existence as a grand old man of English letters. The move to London, even if temporary, restored his health, and he was short with those who suggested otherwise. When one well-meaning friend advised him not to walk from seeing his doctor in Harley Street back to his London home, he responded shortly "Walk! Of course I'll walk. I walk six or seven miles a day. I never wore a pair of glasses in my life and I still feel eighteen."[38]

When he was resident at Eaton Square, attended by his beloved protégée Nancy McIntosh—an American actress who became his and his wife's surrogate daughter—he entertained lavishly, went to the theatre frequently, and enjoyed the life of a literary lion. There was a dinner for a hundred guests at the Savoy to celebrate his knighthood, and his letters to Bertie Sullivan radiate warmth—"an instance of friendship that can never fade from my memory," "the most gratifying compliment that I have ever received"—to a point that some, including Bertie, must have wondered if there was an element of sly exaggeration in the fulsomeness of his compliments.

Nonetheless, Gilbert relished the public aspects of his celebrity. Although the unfortunate Helen Carte continued to receive vitriolic letters about minor details of staging his musicals at the Savoy Theatre,* he was otherwise content to play the modest but successful author. In one address that he gave to Harrow Speech Day in 1908, he stated that, apropos his knighthood, "I am the oldest dramatic author now before the public. . . . I have been rewarded for having brought up a family of 63 plays without ever having had to apply to the relieving officer for parochial assistance. This knighthood I [therefore] take to be a sort of commuted old-age pension."[39] And he was capable of being amusingly caustic about contemporary politics, too. When he was informed that the suffragettes had chained

* Publicly, he defended her, saying "I am sure that Mrs Carte, if left to herself, would have treated me with the courtesy that I have always received at her hands."

themselves to the railings of Downing Street in order to draw attention to their cause, he remarked, "I shall follow suit. I shall chain myself to the railings outside Queen Charlotte's Maternity Hospital and yell 'Beds for Men.'"[40]

There was to be one final operetta, *Fallen Fairies*, which Gilbert wrote with the musician Edward German, and which starred McIntosh in the role of Selene, the Fairy Queen. It was not a success at its premiere on 15 December 1909,* and Gilbert's relationship with its producer, Charles Herbert Workman—who replaced Carte, who understandably declined the chance to work with him**—was catastrophically poor, resulting in McIntosh being fired from the production a week after opening night and a vengeful Gilbert withdrawing the rights from Workman to stage any of his works again.

He did not mince his words to the producer, saying on 22 June 1910, when approached for a parlay, "I do not intend to waste any epithets upon you—you can easily supply them for yourself. It is enough to say that no consideration of any kind would induce me to have dealings with a man of your stamp."[41] Nor was he especially impressed with German, who proved an ineffectual substitute for Sullivan. Gilbert sent the composer an angry letter from Eaton Square on 30 January 1910 saying, "As I wired to you I will most certainly not guarantee that syndicate of rogues and fools against loss. They have paid me nothing since Jan. 1 and of course will pay nothing. A piece treated as that piece has been must necessarily go to pieces and from my point of view the sooner the better, for, as it is, my libretto is held up to ridicule and contempt every time it is played." After saying that he had begun to sue Workman for breach of contract, he concluded that "If you had joined with me in applying for an injunction to restrain them from substituting Miss Evans for Miss McIntosh, I

* Gilbert made a speech to the company after the final dress rehearsal in which he stated, "If the play succeeds, the credit is yours; if it fails, the fault is ours." The sincerity of this was uncertain.

** She commented, with heroic understatement, "I feel that the many anxieties and responsibilities of London management are more than my health and strength allow me to continue."

believe the piece would now be running to £200 houses. The libretto really counts for something."[42]

Gilbert wrote one last play, *The Hooligan*, which was staged at the end of February 1911 at the Coliseum Music Hall. It was atypically serious, revolving around the fate of a young man awaiting execution for the murder of his girlfriend, and was inspired by the recent trial of Dr Crippen. Yet its brooding on existential themes, mainly the inevitability and imminence of death, had its counter in Gilbert's own fears about his health. He was prepared to accept retirement, but quipped to one friend that "old age is the happiest time of a man's life. The worst of it is, there's so little of it."[43]

When he finally expired in the Grim's Dyke lake on 29 May 1911, he at least fulfilled an ambition that he had held for a considerable time. He had commented, "I should like to die upon a summer day in my own garden."[44] Ironically, the protagonist of *The Hooligan* had also died of heart failure, suggesting it was a matter on its writer's mind. The coroner, Sir Gilbert Hogg, found at the inquest that "the evidence made it quite clear that Sir William died in endeavouring to save a young lady in distress. It was a very honourable end to a great and distinguished career." Helen Carte wrote to Gilbert's widow, showing considerable magnanimity in the circumstances, that "It seems to me as if the last great link with the past had gone—it is a very sad thought. Very few have done as great work as he in their lives and it will live after him."[45]

She was correct. Of all the residents of Eaton Square, it is hard to think of many whose work has continued to give such pleasure to millions as Gilbert's. He was, as most would admit, by far the greater talent of the Gilbert and Sullivan duo. Although he could be extraordinarily difficult to deal with, being possessed of a quick temper that could swiftly shade over into aggression and vitriol, he was also kind, witty, and devoid of personal malice. He once said, "I fancy that posterity will know as little of me as I shall of posterity."[46] He was entirely, gloriously incorrect.

As a playwright, he influenced everyone from Oscar Wilde and

George Bernard Shaw to Cole Porter and, most recently, the American screenwriter Aaron Sorkin. It is hard not to agree with the *Cambridge History of English and American Literature*'s judgement that "his lyrical facility and his mastery of metre raised the poetical quality of comic opera to a position that it had never reached before and has not reached since." And as a man, his wit and panache attained Wildean proportions. At one dinner at Eaton Square, he was surrounded by a selection of society women, all of whom enjoyed his sallies and quips. When one of the (perhaps jealous) male guests asked why he was inconstant in his favours and affections, Gilbert smiled and delivered a remark for the ages that also functions as a fitting epitaph. "Because I am too good to be true."

5

Diana Mitford: 2 Eaton Square

"Thuggery, buggery, hunger and war"

It was once said of the Johnson clan—the former British prime minister Boris, his journalist sister Rachel, their environmentalist father Stanley et al., not Samuel—that they were "pleased with themselves, and each other." Their influence on British politics and society may have been decidedly mixed, but they at least follow in the tradition of large, rambunctious families behaving in a self-absorbed way, with ordinary people thrown into the mix as collateral. The same could equally be said about *another* famous, if hardly great, British family, the Mitfords. It is a dynasty that has existed since the time of the Norman Conquest, but they achieved their greatest renown in the thirties and forties, when the children of the intellectually limited and belligerent David Freeman-Mitford, 2nd Baron Redesdale—a man who liked to say that he had read Jack London's *White Fang* and enjoyed it so much he never felt the need to pick up another book again—made their respective marks on the London, and international, scene.

I cannot best the 2007 description of the younger Mitfords by the historian Ben Macintyre, who brilliantly called them, "Diana the Fascist, Jessica the Communist, Unity the Hitler-lover; Nancy the Novelist; Deborah the Duchess and Pamela the unobtrusive poultry connoisseur."[1] (He misses out the sole boy, Tom, who died fighting in Burma in 1945. An admirer of Hitler and fascism, Tom was happy nonetheless to join in on his country's side, but only if he could be posted to the Far East, thence to fight the Japanese.)

Nancy may be the best-known today, thanks to her brilliantly witty comic novels *The Pursuit of Love* and *Love in a Cold Climate*, which were based closely on the lives of her eccentric family; but Deborah, who lived until 2014, managed to befriend a far younger generation of socialites and writers, all of whom remained in awe of her. Pamela was, in the words of the poet John Betjeman, "the rural Mitford," quietly living in the country; and Unity's early death after a botched suicide attempt marked her out as the tragic Mitford. Jessica fled to America, where her communist sympathies could be indulged in the right circumstances and situations; and then, most famously of all, there was Diana, the most beautiful, coldest, and most notorious of all the Mitford sisters.

It might have been expected that David Freeman-Mitford—known as "Farve" by his children—would have maintained a substantial Eaton Square residence as well as the family home in Oxfordshire: first Asthall Manor and then, from 1926, the better-known Swinbrook House. However, Farve instead chose to take on the lease of 26 Rutland Gate in Knightsbridge, which he would then relinquish in the mid-thirties because of the economic downturn caused by the Great Depression. It was not, in any case, a residence that his children remembered with any particular nostalgia; Jessica commented that it was redolent of "comfort and serviceability rather than elegance."[2]

Diana would not live there as an adult, but instead took out a lease on "the Eatonry," 2 Eaton Square, on 1 January 1933. After it had been refurbished, she lived there in what were, for her, modest circumstances, accompanied by her children, Jonathan and Desmond; and a skeleton staff of cook, nanny, housekeeper, and lady's maid. The Grosvenor Estate—by now controlled by the politically simpatico Hugh "Bendor" Grosvenor, 2nd Duke of Westminster since 1899—offered her highly favourable terms: She could live on the square at a reduced rent, provided that she refurbished and redecorated the property, for which she would be allowed a grant. It was not as substantial as Diana's previous home, a Wiltshire mansion called Biddesden House, or her former London residence at 96 Cheyne Walk, where she had lived for less than a year. Yet the grandiosity or luxury of her new home was less important to her than her proximity to the man she had breathlessly called "the Leader": Oswald "Tom" Mosley, the peerlessly charismatic head of the British Union of Fascists (BUF), who maintained a residence in a deconsecrated chapel at 22a Ebury Street, mere minutes from his new mistress.

Of all the Mitford sisters, Diana had already had the most riotously turbulent existence since she was presented at court in 1928, age eighteen. She had met and fallen in love with Bryan Guinness while still a teenager, and Guinness appeared to be the perfect match for her. Heir to the brewery fortune, he was handsome, wealthy, witty, and cultured, if also sometimes shy and diffident. He moved in a worldly, sophisticated culture of predominantly Oxford graduates that saw him and his friends, who included Evelyn Waugh and Harold Acton, labelled, with a mixture of condescension and envy, as the "Bright Young Things." At twenty-three, he was probably the most eligible bachelor in London, but when he saw Diana at a concert at the Albert Hall, he was struck dumb with both admiration and adoration. Her attitude towards him was simpler. He was a way out of Swinbrook and a way into London society.

Anne de Courcy, who wrote the authorised biography of Diana and published it after her death, speculated that her motives in marrying Guinness were nearly entirely mercenary. She told him, after their first embrace, that while she was "very fond" of him, the kiss that they had shared meant nothing, and that, as she put it, "I do it without thinking as I'm used to kissing my family."[3] Guinness persisted in his suit; and, although Diana's parents believed her too young and too fiscally naïve to be joined in matrimony to one of the wealthiest men in London, he was eventually allowed to court her officially.

The unwritten but strict rules about the upper-class dance of potential matrimony were by then well established, and would not be bent until after the war. As I described it in my 2024 book *Power and Glory*:

> In the pre-war days, there was a set expectation of the etiquette required when a young would-be suitor visited his aristocratic inamorata's family home for a weekend. He should be polite and formal, but never dull or silent; well versed in current affairs, but prepared never to contradict his hosts, whatever the outrageousness of their opinions or views; well dressed for a variety of occasions, from shooting to formal dinners, but never ostentatious or peacock-like.

He would be surrounded—some might even say confronted—with a host of fellow guests, who might range from the charming to the choleric, and would be expected to overcome the conversational minefields that their disparate presence could also involve. In other words, if he managed to give a good account of himself in the most unpromising and stressful of situations, then it was likely that he would be given the nod to marry the daughter of the house. If he failed, he could expect a letter curtly informing him of his would-be fiancée's betrothal to another, more accomplished man.[4]

Guinness was accordingly tested with a house party at Elveden Hall in Suffolk, to which George V and Queen Mary were invited, and nerves reduced him to a stuttering wreck, muttering "Yes, sir" whenever his monarch said anything to him. Had Guinness been less well-connected, the event may have been a failure; but his high status, coupled with a reluctant agreement from Farve after lunch at his Piccadilly club the Marlborough, which Guinness called "the most alarming thing I have ever had to do in my whole life,"[5] meant that the he and Diana were married on 30 January 1929 at the fashionable church St Margaret's, Westminster. The honeymoon was in Paris, and the eighteen-year-old Diana became resident thereafter in Guinness's grand house of 10 Buckingham Street, which became a base of operations for the cultured, wealthy lifestyle that she had always aspired to and now had the chance to enjoy.

Diana became one of the most talked-about and photographed women in London society almost overnight. If she had a new hair-style, *Tatler* wrote about it. If she went to a dance that the Prince of Wales was also present at, *Bystander* paid her considerably more attention than the future Edward VIII received. Evelyn Waugh, who inevitably fell in love with her, took advantage of his standing as an *ami de maison* to spend his days at Buckingham Street, making her laugh by wittily dissecting the recent failure of his marriage to "She-Evelyn," Evelyn Gardner.

He would later dedicate his second novel, *Vile Bodies*, to the pair ("To B.G. and D.G."); it would be published on 14 January 1930. On 16 March, Diana's first child, a boy named Jonathan, was born. Her friendship with Waugh soon suffered, and they were no longer speaking by August that year. He later confessed "[it was] pure jealousy. . . . I was infatuated with you. Not of course that I aspired to your bed but I wanted you to myself as especial confidante and comrade. After Jonathan's birth you began to enlarge your circle. I felt lower in your affections than Harold Acton and Robert Byron and I couldn't compete or take a humbler place. That is the sad and sordid truth."[6]*

Diana, meanwhile, now became chatelaine of Biddesden House, a Queen Anne mansion in Wiltshire that tempered its beauty and grandeur by the presence of a malevolent ghost. Although she and Guinness appeared to be a golden couple, her indomitable spirit and family-honed humour were alien to his quiet, adoring whimsicality. They conceived

* She castigated Waugh for what she believed was an unflattering caricature of herself in the abandoned 1942 novel *Work Suspended*, to which he replied, "It was perhaps to some extent a portrait of me in love with you, but there is not a single point in common between you and the heroine except pregnancy."

a second child, Desmond, who was born 8 September 1931, but after their friends the author Lytton Strachey and the artist Dora Carrington died in quick succession (he of stomach cancer on 21 January 1932, bidding the world farewell with the bon mot "If this is dying, I don't think much of it," and she, grief-stricken, using one of Guinness's guns to kill herself, on 11 March) Diana was in desperate need of new distraction and of greater excitement in her life.

She had escaped Swinbrook and her family, only to be, as she saw it, trapped in a marriage of suffocating affection with a man who worshipped her but did not challenge or stimulate her. She was in search of someone who would do so, and this duly arrived in the form of Mosley, a saturnine and beguiling figure whose captivating political oratory was matched by a near-compulsive need to conduct love affairs, preferably concurrently. The two met at a dinner party on 21 February 1932 at the home of society hostess Emerald Cunard, and there was no particular initial spark. She was, in her description, "a Lloyd George Liberal," and he had been courted by the Conservatives and Labour alike, but his primary interest was in as pursuing as many extra-marital entanglements as he could.

Although Mosley was married to Lord Curzon's daughter Cynthia, aka "Cimmie," he approached the seduction of younger women with a single-minded dedication that usually succeeded, even if his spurned lovers regretted their acquiescence. One, Georgia Sitwell, was attracted to his "sunburnt, muscular torso," but later sourly noted, "Of course I went to bed with Tom. We all did, and then felt bad about it afterwards." She, and others, felt all the worse because they were simply conquests, not lovers. Mosley had a routine that he called "flushing the coverts," which was doing the rounds of the London season to make the acquaintance of young, newly married women, who often found that the first weeks or months of their union had not lived up to their breathless hopes, or indeed fears. Enter Mosley to set them on the proper path, which he did dozens of times. Yet his seduction technique was devoid of any genuine feeling or emotion, leaving Georgia to admit, "I wonder if Tom felt anything at all, then or ever?"[7]

Diana was a different proposition altogether. Although she was the same age and social background of his usual prospects, his marriage to Cimmie, who was miserably aware of her husband's antics, had endured because he was able to claim that his dalliances were simply the expression of an overactive libido—one that had already resulted in three children—and implicitly better indulged with women of the right sort than with paid companions. However, her concern was that if Mosley met someone who represented an authentic challenge to her, then he would simply leave. And although he and Diana had only met briefly, the great seducer was already enraptured by her beauty. He would later write in his self-serving memoir *My Life*: "Her starry blue eyes, golden hair and ineffable expression of a Gothic madonna seemed remote from the occasion but strangely enough not entirely inappropriate."[8]

Mosley's compulsive desire—some would call it mania—to sleep with as many women as possible was of a piece with his restless, self-absorbed political instincts. Cimmie sourly called it "his incurable boyishness and *joie de vivre*."[9] Had he been born a century later, he would undoubtedly have been diagnosed with an attention-deficit or obsessive-compulsive disorder, probably both, but his personal charisma was such that those who would have spurned a lesser man were instead enraptured by him. Diana was fortunate, or unlucky, enough to meet him when his political career appeared to be in abeyance. He had served in a Labour government, where he had risen to the office of Chancellor of the Duchy of Lancaster, but this was not the cabinet position that he had craved. In a fit of pique, he formed the short-lived New Party, which failed to see any of its candidates succeed in the 1931 election.

At the time that Mosley and Diana met, he was beginning to believe that there was a future in politics and that the old parties had to be swept away in favour of something new. While a Labour MP, he had ridiculed the British fascists, calling them "black-shirted buffoons, making a cheap imitation of ice-cream sellers" in a 1927 speech. Yet when he had time on his hands, having rejected his friend Lord Beaverbrook's offer of a column in one of his newspapers,

Mosley began to reconsider his opposition to fascism, which he now began to see as the only alternative to an otherwise broken Britain. He invited Diana out to lunch to discuss politics with her, and, to their mutual delight, discovered that her idly received and barely examined liberalism was only skin deep and that she instead believed that England was currently in a dire situation.

Mosley had spent years seducing women with force and physicality, and his good looks and charm were equally welcome as far as Diana was concerned. He was an entirely different physical proposition to Guinness: He was tall, dark, and confident, while Guinness was fair-haired, slight, and insecure. Yet the most appealing aspect of Mosley was his vigour and certainty that something could be done about the rotten state of the world. As Diana later described it, "In 1932 we all—everyone with the slightest intelligence—thought about politics. We believed that our parents' generation had made the war, that by *will* plus *cleverness* its horrible legacy could be cancelled out, and the world could be changed . . . He seemed to me to be a prophet of this changed world one longed for and I thought: if I can help him as he seemed to think I could, then nothing else mattered in the very least."[10]

This "help" soon translated into a full-bore love affair, which left Diana breathless with admiration. "Isn't the Leader *wonderful*!" she informed her bewildered friend Cecilia "Cela" Keppel, who was soon one of the many confidantes and acquaintances who was kept updated as to Diana's adulterous entanglement with one of the most notorious men in London. Guinness, who had recently purchased a Cheyne Walk house in large part because his wife had wanted it, was embarrassed and even angered by his wife's flaunting of what he referred to, for decency's sake, as a "friendship," and wrote to her formally to ask her to end it.

Diana, however, was far too excited by Mosley's magnetic presence even to consider bringing the liaison to a close. On 7 July, she held a party at her new house, to which Mosley and Cimmie were invited. Amidst the evening's bacchanal (the writer Robert Byron quipped that "it was the best party ever given, even by you . . . I feel as if I have been raised from the dead by it") she and Mosley declared their mutual love, even as he made it clear that, whatever the future of their relationship, he would not countenance leaving Cimmie. Nonetheless, she was now able to tell the long-suffering Cela the following day, "I'm in love with the Leader and I want to leave Bryan."

Diana's embrace of Mosley and fascism were inextricable. As she later wrote, "Fascism seemed at the time the only dynamic movement led by the only politician in England who combined the experience, the force, the intellect and all the other essential qualities of leadership to make possible the difficult task of shifting the dead weight of Baldwinites* on the right and MacDonaldites** in the centre with the rump of Labour led by [Clement] Attlee on the left, which was smothering the country with inertia and complacency."[11] Diana, writing with considerable hindsight, had conflated her own personal situation with the national one. After only a few years of marriage to a wealthy, kind, adoring but—in her perception—undynamic man, she had had her head turned by someone she continued to call "the cleverest, most balanced and most honest of English politicians."[12]

It was without undue emotion that she wrote, "Of course I fell in love with him, and decided to throw in my lot with him."[13] She was twenty-two, and Mosley was more than a dozen years older, to say nothing of being the most notorious womaniser in London. The position of mistress to such an eligible (if decidedly married) figure was one fraught with reputational peril but also with sexual and social opportunity. Diana relished the opportunity to encounter Mosley at balls and parties, where their array of mutual friends meant that there could be no hint of scandal, but also arranged numerous clandestine trysts with him at his pied-à-terre on Ebury Street. She even gave him the pet name of "Kit," perhaps to avoid confusing

* Followers of the Conservative leader Stanley Baldwin who was, as we shall see, another Eaton Square resident.
** Admirers of the Labour leader Ramsay MacDonald, who did *not* live in Eaton Square.

him with her brother, Tom. As Diana later wrote, "I had to think of a name for Mosley and called him Kit—why, I have completely forgotten, but so he was known by my Guinness sons, and all young people, and our French friends."[14]

They also took their affair in international directions. Not long after the Cheyne Walk party, Diana and Guinness arrived at the Venice Lido to find Mosley and Cimmie, amongst others, in situ. The presence of the clandestine lovers was no accident, and Guinness and Cimmie were neither stupid nor unobservant. Diana and Mosley, like countless adulterous couples before and since, took an almost perverse delight in carrying on their affair in plain sight, barely bothering to make excuses.

At times, this turned into literal bedroom farce. One of those present was the politician—and future Eaton Square resident—Robert Boothby, who would later become notorious in his own right but then was simply an aspirant backbencher. He was used to facilitating the whims of the powerful—he had served as private secretary to Winston Churchill between 1926 and 1929—but even he may have been surprised to be told by Mosley one night, "Bob, I shall need your room tonight between midnight and 4 a.m." Boothby, assuming that his friend was joking, replied, "But, Tom, where shall I sleep?" That his sexual shenanigans might inconvenience others had clearly not occurred to Mosley, who said, shortly, "On the beach."[15] As Boothby discovered, Mosley was not joking, and the politician spent an uncomfortable few hours on a Lido recliner as rather more passionate events took place in his bedroom.

After Venice, it was impossible for Guinness and Cimmie to keep up even the bare pretence that their spouses were not adulterously entangled with each other. It was also clear that Mosley's interest in fascism was not a passing fad but a committed, reckless abandonment of the existing order in favour of something that he perceived as greater and more lasting. He wrote in a self-serving pamphlet, *The Greater Britain*, that "better the great adventure, better the great attempt for England's sake, better defeat, disaster, better far the end of that trivial thing called a political career than stifling in a uniform of blue and gold, strutting and posturing on the stage of little England amid the scenery of decadence until history." He concluded "We shall win."[16]

Mosley may have been referring to his country, but the parallels with his now open relationship with Diana were impossible not to see. By the time *The Greater Britain* was published in October 1932, he was not only the leader of the British Union of Fascists, which held a triumphant inaugural rally at Trafalgar Square on 15 October, but it was clear that he had lost all interest in his marriage. Although he attempted to manipulate the situation to his advantage, informing Cimmie that they could have "such a lovely life together if his little frolicsome ways did not upset her," it was clear that Diana was a grand passion, not a fling.

Cimmie wrote to him in despair to say, "the feeling you are not telling me, that you do things behind my back, that you are only sweet to me when you want to get away with something, gives me such a feeling of insecurity and anxiety and worry . . . I am more nervy and upset than I ought or need to be." Hideously, she continued to be in love with her husband, despite everything—"Oh darling darling don't let it be like that. I will truly understand if you give me a chance, but I am so kept in the dark"—but this was compromised by the certain knowledge of what was taking place. "That bloody damnable cursed Ebury—how often does she come there?"[17]

With Diana, it was a similar, if less heart-wrenching, story. It was now clear to her and Bryan's friends that the two were destined to part; the time for dignified adultery had long since passed. The author Rosamond Lehmann wrote of how, at one ball they gave at Cheyne Walk, "[Diana and Mosley] looked as though they were magnetized together, she always laughing with her mouth wide open," and how "Bryan was simply totally silent, he danced with me a great deal but never spoke a word. It was the most awful evening. Tom in triumph with this dazzling beauty and Bryan, the host, looking like a shattered white rabbit." She did not find it hard to summarise the experience of a party where the fine food and wine seemed to turn into ash and sulphur for the appalled guests: "Dreadful."[18]

In November 1932, Diana had decided that there was no future for her and Guinness. Mosley was relieved at the prospect of being able to conduct their dalliance without secrecy, although he continued to make clear that he would not leave his wife, and a besotted Diana agreed. At the end of the month, she informed her husband that their marriage was over, and said simply, "I think the only thing is for us to part."[19] The news could not have come as a remote surprise to Guinness, but nonetheless Diana's decision to end the union was a seismic step. The only concession that he wrung from her was not to leave until after Christmas, presumably in an attempt to give the children as normal a festive experience as they could.

Her sister Nancy, who had been apprised of her decision, wrote to her in horror on 27 November from Swinbrook to say, "Mitty [Tom] and I spent the whole of yesterday afternoon discussing your affairs & are having another session in a minute! He is horrified, & says that your social position will be *nil* if you do this." Nancy was compassionate—"whatever happens *I* shall always be on your side as you know & so will anybody who cares for you & perhaps the rest really don't matter"—but also clear-sighted. "Darling I do hope you are making a right decision. You are SO young to begin getting in wrong with the world, if that's what is going to happen."[20]

A couple of days later, Nancy gloomily informed Diana that "Muv & Farve & Tom, Randolph [Churchill], Doris [Castelrosse], Aunt Iris, John [Sutro], Lord Moyne & in fact everybody that you know will band together and somehow stop it. . . . I believe you have a much worse time in store for you than you imagine."[21]

Diana did not care. "I never thought of it as risky, or a great gamble," she said, although she admitted "though all my friends did" and that "although I was convinced of the permanency of what I had decided to do, other people gave it a year at most."[22] The divorce settlement that she discussed with Guinness was trifling—a comparatively paltry £2,000 a year—and, as Nancy told her, "Mitty says £2,000 a year will seem tiny to you & he will urge Farve, as your trustee, to hold out for more."[23]

Yet her errant sister made light of the whole affair. She wrote to Nancy in late November to compliment her on her new book, *Christmas Pudding* ("I read a lot of it to the Leader and we laughed so much we couldn't go on reading") and suggested disingenuously that the separation was an amicable one. "Bryan has now arrived and is in a state of airy bliss and longing for me to start work on his flat. He is in a magnanimous mood. . . . He says I can have the pick of Cheyne Walk furniture and in return I am giving him two or three pictures." She concluded, in what was either self-delusion or a wilful attempt to put a brave face on matters, "The future appears to me to be roseate specially now he is so gay and bright."[24]

This was untrue. Guinness was plunged into a well of loneliness at the prospect of separating from his adored wife, and refused to deal with the inevitable disposal of Cheyne Walk and its contents, leaving Diana to sort matters out. And her father, Lord Redesdale, never a man to be underestimated, knew that he now had to get involved, when he returned home from a lengthy cruise and found his daughter on the verge of a scandalous separation. He and Bryan Guinness's father paid a grim visit by appointment to Mosley at Ebury Street—when asked what he would do by Randolph Churchill, the Leader replied, "wear a balls protector, I suppose"—and, in Nancy's inevitably coloured account, "[Lord Moyne] and Farve went to see [Mosley] (who was dead white and armed with knuckle dusters). They said to him 'Are you prepared to give Diana up now?' 'No.' 'Then,' said Lord M, 'we shall put detectives on you.'"[25]

Diana's wish to obtain a divorce was compromised by her refusal to state publicly that she was the guilty party. Under normal circumstances, the husband would stage an adulterous scene in a hotel that would then be captured by an acquiescent photographer and used in evidence in court, thereby sparing his wife's dignity. However, not only did Guinness refuse to do this, but his father was roused to yet greater ire by the "extraordinary character" that was Lord Redesdale when he remarked, "I suppose you know that my daughter is laying in a store of furs and diamonds against the time when she is divorced." This had been said by Unity—"half out of mischief and half as a joke"—but it turned Lord Moyne into "a fearful rage with Diana whom he was on good terms with before."[26]

The reality was that the greatest extravagance that she wished to obtain from Guinness was a pair of sturdy country shoes, but it no longer mattered. In one of the final letters that Diana sent from Cheyne Walk, she wrote to Nancy on Christmas Day 1932 to sneer at the private detectives Lord Moyne had engaged at huge expense to uncover proof of her adultery with Mosley ("It is rather heavenly to feel that they are around—no pickpockets can approach etc"), and said of her soon-to-be ex-father-in-law "may he burn in hell." She called Nancy her sole ally, but acknowledged "it is vastly lying to suggest you encouraged my sot;* you *always* said it would end in TEARS." She ended by writing, "I am not hurrying to leave because if Bryan leaves *ME* the onus is on *HIM* and so he will."[27]

In the event, the separation was handled swiftly and relatively painlessly. Guinness left London for Switzerland over Christmas and New Year—ironically enough with Diana's parents—and so her departure from the family home for the Eatonry could be accomplished without unnecessary tears or emotional outbursts. Diana would later write in her memoirs, with commendably cool understatement, "Bryan and I were divorced.** We were the recipients of a great deal of advice from friends and relations, but our minds were made up. . . . Advice is given by the unworldly. Perhaps worldly people know from experience that it is never taken."[28] She now embarked upon the Eaton Square phase of her life, and could only hope

* A Mitford term for "foolish behaviour."

** Guinness is dismissed with remarkable nonchalance in Diana's memoir, *A Life of Contrasts*. "Bryan soon married again; a Scotch girl [Elisabeth Nelson, a scion of the Nelson publishing dynasty] who, like me, was one of a big country family. They had many children [nine] and lived happily ever after."

that it was more successful and less controversial than the events that had precipitated it.

> I took a small house at the eastern end of Eaton Square. Nanny was rather pleased because it was within easy reach of the park and the other nannies; she had never cared for Cheyne Walk. Nancy was also quite pleased; she had her room at Eaton Square and we saw more of one another than formerly. Everyone else was cross, predicting disasters. None of my friends approved. However, having delivered a few lectures they soon settled down, and Eaton Square was full of the old familiar faces.[29]

Diana's memoir *A Life of Contrasts* cannot be accused of excessive muckraking when it comes to her past. Given quite how eventful this past was, by the time that she was writing her autobiography in 1977, she can hardly be blamed for choosing to present some events in reasonably terse fashion. However, even by her standards, this paragraph was remarkably coy and verged on the disingenuous. Not only was Diana now openly living as a married man's mistress, but she was also expecting to be sued for divorce by her now estranged husband, which would become scandalous and embarrassing for the family. Although Nancy, who was recovering from the heartbreak of a failed relationship, was a welcome house guest, subsequently claiming that "I'm having a perfectly divine time, it is certainly more fun not being engaged,"[30] everything else verged on the disastrous.

Diana may have hoped that, by presenting London society with her new relationship, it would come to be regarded as a fait accompli. This was not the case. As Cimmie's sister Irene, Baroness Ravensdale, wrote, dispensing with punctuation in her fury, "My heart was in my boots over the hell incarnate beloved Cim is going through over Diana Guinness bitching her life wanting to bolt with Tom and marry him and the whole of London getting at me and Baba with the story he had gone with her and needless to say every Redesdale up in arms and Walter Guinness only wanting to 'crash' him and this blithering cow-faced fool insanely dithering recklessly trying to ruin Cim's life for her 19-year-old crush on that vain insensate ass Tom."[31]

This rush of telegraphese did not obscure Irene's justifiable sense of hurt and betrayal at Diana's selfish and cold actions. Yet Mosley, judged by any standard, was behaving as badly as his new mistress, if not worse. If Diana had thrown in her lot with him out of love, her paramour seemed determined not so much to have his cake and eat it, but to turn the leftovers into trifle and wolf that down, too. At one point, he deputed the long-suffering Boothby to visit Cimmie in order to console her, remarking that she was in a bad way because Oswald had decided to make a clean breast of his affairs and tell her about all the women he had slept with during their marriage.* "*All* of them?" a justifiably aghast Boothby asked. "Well," Mosley mused, "all except her stepmother and her sister."[32]

Diana entered into her relationship with Mosley in the insecure knowledge that attempting to turn him into a faithful consort was about as likely as her father becoming a left-wing newspaper's literary editor. However, Mosley offered little concession to the sacrifice that she had made for him, continuing to lead a lifestyle like a more than usually right-wing Restoration rake. One appointment diary, for 6 January 1933, suggests that he lunched with his wife, had a late afternoon rendezvous with Cimmie's sister Baba [Alexandra Metcalfe], and dined with Diana in the evening. Some of these meetings may have been platonic, but it added to the sense of unease that everyone around Diana and Mosley felt. It remained unclear where he saw his deepest and most important allegiance as lying: Diana, Cimmie, or the BUF.

Diana's family remained convinced that the affair was doomed. She, however, decided not to care, shrugging, in response to her

* Cimmie, understandably, complained that "They are all my best friends!" The bonds of amity, however, could not withstand Mosley's irresistible sexual drive.

father's furious bellow, "That man will just cast you aside!" with "If he does, that's too bad." With the exception of the ever-loyal Nancy, most of her friends had privately sided with the wronged parties of Guinness and Cimmie, but Diana held the belief that Mosley was not just a successful and impressive lover but one of history's Great Men.

She later observed, "It was this which gave me the courage to survive ostracism, the anger of my parents (who did not allow [Deborah] or [Unity] to come and see me), the disapproval of absolutely everyone—the fonder they were of me, the more they disapproved."[33] She claimed to be unaware of the misery that Cimmie was undergoing, either perhaps because she was genuinely ignorant, or, more likely, she was so swept up in her own passion for Mosley that she regarded his spurned wife as mere collateral baggage in the grand affair.

Guinness was reduced to asking his former wife not to be seen in public with her lover. ("I cannot consent to your associating with Mosley, either at Cheyne Walk or anywhere else . . . I do not mean that I shall send a policeman to fling him out but I cannot in any way condone your meeting him.")[34] It was he who had to deal with the tedious admin that is occasioned by any separation—shutting up the house he had shared with his wife; allowing the Biddesden cook to go to Eaton Square with Diana; and, worst of all, having to deal with society knowing that he was the highest-profile cuckold in London.

He sent Diana a desperate, heartfelt appeal to return to him on 5 February, asking, "Don't you find that I am the one you will miss most?" and noted of Mosley, "his weakness may lie in his power and his charm, which enable him to do without you." Unfortunately, by the time that Guinness was writing "I have this strong feeling that we both belong to one another, that we are bound by our mutually broken virginity,"[35] he must have realised that he was only succeeding in destroying what remained of his dignity. Diana continued to reside in the Eatonry, Mosley enjoyed his simultaneous supremacy over the BUF and his romantic attachments alike, and Guinness was driven to remark to Nancy, "I am determined to control dismal associations as far as I can."[36] There was little else he could do.

When Diana moved to Eaton Square, it was with the expectation of remaining a mistress rather than becoming a wife. As she later wrote, "For me there was no question of marriage, for M. was married already. I looked forward to a long life alone, seeing my beloved M. when he could spare time from his all-absorbing political work and the family to which he was devoted."[37] In any case, for all of her dedication to Mosley, it was Cimmie who he took with him on a trip to Italy in April for the International Fascist Exhibition, where he was hosted by Mussolini. The event reaffirmed his dedication to fascism, which he pronounced "the greatest creed that Western civilisation has ever given to the world" in the BUF newspaper *Blackshirt*. Yet a few weeks later, a deus ex machina occurred that provided a solution of sorts to his increasingly tortuous domestic entanglements.

After their return from Italy, Cimmie's health declined, and she complained about feeling "all in with sickness and crashing back and tummy ache." She had suffered from a congenital curvature of the spine, and had been feeling more than usually unwell, not least through the stress of essentially sharing her husband with another woman. However, her final decline was heralded by an attack of appendicitis, which developed into peritonitis. On 16 May, at the age of thirty-four, Cimmie died, leaving Mosley free to marry again.

He informed Diana of his wife's death within moments of its taking place. When they next met at the Eatonry, Mosley made it clear to her that, for a decent interval of mourning, they would have to stay apart. She was devastated, both by the event itself and the consequences, calling it "a harbinger of unhappiness." Cimmie's family believed—and continued to believe—that Diana was the direct cause of Cimmie's death, with the stress and misery of having to observe Diana's affair with Mosley leading to an irreversible decline in her health.

When Diana was not pining for her lover or dodging the

brickbats of outraged society members, she took pleasure in her new life at 2 Eaton Square. She called it "a comfortable, sunny little house looking down the length of the square gardens." Although she could only entertain half a dozen at a time in her small dining room ("three a side on red velvet banquettes"), she soon found that the same members of London society who had gossiped so furiously about her wickedness were equally willing to dine with her.

One of these visitors, brought by John Betjeman, was none other than Oscar Wilde's now-aged lover Lord Alfred Douglas—a remnant of the rival court of Tite Street—whom Diana detested. "We tried hard to like him, but we failed. We tried, because he had been ostracized for so many years; we failed, because he was a self-centred bore. All traces of the beauty which had so entranced Oscar Wilde were vanished. Lord Alfred, prompted by us, spoke freely about Wilde, whom he called 'O. W.', but he had nothing of interest to tell; it was a well-worn twice-told tale." Betjeman, typically, "looked upon him as an ancient, though minor, Victorian monument,"[38] a Gothic Revival gargoyle come to life.

Other Eaton Square characters offered distraction from Mosley and fascism, as well as light relief. There was Gladys, Duchess of Marlborough, who was a frequent visitor to the house and who was married to a man whom she despised, and dismissively referred to as "Little Ogpu." She was "the victim of an early and disastrous attempt at facelifting," with a face that "looked like a collapsed balloon," and who eventually went mad. Another neighbour was the industrialist, and former prime minister, Stanley Baldwin, whom she loathed. Diana later wrote of him that "the waste of the talents of gifted, inventive and hard-working people under leaders like MacDonald and Baldwin made one almost as angry as did their surely unnecessary privations."[39] It was, from her perspective, inevitably time for wide-reaching political change, and this could only come courtesy Mosley and the BUF.

The relationship between Mosley and Diana remained becalmed throughout 1933. She obtained a relatively scandal-free divorce from Guinness in June, although—as Edward VIII and Wallis Simpson would discover a few years later—Guinness's gentlemanly decision to fake evidence of his adultery and thereby take responsibility for the separation was haunted by the knowledge that the King's Proctor, who oversaw all divorce cases, could step in and nullify the decree nisi agreement if there was any evidence of collusion or the petitioner committing adultery themselves. Although in practice this seldom happened, high-profile and indiscreet extra-marital relationships were unusually susceptible to investigation, and it was no wonder that Diana suggested, "The King's Proctor haunted us all."[40]

Diana was angered by Mosley's flippancy when it came to her divorce—he suavely asked, "Have you jumped your little hurdle yet?" which led to a cataclysmic row between the two*—and in any case his ongoing relationship with Baba Metcalfe made it hideously clear that he was not prepared to change. Although he persuaded a reluctant Diana that Baba served as a beard during the six months between the decree nisi and its granting at the end of the year, the continued affair—conducted, it must be remembered, with his late wife's sister—was an inevitable source of misery to Diana, as well as a reminder who her lover was. Perhaps out of guilt, she took relatively little from Guinness in the eventual divorce settlement, accepting the already reduced annual settlement of £2,500 (around £230,000 today) and retaining only the items of jewellery that she had been given during their three-year marriage.

Despite her inevitable ructions and disagreements on a personal level with Mosley, Diana was as committed to the "noble cause" of fascism as she had ever been. Her nineteen-year-old sister, Unity, shared her fascination with both Mosley and the BUF, and the two visited Germany in September 1933. They attended the Nuremberg Rally, which Hitler intended to showcase his election as Chancellor at the end of January earlier that year and his consequent seizure of total power over the country. Diana's horrified father called the Nazis

* Diana denied this, claiming the story had been invented by a jealous Irene Curzon.

"a murderous gang of pests" and lamented "that you should associate yourself with such people is a source of utter misery to us."[41]

However, several of their daughters—including, briefly, Nancy—were in thrall to fascist ideas, loudly applauding at BUF meetings and proudly sporting the organisation's obligatory outfit of black shirts. Mosley's good standing with politicians and newspapermen alike saw the organisation attract some high-profile endorsements. To its subsequent cost, Lord Rothermere's *Daily Mail* published a signed editorial by its proprietor, headlined "Hurrah for the Blackshirts," on 15 January 1934, which defined fascism not as an undesirable foreign import but as "the organised effort of the younger generation to break the stranglehold which senile politicians have so long maintained on our public affairs."[42] A week later, Rothermere went even further, announcing, "The hysterical abuse and misrepresentation at present being poured out on the British Blackshirt movement have had their counterpart at each successive stage of our constitutional progress" and that it was the patriotic duty of the young to stand up for fascism. He declared, "I appeal to them not just to stand idly by but to take a share in this great task by giving the Blackshirts a helping hand."[43]

The year 1934 also represented a renewal of the relationship between Diana and Mosley, which had suffered under various pressures and woes the previous year. Now divorced and bereaved, respectively, they could at least associate on legal, if hardly respectable, terms, and they spent a clandestine period together in Provence as he recovered from an attack of deep vein thrombosis. Diana would not, at Mosley's behest, take active part in the BUF, but she thrilled to the set piece events that he would address.

A bout of stomach flu, however, kept her away from the largest and best attended, which took place at the Olympia exhibition centre in Kensington on 7 June and saw an audience of twelve thousand come out to see Mosley speak, as well as an opposing faction participate in anti-fascist protests against "thuggery, buggery, hunger and war."

As Nancy abandoned her flirtation with the BUF, horrified by the violence, so, too, did the *Daily Mail* and Rothermere. The proprietor made it clear to Mosley on 14 July that "I have never thought that a movement calling itself 'fascist' could be successful in this country and I have also made it quite clear in my conversations with you that I could never support any movement with an anti-semitic bias, any movement which had dictatorship as one of its objectives, or any movement which will substitute a 'Corporate State' for the Parliamentary institutions of this country."[44]

In retrospect, it is easy to see that the BUF peaked half a decade before war broke out, and that, for all Mosley's undisputed charisma and powers of oratory—he aimed to seduce every audience member as consummately as he did the women he bedded—he would never be able to enjoy the support of a major newspaper or its owner. He was friends with Lord Beaverbrook, publisher of the *Daily Express*, but Beaverbrook, who had given Mosley platforms in his newspapers to expound his political views when he was still a Labour MP, was fearful of the politician's independent-minded and unaccountable impulses. The magnate therefore shied away from offering either explicit or implicit support to Mosley, just as he had refused to back the short-lived New Party.

All the same, it was through Unity, rather than her lover, that Diana made the acquaintance of Hitler. She found him impressive and amusing, praising his wit—"he did imitations of marvellous drollery which showed how acutely observant he was"[45]—and his good manners, which she recorded in great detail in her memoirs as a corrective to the received wisdom that the Führer was a power-mad dictator. She spent a considerable amount of time in Germany in the autumn of 1934, living in Munich and enjoying the contrast of life there to her existence in Eaton Square. Unity formed a closer friendship with Hitler, who may not have had Mosley's looks or sexual vitality but possessed a similar degree of magnetic charm, which had its own aphrodisiac effect. Rumours persisted—as they do to this day, not quashed by the release of Unity's diaries in January 2025—that she and Hitler had a love affair, but theirs was no Diana–Mosley embrace of mutual longing. The Führer, after all, loved one person above all others, himself.

When Mosley first witnessed Hitler in April 1935, he called him "quite a man," and remarked, "he seemed to me to be a calm, cool customer, certainly ruthless, but in no way neurotic."[46] Even as Unity became more and more extreme in her adulation for Hitler and consequent antisemitism—"Hitler is so kind and so divine I suddenly thought that I would not only like to kill all who say things against him but also torture them . . . I want everyone to know I am a Jew hater"[47]—Diana found herself torn between her intrinsic dislike for such extreme statements and the knowledge that the new order that Mosley represented was one in which she had chosen to participate wholeheartedly.

When Nancy satirised British fascism and Mosley ("Captain Jack") in her 1935 novel *Wigs on the Green* it led to a froideur between her and Diana for years. Even as Nancy unbelievably claimed, "I still maintain that it is far more in favour of Fascism than otherwise,"[48] Diana correctly believed that her ever-observant sister had used her privileged position at Eaton Square and elsewhere, to view the vicissitudes of the movement that she and Mosley so vigorously espoused and to present it in a comical, rather than approving, light. Nancy called what she had done "Leaderteasing," and Mosley's responses to her satire went unrecorded, but the writer knew that she had transgressed. She wrote to Unity in June 1935, "I'm going to Oxford with [Diana] tomorrow, our last day together I suppose before the clouds of her displeasure burst over me." The letter concluded, understandably enough, "OH DEAR!"[49]

However, before Diana could direct her anger towards Nancy, a series of events occurred that would alter her life and eventually lead to her departure from the Eatonry. The first of these was an unpleasant car crash in July 1935 just outside Eaton Square, in which her self-consciously chic vehicle, a Voisin, was bashed into by a Rolls-Royce. Diana overheard two passers-by say, of the mayhem, "Don't look, it's too horrible," and later wrote "This struck me as comic; I was an 'accident,' too horrible to look at, drenched in blood."[50]

Somewhat unbelievably, Guinness and his father came to her rescue, hiring the country's best plastic surgeon, Sir Harold Gillies, to operate on her, and by dint of strict instructions—"he told me not to talk or laugh more than I was obliged"[51]—she was left without any visible scarring, her legendary beauty intact. That her ex-husband, rather than current beau, was responsible for her deliverance was merely regarded by Diana as a fitting testament to her continued charms.*

Mosley was in Italy when the accident took place, and sent Diana a letter that mixed charm with self-absorption. He wrote to her that she should "Hurry up and get well as this place is lovely . . . I feel so badly being away while you are bad."[52] It had the desired effect, and Diana soon discharged herself from hospital to be with her lover. It was either during this Italian holiday or shortly beforehand that she discovered she was pregnant with Mosley's baby. She was immediately torn between her desire to keep the child—not least because she imagined that he would be more invested in their relationship if there was tangible proof of it—and the knowledge that it would be a significant scandal at a time that her family could have done without further calumny. She therefore had an abortion, a risky and unlicensed procedure, and, after a tempestuous, largely unenjoyable 1935, took a considered look at her life.

Diana later wrote, "As regards my personal position, I loved Kit but never considered marrying him. Marriage as such meant little to me; yet three years after his wife's death we did marry, because we wanted children, and in those days it was supposed to be better for children to be born in wedlock."[53] As she described it, 1936 "was a watershed year for Kit and I."[54] For reasons of propriety on both of their parts, matrimony seemed the correct solution, which would

* Guinness continued to write beseeching letters to Diana, begging her to return to him. They were ignored.

also necessitate space for an early, aristocratic version of a blended family. Diana had her two sons, Mosley three of his own children, and they leased a country house, Wootton Lodge in Staffordshire, that would be suitable for the seven of them.

A strange mixed existence now ensued. In the country, Diana led a happy life not very far from her upbringing at Swinbrook. Her diary was full of remarks like, "Perfect day with Kit," but it was also put into relief by Mosley's responsibilities towards the BUF, which he was now funding himself. The violence that had taken place at Olympia had turned the organisation from a near-mainstream concern into a fringe one, and wealthy supporters had been scared away. It was therefore inevitable that Diana and Mosley would spend an increasing amount of time in Germany, attempting to raise funds for their endeavours directly or indirectly. Diana had the innovative idea of setting up a Germany-based radio station that would broadcast to Britain, as a commercial enterprise, and play the popular songs of the day that the BBC refused to acknowledge or broadcast.

It came to nothing, but meant that they both became intimate members of the inner circle of the Nazi party, along with Unity. The strikingly beautiful, blond sisters were venerated in Germany; and Diana became particularly close to Hitler's powerful propaganda minister, Joseph Goebbels, and his wife, Magda. It was to Frau Goebbels that Diana confided the difficulty that she and Mosley had in finding a suitable location for their planned wedding, which they wanted to conduct discreetly and without publicity. Paris was initially mooted, but it became impossible because the details of the marriage would be posted outside the consulate. As Diana later wrote, "it was no better than a London registry office as far as journalists were concerned."[55]

Magda then made a suggestion that appeared altruistic but in fact bore the fingerprint of her husband. Given the difficulties that Mosley and Diana faced in Britain and France, why not have the wedding at the Goebbelses' home in Berlin? A reciprocal arrangement then existed that allowed British subjects to be married by a German registrar; and, as long as the British consul was informed, any further news of the union could be kept private. The couple agreed, and, on 6 October 1936, they were married, with none other than Hitler as guest of honour.* It was a small, rather desultory wedding for a couple with such a high public profile, and the presence of Mosley's friend Bill Allen, who was an undercover agent for MI5, ensured that the British government would soon come to know what had happened. The company then celebrated by watching Hitler address a crowd of twenty thousand at the nearby Sportsplatz, after which Mosley and Diana ended their wedding day by having an argument in the luxurious Hotel Kaiserhof. The following day, they returned to Wootton.

Somewhat surprisingly, Mosley and Diana's marriage lasted to his death in 1980. She outlived him by twenty-three years and never remarried. Their union weathered his imprisonment during World War II and public disgrace, Mosley's failed attempts to launch new political parties, and Diana's later career as a publisher and memoirist. She remained unwaveringly loyal to her late husband, who had continued to have love affairs throughout their marriage, and Diana was regarded with a mixture of admiration and distaste by latter-day literary London. They simultaneously lionised her beauty and elegance and damned her unrepentant adherence to fascism. She never returned to the Eatonry, which became yet another part of the Mitford legend, one of the near-countless glamorous houses and apartments that still trade off their vicarious associations with this famous, frustrating family.

Had she done so shortly after her marriage, however, she may have encountered a new neighbour who shared several of her views.

* His gift to the happy couple was a signed photograph of himself in a silver frame embossed with an eagle.

6

Neville Chamberlain, Stanley Baldwin, Lord Halifax, Joachim von Ribbentrop, and Bendor Grosvenor: 37, 86, and 93 Eaton Square

"A tough time in London"

When I was writing my 2020 account of the 1936 abdication crisis, *The Crown in Crisis*, one of the difficulties that I faced was a superabundance of interesting characters to write about. My focus had to be naturally on the not quite star-crossed lovers, Edward VIII and Wallis Simpson, whose all-consuming (on his part, at least) relationship led to a constitutional crisis and the first voluntary royal abdication. However, there were many fascinating characters lurking on the periphery, many of whom deserved their own books. There was the indefatigable lawyer Walter Monckton, the society wit Diana Cooper, and the perpetually disapproving royal private secretary Alec Hardinge. And, most gloriously of all, there was Joachim von Ribbentrop: former champagne salesman turned German ambassador to Britain, close confidant of Hitler, and an arrogant buffoon.

Any writer has to kill their darlings, and I reluctantly forewent page after page of detail about Ribbentrop's antics in London on the grounds both of irrelevance and narrative expediency. Ribbentrop was friends with both Edward and Wallis, which justified his inclusion, but he was also fascinatingly, hilariously awful, the worst possible choice for a sensitive diplomatic position and subject to the contempt of both the British and the Nazis alike.

Edward's official biographer, Philip Ziegler, described him in an *Evening Standard* review of Michael Bloch's 1992 life of Ribbentrop as "spiritually barren, intellectually negligible, yet never quite a monster," which is broadly fair: He was too stupid and too shortsighted to sink into the true depths of monstrosity which most of those around him plumbed. Instead, Ribbentrop was a figure worthy of W. S. Gilbert's satire, who inadvertently found himself, when he arrived at his London home of 37 Eaton Square on 26 October 1936, at the centre of several different power struggles. Hitler's parting words to him, when he was dispatched to London, were: "Ribbentrop, bring me the English alliance."[1] He was utterly inadequate to such a task; the new ambassador was barely capable of tying his own shoelaces. Yet he had built his considerable power and prestige by flattering Hitler and telling the Führer precisely what he wanted to hear, and so he was the wrong man in the right place.

When Ribbentrop established himself in Eaton Square, he may or may not have been briefed that, by 1936, it was home to three of the most significant Conservative politicians in the country. Stanley Baldwin, who was then serving as prime minister for the third and final occasion, lived at number 93. His rival and eventual successor Neville Chamberlain was the usual inhabitant of 37, but he leased his house out when he did not need to use it. Meanwhile, Lord Halifax, leader of the House of Lords and Lord Privy Seal, resided between the two, at 86 Eaton Square.

It would have been a pleasing image if the three powerful men had all been on jocular terms together, regularly popping round to each other's palatial residences for cups of tea and light-hearted badinage about the state of the country. Unfortunately, power has a habit of turning even potential friendships into rivalries; and the tensions among the three ambitious, successful politicians—two of whom became prime minister, and the other who wished to do so—meant that, by the time that the new German ambassador made himself known in and around London, there was already a powder keg of ambition in this particular corner of SW1, primed and ready to explode.

None of the three were young. When Ribbentrop moved into 37 Eaton Square, Baldwin was sixty-nine; Chamberlain sixty-seven; and Halifax, the junior of the trio, was a mere fifty-five. All of them had already had long, distinguished careers in politics. Baldwin had entered the Commons in 1908, Halifax in 1910—where he remained until he was elevated into the Lords in 1925, prior to becoming viceroy of India—and Chamberlain in 1918. Collectively, they had served through the premierships of Herbert Asquith, David Lloyd George, Andrew Bonar Law, and James Ramsay MacDonald (twice), and brought an invaluable amount of collected experience into both the Commons and the Lords.

It was an oddity of Baldwin's political career that he first served under Chamberlain's half-brother, Austen, who might realistically have expected to become prime minister himself. He served as leader of the Conservatives between 1921 and 1922 but ceded power to Law, who was then himself succeeded by Baldwin as prime minister, an office that he served in briefly from 22 May 1923 to 22 January 1924, and then more significantly from 4 November 1924 to 4 June 1929. Baldwin had a good opinion of Austen Chamberlain, writing to his mother: "I anticipate that [he] will be my new chief, an appointment that will meet with a good deal of criticism."[2] He was right on both counts.

The brothers Chamberlain were both in Parliament together for a considerable period, and it was the ill fortune of Austen to be in thrall to Baldwin, a man who he regarded as his junior, even his subordinate. Austen therefore adopted an almost self-consciously Victorian form of dress, wearing a monocle, top hat, and frock coat in the Commons well into the thirties, even as he seethed at the way in which he had been unable to take the highest office in the country. When he was offered the post of ambassador to Washington by Baldwin rather than the role of Chancellor of the Exchequer that he expected, he refused angrily, writing to Neville to say, "The discourtesy shown to me, down to the last detail . . . was not expected and I profoundly resent it."[3]

Baldwin may have been able to wield power in any fashion that he pleased, but even he realised that becoming prime minister was not simply, in Shakespeare's words, "an honour snatched with boisterous hand" but a serious, life-changing responsibility. When he left Eaton Square for Downing Street, it was with an air of reluctance. He wrote to his mother to say, "I am not a bit excited and don't realise it in the least," although he was more equivocal when he shared his thoughts with his friend and neighbour Phyllis Broome. "Here is the biggest job in the world and if I fail I share the fate of many a bigger man than I. But it's a fine thought, isn't it? And one may do something before one cracks up."[4]

It is debatable as to whether Baldwin did, in the event, crack up, but if there was a single man who may have served as his nemesis, it was Neville Chamberlain, who became Chancellor in his first, short-lived administration. After it fell apart, succeeded by an even shorter-lived MacDonald-led minority Labour government, Chamberlain did not turn against Baldwin but instead supported him, although with a careful eye on his own position should the leader topple. In any case, Baldwin was briefly glad to be relieved of office, saying, "I have not felt so well for a long time" before the imminent collapse of his government on 21 January 1924, both in the anticipation of a rest and the likely end of the precarious MacDonald tenure.

The latter duly came on 29 October 1924, and Baldwin returned triumphantly to power with a landslide majority of 209, apparently making his position impregnable. Yet Chamberlain had seen this happen repeatedly before; it was the third general election in less than two years, demonstrating the instability that the country found itself in. He wrote to his sister Ida on 1 November to say, "What alarms me now is the size of our majority, which is most dangerous . . . Unless we leave our mark as Social Reformers the country will take it out of us hereafter, but what we do will depend on how the Cabinet is made up." He ended by saying, without the sympathy that the words suggested, "Poor S.B!"[5]

Rather than return to the chancellorship, Chamberlain took on the safer, less high-profile position of minister of health, and watched Baldwin appoint Winston Churchill to the role instead: an inevitably controversial move, as Churchill had served as a Liberal for two decades beforehand. In any case, Baldwin's government was not a success; and although it lasted a full term, it was narrowly defeated by a resurgent MacDonald and his National Labour government, which held office between June 1929 and June 1935.

At this point, Chamberlain may have been expected to act against Baldwin and secure the leadership of the party himself, but he continued to wait, mindful of the old adage: "He who wields the knife never wears the crown." He was, however, prepared to be far more openly critical of Baldwin's perceived shortcomings when the party was in opposition, writing to his sister Hilda in October 1929: "I told [Baldwin] of the criticisms that were reaching me from all quarters about his want of leadership and told him that he must give a lead and be a bit more aggressive if the Party was to be held together. . . . It is all very depressing and particularly embarrassing for me because everyone I meet tells me of S.B.'s failings and many suggest that I should do better in his place."[6]

Having thus stated his credentials, Chamberlain rubbished the idea—"Heaven knows I don't want the job. It is a thankless one at any time and never more so than now when the Party is all to pieces"—and claimed amity with his leader, writing, "Moreover S.B. is my friend as well as my leader and I would not on any account play [Lloyd George] to his Asquith."* This was disingenuous. His and Austen's father, Joseph Chamberlain, was mayor of Birmingham and arguably the most powerful and influential political figure of the twentieth century never to become prime minister. Even Churchill

* Lloyd George forced the collapse of his fellow Liberal Asquith's government in 1916 by insisting that the premier hand over administration to a War Cabinet, or alternatively threatening to resign himself.

acknowledged that Joseph was "the man who made the weather." After he died of a stroke in 1914, he left a legacy for his sons not only to continue but to take to its logical conclusion. Austen had served successfully as foreign secretary in Baldwin's administration, and now returned to being a backbencher. If anyone would become the first Chamberlain to enter Number 10, it would be Neville.

Baldwin, meanwhile, was surprised to have been ejected from office, and indeed had failed to make preparations to return to Eaton Square, which he had leased out while he was in Downing Street. After moving into temporary lodgings in Upper Brook Street, he found himself under consistent attack from the two most powerful newspaper barons of the day, Lords Rothermere and Beaverbrook. They both regarded Baldwin's continuing to lead the Conservative party as an affront to normal standards of political life—not least because neither regarded him as a sufficiently biddable figure—and so he was criticised on a near-daily basis in the editorials of both major papers.

At last, after being accused of running "an insolvent plutocracy," he struck back. He gave a speech on 12 March 1931 in which he railed against his tormentors, saying, "The papers conducted by Lord Rothermere and Lord Beaverbrook are not newspapers in the ordinary acceptance of the term. They are engines of propaganda for the constantly changing policies, desires, personal wishes, personal likes and dislikes of two men. What are their methods? Their methods are direct falsehood, misrepresentation, half-truths, the alteration of the speaker's meaning by publishing a sentence apart from the context." He then concluded with a famous line written by his cousin Rudyard Kipling, in which he sneered at the lordly newspapermen for desiring power, but "power without responsibility—the prerogative of the harlot throughout the ages."

It was a brilliant, furious riposte, and ensured that he made a lifelong enemy of two extremely powerful and influential men, both of whom then set out to find a more amenable successor. They found this in Chamberlain, who brokered an informal peace agreement with Beaverbrook a couple of weeks later, agreeing that the *Daily Express* would continue to support the Conservatives in the next election in exchange for some concessions about agricultural production. He was able to write to his sister Ida in triumph on 5 April, "I have been overwhelmed with congratulations which have come from all quarters (except S.B. who can't bear the thought of making it up with the Press Lords and doesn't see how it has helped his own position)".[7]

The inference was clear. Chamberlain may have been only two years younger than Baldwin, but he represented a new age, in which he understood the power of media and the necessity of doing deals with magnates rather than loftily insulting them. Beaverbrook, in particular, looked to anoint the next leader of the Conservative party, then have his papers support him loyally. Chamberlain did not need to jeopardise his own political future by acting against Baldwin. Instead, time and gravity would do his work for him, and the newspapers would finish the beleaguered, exhausted leader off instead.

Chamberlain was also mindful that he had tried, and failed, to persuade Baldwin to quit earlier that year. On 1 March, he suggested that it was time for the leader to step down, and expected argument and equivocation. He was therefore surprised when Baldwin appeared to agree, asking only for the grace of a day so that he could bid farewell to his colleagues in person. Chamberlain duly briefed *The Times* on the welcome news, but when he turned up to hear his colleague's departing words, he was shocked to discover that he had been outmanoeuvred.

Baldwin now announced that he would not stand down, but instead contest the by-election of St George's, Westminster, against a candidate put up by Beaverbrook, thereby enabling him to stand against his hated nemesis by proxy. When he told Chamberlain this, the Chancellor, horrified, said "S.B., you can't do that . . . Think of the effect on your successor." Baldwin calmly replied "I don't give a damn about my successor."[8] The only hint of compromise he offered was that he would not stand in the seat himself, but would instead put up a protégé in the form of Duff Cooper, who ran on an explicitly pro-Baldwin platform. It was during this campaign that Baldwin made his famous remarks about "power without responsibility," and the phrase made the reporters—Beaverbrook's and otherwise—leap up and pay attention. Cooper was duly elected with a majority of five thousand.

Baldwin himself called 1931 "the year my party tried to get rid of me."[9] They, and Chamberlain in particular, had failed; and even Beaverbrook remarked, not without admiration, "He always beats me—the toughest and most unscrupulous politician you could find—cold, merciless in his dislikes."[10] There was no big beast who the beleaguered Conservatives could turn to, and Baldwin remained as leader of the opposition. Chamberlain, however, may not have taken charge of the party, even going so far as to resign as party chairman, but he was instead persuaded to join a coalition government formed in October 1931, led by MacDonald but with a ragtag band of Conservatives, Liberals, and Labour supporters in its ranks. He once again assumed the position of Chancellor of the Exchequer, with Baldwin as Lord President of the Council, rather than prime minister.

The government was therefore led by a triumvirate of sorts. MacDonald, approaching seventy as the administration wore on, was an increasingly woeful figure, suffering a decline in his eyesight, coherence, and memory. He was nicknamed "Ramshackle Mac"; and Baldwin's biographer Roy Jenkins said of him, "In the House of Commons he became an embarrassing joke, and in Downing Street a guarantee of indecision."[11] That was one of the kinder judgements. MacDonald was reckoned to "outlive himself not in retirement but in office,"[12] and it fell to his colleagues to pick up the slack. Baldwin himself remarked, "It was tragic to see him in his closing days as Prime Minister, losing the thread of his speech and turning to ask a colleague why people were laughing."[13] Privately, he vowed that the same thing would not happen to him, but determined to go out on a high, rather than a humiliating defeat.

Meanwhile, Chamberlain began to tire of his duties: less power without responsibility and more its reverse, the prerogative of the drudge throughout the ages.

He observed to his sister Hilda in early 1935: "I am more and more carrying this Government on my back. . . . It is certainly time there was a change,"[14] and implied to her on 23 March that he should be the instrument of this change. "I have become a sort of Acting P.M.—only without the actual power of the P.M. I have to say 'Have you thought' or 'What would you say' when it would be quicker to say 'This is what you must do.'"[15] It was clear that MacDonald could not last as leader, and so he informed George V on 16 May that it was time for him to resign. Few disagreed. The only question that arose was who would replace him.

Had Chamberlain now made another move against Baldwin, it is more likely than not that he would have become premier. There was no other outstanding candidate for the highest office—Churchill was still regarded with distrust and contempt by his party a decade after he had returned to it from the Liberals—and Britain, struggling with economic downturn and high levels of unemployment, was a country that was crying out for strong, certain leadership. One reason for Oswald Mosley's initial success, and the ten-thousand-strong membership of the BUF, is that he provided this strength and certainty while other democratically elected politicians vacillated between makeshift solutions and despair. Germany was flourishing under Hitler and Europe appeared to be teetering towards conflict once again. Chamberlain therefore saw himself as the responsible, guiding statesman, arguing for an inevitably expensive programme of rearmament. Memories of his failed coup had not faded, and he could only hope that Baldwin would stand down of his own accord before the next election.

He may have been both surprised and horrified, then, that Baldwin won re-election on an explicitly anti-defence platform, arguing that "not a penny more than was absolutely necessary"[16] would be spent on armaments, and shooting down Labour's arguments that the Conservatives would be "a danger to the peace of the world, to the security of this country."[17] The National Government was re-elected with a strongly Conservative, anti-armament ethos at its centre on 7 June 1935. It was Baldwin's personal victory, not that of the Conservatives. Churchill, who had explicitly argued for rearmament at any cost, was an even more diminished figure after it, reduced to scowling on the backbenches.

Yet Baldwin did not have long to savour his triumph. That autumn, Mussolini invaded Abyssinia, a display of fascist aggression that Chamberlain labelled "barbarous" and which threatened to precipitate war, if the League of Nations agreed to support such a decision. They did not, and in the end half-hearted sanctions were all that could be agreed upon, meaning that Mussolini was free to annex the whole of the country the following May. Halifax, who had briefly served as secretary of state for war but became leader of the House of the Lords in November 1935, watched the shift with interest but without any desire on his part to usurp his friend Baldwin's position. It was quite clear that Britain was not ready for an expensive, gruelling war, lacking both the arms and manpower to do so.

It was therefore undesirable but essential that peace had to be maintained at all costs, and the irresistible rise of Adolf Hitler, which had been dominating world affairs throughout the thirties, had to be tolerated. As could be seen by the initial success that the BUF had enjoyed, many influential and aristocratic figures in Britain were pro-Hitler, seeing him as a vigorous reformer who could bring a lasting peace to Europe, if his territorial ambitions were either indulged or, at the very least, not blocked. Baldwin himself declared in April 1936: "Hitler, the dictator of Germany, has it in his power today to do more at this moment to lift the black shadow of fear from Europe than any other man living . . . God grant that he may have the will."[18]

Privately, Baldwin did not believe Hitler wanted war; and if he did, Baldwin imagined that his truer opponent would be Stalin and communism. Baldwin explicitly told Churchill: "I am not going to get this country into a war with anybody for the League of Nations or anybody else or for anything else. If there is any fighting to be done in Europe, I should like to see the Bolsheviks and the Nazis doing it."[19]

Two potentially decisive matters then occurred in 1936 that allowed Baldwin and Chamberlain to see that the status quo that they had been intimately involved in for decades was being brutally and terminally upended. The death of George V on 20 January 1936, from chronic bronchitis, was not unexpected—the king's personal doctor Lord Dawson had told Baldwin the previous year that George was in the process of leaving this earth—but it precipitated the arrival of Edward VIII to the throne, which horrified most of those who had had dealings with him previously.

Chamberlain remarked that unless the king "pulled up his socks he will soon pull down the throne."[20] Baldwin had gone even further. The courtier Alan "Tommy" Lascelles, who had had the misfortune to serve as Edward's private secretary, made the treacherous but understandable admission to the politician in 1927 that he sometimes hoped that the then Prince of Wales would fall off his horse and break his neck while riding in a race, to which Baldwin replied, "God help me, so do I."[21]

The new and very much alive king was an arrogant, self-absorbed playboy who was notorious both for his adulterous affair with the twice-married American Wallis Simpson and for his pro-German, even pro-Nazi, sympathies. He had declared in a visit to the German embassy the previous year that "the hand of friendship" should be outstretched to the Germans by former soldiers "who fought them and have now forgotten all about it and the Great War," to the disbelief of those veterans who had certainly not forgotten about the events of two decades previously. When he was challenged about his forthright views shortly after ascending the throne, Edward sharply retorted, "Who is King here? Baldwin or I?

I myself wish to talk to Hitler, and will do so here or in Germany. Tell him that, please."[22]

It was out of the question that the new king should meet Hitler except in an official capacity; but it was good, or bad, fortune that he had been befriended in a somewhat forward fashion by Ribbentrop, who had been introduced to Edward and Wallis at a lunch given by the society hostess Emerald Cunard in June 1935. Ribbentrop was, as the delighted Cunard put it, "a real, live Nazi," and the king's private secretary Lord Wigram offered a disparaging account of the lunch. "Ribbentrop poured out all the German propaganda, which I expect bored HRH. However, I am told that Ribbentrop telegraphed to Germany that the Prince entirely agreed with his views, and that HRH added that after all he was half a German." He qualified this by writing that "I cannot believe there is any truth in this,"* but also complained that "This is the result of accepting invitations from people like Lady Cunard to meet such men as German propagandists."[23]

Edward was hardly an innocent when it came to such associations. He had met Mosley earlier that year, and had admiringly enquired about the "strength and policy" of the BUF. Ribbentrop himself said of the new king: "He desired good Anglo-German relations . . . King Edward VIII had shown his sympathy for Germany on several occasions [and] had warmly supported a meeting of German and British leaders of ex-servicemen's organisations."[24] He had also endeared himself to Hitler by suggesting that the monarch was "a kind of English national socialist," and someone who could look on their activities favourably.

* * *

* Unfortunately, there was. Wigram had to acknowledge that "Evidently Ribbentrop had telegraphed to Germany the most favourable account of the Prince of Wales' speech and also, I gather, of a conversation which he had had with His Royal Highness . . . There is no doubt that this indiscretion has been most embarrassing to the Foreign Office."

Under normal circumstances, Ribbentrop would have been an unlikely, even inconceivable choice for the diplomatically sensitive and politically crucial post of British ambassador. Only a few years ago, he had been a successful dealer in wines and spirits, which led to his being caricatured as a mere champagne salesman, but he was hardly a lifelong adherent to national socialism, or any other political ideology. The most notable thing about him was that he was fluent in English, having spent nearly a year in London between 1909 and 1910 and then having travelled to Montreal, where he worked as a bank clerk for eighteen months, and New York, where he claimed to have spent time as a reporter for various newspapers.

These claims, which he made in his self-serving memoirs, written while he awaited execution at Nuremberg, may or may not have been true, but what was undeniably the case was that his experience and knowledge of England interested Hitler, and marked Ribbentrop out as someone who was unusually useful to him. The former ambassador wrote that "what he wanted above all else was a permanent and clear settlement with Britain. . . . Hitler could not hear enough about England. Everything interested him: her way of life, parliamentary institutions, the City with its trade, and Empire policy. . . . Hitler was particularly interested in what influential Englishmen thought about National Socialism."

In this area, Ribbentrop had to disappoint him, though had he visited the country more recently, he would have found a greater degree of sympathy and interest than a decade previously. Nonetheless, he was able to write, albeit with the benefit of some hindsight, "It was the harmony of our views about England which, on this first evening spent together, created the seed of confidence between Hitler and myself."[25]

The politician Anthony Eden described Ribbentrop, clear-sightedly, as "essentially a salesman, and his ideas of statesmanship and diplomacy began and ended there. His task was to sell Hitler's Germany but above all Hitler."[26] His greatest talent was selling himself. He made repeated visits to Britain in the early 1930s, when he obtained the ear of the pro-German Lord Rothermere, and was able to report to the Führer that the greatest obstacle to greater understanding between their two countries was "a pro-French clique led by the Foreign Office." Hitler was nonetheless assured that "the people would rather like to go in our direction."[27]

The Führer was pleased to hear the good news from Ribbentrop, not least because it ran counter to everything else that he was hearing. The incumbent German ambassador, Leopold von Hoesch, a popular figure who was quietly opposed to Hitler and fascism, was both surprised and appalled by Ribbentrop's increasingly regular visits to London, where he operated almost as a minister without portfolio, organising high-profile meetings with politicians, clergymen, and journalists without any authorisation.

After Ribbentrop entirely misrepresented a meeting that he had with Anthony Eden to Hitler, describing a civil but strained formal encounter as "a way of strengthening the confidence of British statesmen in the broad outlines of German foreign policy," Hoesch, briefed "very frankly and as friends" by Eden, wrote to the German foreign minister Konstantin von Neurath to apprise him of the situation and to ask that Ribbentrop's freelance activities cease.

Neurath, both perturbed and angered by the potential for diplomatic chaos, wrote to Hitler to say, "From reports in the English press and from private correspondence which has reached me from England, I had already formed the impression that Ribbentrop's trip had been a complete disaster." He concluded that "I believe there should be no repetition of this visit, at least not in the near future."[28] Hitler, however, had faith in his protégé, and chose him to be his chief negotiator in the Anglo-German Naval Agreement of the following year, that would cap the German navy at no greater a size than 35 per cent of the British navy: an apparent concession that nevertheless meant that German sea power would be three times the size fixed upon at the Versailles Agreement in 1919. Ribbentrop then presented this as a fait accompli, unnegotiable and final. The British side blanched, and then accepted it, believing that it was worth maintaining peace with Germany at this particular cost.

Inadvertently, they had handed the ambitious salesman a personal triumph. He later wrote in his memoirs: "I was very satisfied with the result of my London mission, and so was [Hitler] . . . [who] called this day the happiest day of his life." Ribbentrop was warmly congratulated by Rothermere and others, one of whom reportedly said, "Perhaps you don't know what it means to have concluded such an agreement with the British Navy which means everything to Britain."[29]

The Foreign Secretary, Sir Samuel Hoare—aka "Soapy Sam"—vetoed any pomp or pageantry to signify the agreement, recognising that "Ribbentrop wished to turn the occasion into an impressive ceremony for the glorification of his country, and still more, a personal triumph for himself." Although Hoare insisted: "I had no intention of pandering to his vanity,"[30] it was a propaganda coup for Ribbentrop, who triumphantly returned to Germany to be embraced by Hitler, promoted to the rank of brigadier, and welcomed into the heart of the Nazi hierarchy, which his enemies had previously managed to keep him away from. It was murmured that he was a certainty to replace Neurath as foreign minister when his term ended in 1938, but in the meantime, Ribbentrop had obtained a near-sacred reverence as the man who could get things done in England, despite obvious and consistent evidence to the contrary.

In the event, it was Neurath's idea that Ribbentrop should be offered the post of ambassador to Britain, thanks to his "special knowledge of the British," after Hoesch's death from a heart attack in April 1936. Neurath knew that it would be a collision of cultures and approaches, remarking privately that "After three months in London, Ribbentrop will be done for. They can't stand him there and we will be rid of him for good and all."[31] Ribbentrop did not wish for the position—he hoped for something higher and based in Germany—but Hitler was pleased with the idea and made his formal appointment on 24 July, over the protests of many in his inner circle.* Ribbentrop would take up his embassy in the autumn—a progress delayed by protestations of ill health—and he finally arrived at Victoria station on 26 October, bound for 37 Eaton Square, and what would become a very eventful ambassadorship.

THE MITFORD SISTERS WERE HORRIFIED at the idea of Ribbentrop as German ambassador. Diana and Unity slightingly referred to him as "Joan Glover," an allusion to a medieval song about a persistent lover—presumably a dig at his closeness to Hitler—and Unity made it plain to the Führer, when they attended a lunch party at the Goebbelses' home in late 1936, that she disapproved of the appointment, saying that she believed that he was wholly the wrong man for the job. Hitler would undoubtedly have been offended had anyone else made such a remark, with its implied dig at his poor judgement, but such was his admiration for the beautiful Unity that she was indulged, and he attached no great importance to it. Diana, however, was delighted, and wrote to her to say, "Magda [Goebbels] is being an *angel*, and she can talk of nothing but your marvellous attack on Joan Glover and how pleased they all were with you for doing it."[32]

Baldwin, meanwhile, had first encountered Ribbentrop in Westminster in late 1933 at a luncheon party. The meeting was not a great success. Baldwin's friend J. C. C. Davidson, who was present, observed that "S.B., never at his best with foreigners, did not really take to Ribbentrop," although Davidson also noted that Ribbentrop "was not at this time . . . the unpleasant creature that he afterwards became."[33] Still, Baldwin was sufficiently aware that Ribbentrop could be the coming man to invite him to tea at Downing Street early the next year, where he introduced him to MacDonald. Later in his premiership, with the prospect of Hitler seeming ever larger, the prime minister began to despair. His biographer H. Montgomery

* When Hitler boasted to Goebbels about how Ribbentrop knew such-and-such a lord or politician, Goebbels sharply replied, "Yes—the trouble is, they know Ribbentrop."

Hyde cited his saying to Anthony Eden, by then foreign secretary, that he wished for better relations with Hitler, and quoted him remarking "We must get nearer to Germany." When Eden, reasonably enough, asked "How?," Baldwin shrugged. "I have no idea. That is your job."[34]

When it became likely that Ribbentrop was Hitler's pick to be the next ambassador, Baldwin's right-hand man, Tom Jones, attempted to give the premier some useful advice. Although Jones was wholly aware that Ribbentrop could seem like a fool—or, in Jones's parlance, "an ass"—he also stated, "At the very least, he is a reliable telephone from Hitler and the likelihood is that he is much more."[35] It was to this end that Ribbentrop attempted to broker a meeting between Baldwin and Hitler in late 1936, but it came to nothing, with Ribbentrop's "telephone" proving to have a perpetual busy signal.

In any case, although Baldwin was prime minister, it was Chamberlain who proved to have an unusually close connection with the new ambassador, in part because he had leased his home to him. Up until the previous year, despite serving as Chancellor of the Exchequer and therefore being entitled to live at 11 Downing Street, Chamberlain had remained in Eaton Square, preferring the familiarity of his family home to what were, essentially, lodgings above an office. However, as Baldwin was making it increasingly clear that he had retirement in mind, it seemed inevitable that Chamberlain would be moving in next door in time, rendering his former home superfluous.

Certainly, the decision to lease it to the ambassador had not been done out of any pro-German or pro-Ribbentrop sentiment but from financial necessity. Earlier that year, he had complained that his own circumstances "went from bad to worse as the country gets back to prosperity,"[36] so he had to take any opportunity that was offered. Chamberlain was no admirer of Ribbentrop or his country, and had once exclaimed, "How I loathe the Germans," while reluctantly holidaying in the Black Forest. He wrote to his sister Hilda on 25 September to inform her of the identity of his house's new tenant with a certain degree of black humour. "Did I tell you that we have let Eaton Square to Ribbentrop?" he wrote. "Amusing, considering my affection for Germans in general, and R. in particular."[37] On another occasion, Chamberlain had called him "so stupid, so shallow, so self-centred and self-satisfied, so totally devoid of intellectual capacity that he never seems to take in what is said to him."[38]

The stupid, shallow, and self-centred one arrived in London with his wife, Annelies and his five children, including his son Rudolf. While initially Ribbentrop had imagined that his stay in the capital would be a blissful whirligig of socialising and good favour—"from London alone I expected a minor invasion of friends"[39]—it was made clear to him by the diplomat Robert Vansittart that his advent was not a welcome one, and he wrote despondently, and accurately: "I could see I would have a tough time in London."[40] As if in anticipation of his unpopularity, he decided to greet the waiting journalists at Victoria with a Nazi salute, before declaring, "Germany wants to be friends with Great Britain and, I think, the British people also wish for German friendship. The Führer is convinced that there is only one real danger to Europe and to the British Empire as well, and that is the spreading further of communism, this most terrible of diseases." He concluded that "a closer collaboration in this sense between our two countries is not only important but a vital necessity in the common struggle for the upholding of our civilisation and our culture."[41]

It was considered unprecedented for ambassadorial policy to be made up on the spot, so this was received badly by German and British sources alike. Matters soon worsened. Ribbentrop's eventual London home was to be the Carlton House Terrace location of the German embassy, but it needed a degree of refurbishment and renovation which, in the spirit of exceptionalism, Ribbentrop ordered be done entirely by German companies and craftsmen. When Göring dared to raise an objection to this, Ribbentrop merely muttered, "What insolence" and ignored his letter of complaint. By then, he had already intimidated the 150 embassy employees—many of whom were not Nazis or even sympathetic to the cause—by describing their loyalty as being to the "beloved Führer" before insisting on a loud declaration of "Sieg heil!"

He seemed to be intent on making himself as unpopular as possible in London, as swiftly as he could. When he informed Eden, "what an advantage it was going to be for us to have an Ambassador in London who knew [Hitler] so closely and could give us his thought," Eden responded suavely, "[We] have an Ambassador in Berlin whose duty it was to report to us the opinions of the German Government." He suggested instead that Ribbentrop's task was to "report to his Government the views of His Majesty's Government," something that Eden noted was "received in sulky acquiescence."[42]

Even a meeting with his supposed friend Edward VIII did not go according to plan. Edward later wrote that "the occasion was not without strain. . . . the appointment of this polished but bombastic opportunist was not calculated to ease British apprehensions."[43] Finally, as if in confirmation that he did not have a clue as to how to conduct himself in public, Ribbentrop attended a service at Durham Cathedral while visiting his friend Lord Londonderry's nearby estate. When the hymn "Glorious things of thee are spoken" began, Ribbentrop, believing that the organist had begun a rendition of "Deutschland über alles," which has the same tune, attempted to give a Nazi salute and had to be forcibly restrained by those around him for his act of impropriety. This and other regrettable faux pas led the *Evening Standard* cartoonist David Low to christen him "Brickendrop," a name that stuck and became the standard means of referring to the increasingly hapless ambassador.

As a family man, Ribbentrop left a great deal to be desired, too. He insisted that his eldest daughter take intensive lessons in golf, despite the local club being much frequented by Jews, on the grounds that "to conquer England, it was indispensable for the younger members of his family to play golf." This was greeted with contempt by Sir Eric Phipps, ambassador to Germany, who wrote, "[He is] a tremendous snob, [who] is convinced that what counts in England is equally snobbish . . . a lightweight . . . irritating, ignorant and boundlessly conceited." Phipps concluded that "I cannot help thinking that before his own game has gone very far he himself will get rather badly bunkered."[44]

Ribbentrop had wished for his eldest son, Rudolf, to attend Eton on the grounds that "he will be able to teach the Hitler Youth," but the school rejected him, ostensibly on the grounds that at fifteen he was too old and that there was no space for him, but almost certainly because they did not want to be associated with such a controversial figure. Westminster, however, had no such scruples, and he was admitted there from the autumn term of 1936.

There is a famous photograph that exists of the young Rudolf leaving Eaton Square bound for school, dressed in the uniform of top hat, morning coat, and umbrella. He looks as if he is going to take over the world, and the expression on his face—half-nervous, half-proud—combines the natural recalcitrance of a teenager with the inherent belief of his family and country's greatness that had been drilled into him since birth. After an initial attempt to pose for photographs outside the house went badly—"when my likeness appeared in the papers the next day, I was shocked at how unfriendly the photo was"—he believed that he "smiled amiably" on future occasions, only to be castigated by his father for "posing for the press."[45]

He proved to be equally unpopular at Westminster, where he did little of worth other than extol the glories of Hitler's Germany and give Nazi salutes at every opportunity. Rudolf was tolerated because of his athletic prowess, and spared corporal punishment because of his exalted position, but was regarded with suspicion and distaste by pupils and teachers alike. On one occasion, a teacher enquired whether Rudolf would be interested in joining the Officers' Training Corps, which might have allowed for the unparalleled spectacle of the German ambassador's son dressing up in the uniform of a British officer-in-waiting, even as conflict seemed ever likelier. Sadly, Rudolf was wise to the trap ("the British press would not forgo the joke of publishing a spread in enlargement of the son of the German ambassador in British infantry uniform"[46]) and asked instead, at his father's instigation, whether he would be able to wear Nazi attire instead, which Westminster was not prepared to acquiesce to.

As his son pretended to be an officer and a gentleman, Ribbentrop's presence in London proved to be increasingly disastrous. Even his military attaché Leo Geyr von Schweppenburg sighed at his uselessness, complaining, "If one asks what his policy consisted of, the answer would probably be that he himself hadn't a clue, except the idée fixe of doing nothing that might displease Hitler. He managed to obstruct the British in almost every direction, and thought that was the right way to deal with them." Ribbentrop attempted a mixture of bluntness and aggression with men of influence, and treated his subordinates rudely and pompously. ("His ignorance was limitless," complained one of the half-dozen who eventually wrote memoirs about the horrors of having to deal with Ribbentrop.) The only occasions that work was ever done was when the ambassador retired to his bed, a period known by his staff as "*tango nocturno*," and which allowed them to get on with their tasks without ill-intended and unwelcome instruction.

Those around Ribbentrop either mocked him to his face—Nancy Astor asked bluntly, "Aren't you a damned bad ambassador?" and accused him of lacking the sense of humour essential for the job, which provoked the thin-skinned one into saying, "You should see me telling jokes to Hitler, and how we both roar with laughter"[47]—or cowered from his stagy outbursts of anger, a technique learnt from his master. As his private secretary Reinhard Spitzy later wrote, "When the chief rang the bell, everyone [at Eaton Square] turned pale and fell silent. The summoned victim left the room with a helpless backward glance . . . He would return disturbed and perspiring, falling into a chair with a despairing heavenward look."[48]

His unpopularity, viciousness, and incompetence would have all been redeemed, however, if he had managed to accomplish one of the key tasks of his ambassadorship: namely parlaying his supposed friendship with Edward VIII into inside knowledge not only of his relationship with Wallis Simpson but also of how this would affect a putative alliance with Germany. Yet Ribbentrop barely had anything to do with the king, who was, in any case, rather more preoccupied with attempting to keep both Wallis and his throne.

If Ribbentrop had failed to make headway with the king, there remained another option. Ribbentrop had met Wallis Simpson at the same lunch where he had first encountered Edward, then Prince of Wales, and rumours of an affair between the two developed subsequently, fanned by Ribbentrop's penchant for sending her seventeen roses at regular intervals (allegedly the number of times the two had slept together).* Although Wallis's political leanings were to the left of Edward's, Ribbentrop had a certain Teutonic charisma, and it is likely that the two became friendly, at the very least. Yet the rumour of a full-blown affair seems implausible, as the notably uxorious Ribbentrop was unlikely to jeopardise his career, marriage, and the chance of the English alliance for such a liaison. If Wallis could serve any greater purpose, it was as a conduit to her lover.

Yet if this was his intention in patronising Belgravia's finest florists, it did not succeed. The ambassador bemoaned their "brief talks," and complained that he had failed to "establish any special contact with Edward VIII . . . Something unforeseen always intervened"[49] Yet when his press attaché Fritz Hesse dared to suggest that, if Edward abdicated, he would become irrelevant, Ribbentrop responded furiously, declaring, "Don't you know what expectations the Führer has placed on the king's support in the coming negotiations? He's our greatest hope! Don't you think that the whole affair is an intrigue of our enemies to rob us of one of the last two big positions we hold in this country?" He even blustered, "You'll see, the King will marry Wally and the two will tell Baldwin and his whole gang to go to the devil."[50]

In this matter, as in so many others, Ribbentrop was misinformed.

---

* This curious, and unreliable, information was derived from a Benedictine monk named Father Odo, the former Duke of Württemberg who supposedly confided it to FBI agents.

Right up until Edward abdicated on 11 December, the ambassador was still deluding himself as to the seriousness and implications of the constitutional crisis, claiming that "the whole affair will go up in smoke, and the King will be grateful to us for having treated the crisis with such tactful reticence."[51] When this did not materialise, Ribbentrop gloomily prophesised that there would be shooting in the streets and that Edward would eventually be restored to the throne, by force if necessary.

Davidson, the recipient of these confidences, wrote, "He talked more nonsense than I have ever heard from anybody in a responsible position of the level of Ambassador . . . It was quite obvious that he had been stuffing Hitler with the idea that the [Abdication] Bill would be defeated and that a more pacifist government would replace it." In fact, a bravura speech by Baldwin in the Commons on 10 December ensured that the Bill passed with virtually no opposition, and meant that the abdication received rare cross-party support. Davidson therefore was able to say, happily, "I had some pleasure in disabusing Ribbentrop of these illusions, and the Ambassador was not gratified by what I had to say."[52]

Ribbentrop saved his skin, and career, by convincing Hitler that the king had been deposed by a wicked coalition led by the Jews and Freemasons, and therefore the irrelevance of his negligible influence was not called into question. He returned to Germany on 19 December 1936, and although he still held the title of ambassador until 4 February 1938,* he spent as much time back in Germany as he did in London, fearful that his absence from Hitler's side might mean that another, similarly ambitious man might usurp his influence.

Thankfully for him, his regular visits back to his home country,

* He was not merely ridiculed by his colleagues but by schoolboys. During George VI's coronation, dignitaries had to raise their arm if they needed to head to the toilet, but the Westminster schoolboys deputed to lead them out refused to acknowledge Ribbentrop's quasi-Nazi salutes, meaning that at least one member of the congregation spent the ceremony in a state of squirming discomfort.

and increasingly lackadaisical commitment to his post, meant that his position as Hitler's right-hand man only grew after the outbreak of war. He remained committed to his master right up until his execution at Nuremberg on 16 October 1946. It was almost a decade to the day in which he had first arrived at Eaton Square, bound on one of the least successful embassies that any diplomat has ever undertaken in modern times. His final words, delivered to the pastor officiating at his hanging, were "I'll see you again."* Appropriately enough, his hanging was botched, like so much else in his life: He squirmed in agony for nearly twenty minutes.

As for the other residents of Eaton Square, Baldwin retired in May 1937, and initially appeared to be one of the most popular former prime ministers (his friend Sir Harold Nicolson commented, "No man has ever left in such a blaze of affection") but this was soon dispelled by changing public attitudes towards appeasement and rearmament. What had once looked like principled, even canny, opposition to warmongering now became regarded as little more than vacillation. Baldwin was pilloried in a 1940 bestseller *Guilty Men*, by the pseudonymous "Cato" that criticised him as one of those responsible for inadequate preparations for war.

Another of those similarly attacked was Neville Chamberlain, whose long-anticipated tenure as prime minister began on 28 May 1937 and ended in opprobrium and war on 10 May 1940, a couple of months before *Guilty Men* was published. Their Eaton Square neighbour Lord Halifax might have been expected to have become premier, but a combination of his standing in the Lords and his own belief that Churchill would make for a more effective and focused leader in wartime meant that he did not seek the position. He was given the role of ambassador to the United States instead, ostensibly a sinecure but in reality a clever means of removing a rival from the country. Yet he, too, had been blamed in *Guilty*

* When I realised that I would have to write about this particular Eaton Square resident once again, this particular line seemed prophetic.

Men, along with others including Hoare, MacDonald, and Chamberlain's successor as Chancellor, Sir John Simon. Anyone, in other words, who had taken a pro-appeasement stance would eventually be punished for it.

During the war that the actions of these various Eaton Square residents had caused, indirectly and directly alike, the square was damaged by bombs. The perennially unfortunate St Peter's church was bombed heavily at the height of the Blitz, and on 16 April 1941, its long-serving vicar Austin Thompson died while firewatching in its porch. The incendiary device that killed him also destroyed, ironically enough, a memorial that had been erected to those residents of the square who had died in World War I. His successor, Prebendary Kirk, wrote a glum account of the total damage that had been wrought. "All the large stained windows with the exception of the east window were destroyed. The roof was slightly damaged, part of the ceiling of the portico fell and two of the three large west doors were smashed. No trace remains of the War Memorial in the garden at the south-west side of the Church, and the Crucifix which hangs over the Roll of Honour is badly broken."[53]

Many of the houses on the square suffered similar depredations. An air raid shelter was built in one of the formal gardens, and residents scuttled down there, night after night, hoping that the worst damage that would be wrought upon their homes was that the windows would be shattered and the masonry cracked. Some of them were fortunate, others less so. Two Eaton Square, in particular—the former residence of Diana Mitford—was especially badly hit and needed to be almost totally rebuilt after the war, making a mockery of the expensive refurbishment that she had undertaken during her residence there in the early thirties.

There was an irony that the ultimate owner of Eaton Square, Hugh "Bendor" Grosvenor was, by a considerable distance, not only the most controversial member of the family but also the most fervently pro-Nazi and right wing.* He has been pilloried by history for being an unscrupulous adulterer who famously had an affair with the designer Coco Chanel, who he lavished with expensive jewellery and gifts, but also a supposed antisemite and homophobe who was responsible for the downfall of his brother-in-law William Lygon, whose liberal politics were the opposite of his own. An apocryphal story exists that, after Lygon was driven into exile—becoming the model for *Brideshead Revisited*'s Lord Marchmain in the process—Bendor sent him a spiteful letter in which he wrote: "Dear Bugger-in-law, you got what you deserved. Yours, Westminster."

Diana Newton and Jonathan Lumby's authorised publication, *The Grosvenors of Eaton: The Dukes of Westminster and Their Forebears*, presents—as can be imagined—the various Grosvenors in as positive a light as they could hope for. Newton and Lumby's description of how Bendor "travelled to the political right [and] joined The Link, a society which admired continental fascism" is as close as they come to overt criticism of any of the Grosvenors, although it is swiftly qualified by their statement: "Once war broke out, however, Bendor reverted to being utterly and generously patriotic." This may be taken in the context of Bendor's committed antisemitism. He possessed a copy of a book called *The Jews' Who's Who*, which purported "to tell the exact quantity of Jewish blood coursing through the veins of the aristocratic families of England," and made frequent, slighting remarks against Jews in his surviving correspondence. He also visited Nazi Germany in 1937, around the same time that the Duke and Duchess of Windsor made their ill-fated visit there,** and was similarly warmly received.

Bendor was not himself a fascist in the Mosleyite vein, being too lazy or unfocused to take up active membership of a political party, let alone any leading role within it. Yet he was a fervent appeaser,

* I am, however, indebted to the careful research of Christina Sykes, whose 2021 doctoral thesis is an exhaustive reappraisal-cum-defence of Bendor, who she punctiliously refers to as "Bend'Or" throughout.

** See *The Windsors at War* for full details of this.

even after war was declared. His stance may have been dictated in part by a wish to avoid unnecessary bloodshed, or simply because he feared—correctly—that his substantial London property holdings ran the risk of damage in the event of warfare. He was friendly with Chamberlain, with both sharing a pro-appeasement perspective, and continued to argue that Germany was Britain's natural friend and ally, rather than its enemy, during the so-called Phony War that lasted up until 1940. Even before Churchill succeeded Chamberlain as prime minister, he wrote to Bendor to suggest that it was time that he abandon his views: "In my view, in time of peace, people in a free country have a right to form their views about foreign policy: but when the country is fighting for its life against a deadly enemy, there are grave dangers in taking a hostile line to the decided plan."[54]

Whether reluctantly or not, Bendor fell into line, and refrained from making any overtly pro-German or anti-Jewish statements in public. Yet before he died, his Eaton Square leaseholder Chamberlain, who may have been a poor judge of character when it came to Hitler but was rather better equipped to see his aristocratic landlord for who he was, described him to his sister as "extraordinarily hospitable, generous and kind hearted." He also acknowledged, however, that Bendor had been corrupted by the sheer amount of wealth that he was the possessor of. Shortly after he became prime minister, Chamberlain said "to have withstood all that [immense wealth and a dukedom] [. . .] poor Westminster would have had to be a hero & he is not that: only a good fellow without any great strength of character."[55]

The diarist Chips Channon described him in a similar, yet ultimately rather harsher, manner. He wrote that Bendor was "magnificent, courteous, a mixture of Henry VIII and Lorenzo Il Magnifico, he lived for pleasure—and women—for 74 years. His wealth was incalculable; his charm overwhelming; he was restless, spoilt, irritable and rather splendid in a very English way. He was fair, handsome, lavish; yet his life was an empty failure; he did few kindnesses, leaves no monument."[56] Yet Channon, for all his usual witty waspishness, overlooked one crucial factor. Eaton Square, in all its multifaceted glories and secrets, was a monument not just to its residents but to the family that owned it. Before World War II, it had been the preserve of the discreet, the aristocratic, and the highest in Britain. But after the depredations of a war that Bendor, and others, had tried to stop happening, a more democratic—and moneyed—demographic would join the life of the square, too.

7

Rex Harrison and Vivien Leigh: 54 and 75 Eaton Square

"Decent indecency"

Amidst the countless public interviews that the actor and raconteur Rex Harrison gave, one of the most bizarre is a brief conversation between him and a reporter from British Pathé that occurred on the steps of his home at 75 Eaton Square in 1969. Harrison, apparently unprepared for an interview, is doorstepped by the eager journalist ("Can I call you Rex?"), who briefly explains that, in those pre-paparazzi days, it was the job of television broadcasters to roam the streets of London to find and gently harass their well-known residents.

Harrison takes it in his stride. He says of his Eaton Square residence that "it's just a furnished pad," and when the woebegone interviewer asks "Are things bad?" replies, as many inhabitants of the square might have done before or since, "No, things are very good." (This, as we shall see later, was not entirely true.) Harrison conveys his distaste for the hotel life expected of celebrities—"I don't like going in and out of foyers being stared at by lots of people"—and, when the reporter, growing bolder, describes Eaton Square as "rather a crummy place these days," Harrison replies, "I had another furnished pad about ten years ago, which belonged to the late Vivien Leigh. I'm not an habitué of this square, but I think it's the last bulwark of 'decent indecency.'"

There is then some small talk about a couple of films that Harrison wished to produce, rather than act in, and then he is ushered into a waiting limousine, complete with chauffeur, the interview obviously at an end. The sixty-one-year-old actor was clearly in a reasonable mood that day—there is an unusual amount of smiling and arm patting—and only the fleeting, slightly cool reference to Leigh, who had died two years previously, could suggest any difficulty or angst lurking beneath Harrison's smooth, assured surface.

The two had first acted together in the 1937 Scotland-set romantic comedy film *Storm in a Teacup*, when they were both at the beginning of their careers. Harrison played a newspaper reporter, described at one point as "a cheeky little rotter from London," and Leigh was the local dignitary's daughter. Both had had recent high-profile successes: Harrison with the Terence Rattigan comedy *French Without Tears*, which had been a West End hit, and Leigh had starred opposite her future husband Laurence Olivier in the Elizabethan potboiler *Fire Over England*, which had given the two a romantic subplot that diverted attention from the supposedly patriotic account of the Spanish Armada. Leigh and Olivier were married to other people, but such entanglements could swiftly be forgotten in the intense, exciting world of film.

Years later, Harrison described the experience of working with her as wholly enjoyable. "Vivien was a talented comedienne, with a very special and endearing quality hard to define. It wasn't just the kind of pertness someone so ravishingly pretty would be expected to have, it was a very special sense of gaiety perhaps best described as insouciance."[1] The twenty-nine-year-old actor, who had already established a reputation as a lothario, despite not appearing to like women very much,* hoped that he would begin an affair with her; but it was not to be, due to the dashing presence of Olivier in the

* He announced himself as an on- and off-screen seducer in the 1937 film *School for Husbands*, in which, when one coquettish flapper says, "I hear you've made love to women on the slightest provocation," Harrison smirks and replies, "That's quite untrue. In fact, I seldom need any provocation at all."

wings. "All she wanted to do was talk about Larry, and so I went along with that, gazing on that beautiful face with unhopeful ardour. I loved Vivien. Although we never so much as held hands, I cannot say my love was platonic. It was more exciting than that."[2]

Although Harrison called Leigh "an old friend of mine [and someone] I was enormously fond of"[3] in his 1990 memoir *A Damned Serious Business*, this amity did not persist once his hopes had been frustrated. Although he had hopes that the romance with Olivier would come to nothing—"there was a great temperamental difference between them which both found hard to take"[4]—there was no opportunity offered to R. Harrison, Esq., although some optimistic critics suggested that he and Leigh might become the British equivalent of William Powell and Myrna Loy, the glamorous (and similarly platonic) stars of the *Thin Man* series.

When the two collaborated again on the following year on the film *St Martin's Lane*, a Charles Laughton vehicle in which she was cast as an unusually glamorous pickpocket and Harrison played the supporting role of a successful songwriter-performer in the Ivor Novello mode, there was, again, no sexual spark. Olivier would appear meaningfully on set during what few love scenes they had before exercising his droit du seigneur with Leigh in her dressing room between takes.

Harrison caddishly attempted to have the object of his unrequited lust fired in favour of the more amenable Diana Churchill, telling her, "I like working with you rather than having to make another picture with that Leigh girl who can't act."[5] The now-forgotten film seems to have been a generally unhappy experience all round. Harrison later sighed that "[Laughton] was a very large and very extrovert actor, and everybody thought he was a genius. I didn't. I thought he was more of a show-off, really."[6] That almost the exact thing might be said of him, and with fewer people suggesting that Harrison possessed similar brilliance, was not something that appeared to occur to the actor.

In any case, the two went off separately to far greater success.

Leigh secured the most-coveted role of the thirties, Scarlett O'Hara in *Gone with the Wind*, despite being neither American nor Southern, and won an Oscar for her performance. And Harrison became one of the most celebrated British light comic leading men of his generation, albeit with an aggressively sexual edge that, say, David Niven did not possess. By the time that he was cast in the lead of the 1945 comedy-drama *The Rake's Progress* as an upper-class roué, there were suggestions that the only role that he was suited to was that of a variation on himself: the smooth-talking, amoral charmer who persuades women to fall in love with him before discarding them with no more interest than he has displayed in the omnipresent cigarette he has been wielding as he seduces them. His biographer Alexander Walker wrote, "It defined him as an incorrigible cad who pursued his pleasures selfishly and did not think twice about the tragedies he brought to others."[7]

It would be more accurate to describe Harrison and Leigh as friendly, in the manner of acquaintances bound together by their separate fame, than friends. (If anything, Harrison was closer to Olivier.) By the early fifties, both were amongst the best-known and most-recognisable British actors in the world, although Leigh's Oscar wins for *Gone with the Wind* and her defining, tragic role in the 1951 film of Tennessee Williams's *A Streetcar Named Desire* gave her a significant edge when it came to critical respect.

Harrison—always a man deeply concerned with money—began a successful stint working in America, sometimes in classics (1947's *The Ghost and Mrs. Muir*) and sometimes in potboilers, such as 1954's risible historical epic *King Richard and the Crusaders*, in which the actor wore brownface to play Saladin and, unsurprisingly, disowned the "absolutely rotten" picture. On-screen, he was gentlemanly, dashing, and humorous, if always with the raised eyebrow of cherchez la femme. Off-screen, he was a committed, shameless adulterer, who, by the time that he was cast in the 1948 musical comedy *Unfaithfully Yours*, seemed to be asking his audience to become complicit in the joke. Despite his regular, often unflattering, appearances in the gossip columns, he took a lordly attitude towards his paramours, once commenting, "Women . . . always leave them beholden."[8]

Leigh, who would move to 54 Eaton Square in 1957 after living at 4 Christchurch Street in Chelsea, aka "Durham Cottage," with Olivier, was not prepared to be beholden to anyone, least of all her husband and those around her. As her career wore on, her eventual marriage to Olivier became one of the most discussed and analysed relationships in show business circles. What began as occasional bouts of depression and anxiety soon worsened and turned into full-scale bipolar disorder, exacerbated by a miscarriage that she had during the filming of the 1945 adaptation of George Bernard Shaw's *Caesar and Cleopatra*. Although she was able to return to work and complete the film, she now largely eschewed the cinema, only making a further five pictures over the next two decades. Instead, she preferred to work on-stage, often opposite Olivier, which she continued to do throughout her life, before retreating to her Buckinghamshire country home of Notley Abbey when exhaustion, stress, and mental illness all became too much for her.

The journalist Godfrey Winn, who was once invited to a weekend house party there in August 1951—at which Harrison, Leigh, Olivier, Orson Welles, and others were present—recorded fascinating vignettes of how they interacted with one another. He called it, "like being part of an exquisite charade, performed by an all-star cast."[9] Olivier and Leigh would host elaborate candlelit dinners at one in the morning, after returning from appearing on-stage in London, at which the assembled celebrities would make small talk. Welles asked Olivier when he would take on the role of Iago, suggesting that he lacked the deep bass voice (and, indeed, skin colour) that Othello required. Leigh, who was an admirer of Harrison's performance in T. S. Eliot's play *The Cocktail Party*, earnestly implored him to explain an apparently crucial acting choice he made of clenching and unclasping his left hand repeatedly and cracking his knuckles. She was disappointed when Harrison explained that this was because he was suffering from a cramp and was trying to relieve it, rather than delving into some hidden subtext of Eliot's.

Winn was keenly aware of the dynamic within the Oliviers' marriage, one where he was the great star of stage and screen whereas she, at thirty-seven, was too old to be the ingénue and too young to be the grande dame. Although Olivier was only seven years older than Leigh, he inevitably took on a paternalistic role to the woman he called "Pussy." The continual demands that she consequently placed upon him—to provide endless drinks, to entertain her and their guests, and to be as charismatic off-stage as he was when on—led him, in Winn's account, to "cry beseechingly" when alone in his study: "I have ten more years of my career, and I *must* have sleep."[10]

Harrison, meanwhile, was able to observe his erstwhile co-star-turned-international celebrity closely, and his opinion of her was not a flattering one. "Vivien's energy had always been manic, of course, but now the manic-depressive condition was taking its dreadful toll, and she seemed more than ever like a beautiful Dresden shepherdess, exquisite, and only too easily breakable."[11] When, on one occasion, Leigh tripped and fell during an impromptu cabaret act, Harrison observed Olivier carry her upstairs and return in a state of terror, "because a slight accident like that could apparently trigger off a bout of her illness, which could last for weeks. We all spent the rest of the evening willing her recovery."[12]

Over the next few years, Harrison and Leigh would both give their career-defining performances. He created the role of Henry Higgins in the Lerner and Loewe musical *My Fair Lady* on Broadway in 1956, opposite Julie Andrews as the Cockney flower-girl Eliza Doolittle, who he seeks to turn into a lady. The musical, based on Shaw's *Pygmalion*, was a much-admired box office success that ran for years in both New York and London, and won Harrison a Tony for Best Actor. When he later reprised the role for the 1964 film—opposite Audrey Hepburn, who replaced Andrews at producer Jack

Warner's insistence—he won an Oscar,* and later wrote that "the only thing that I was not delighted with was that [Andrews] didn't do the film with me, and that was only partly because it would have been much easier for me if she had."[13]

Leigh, meanwhile, was cast in the lead role of the film adaptation *A Streetcar Named Desire*, playing the tragic, doomed Southern belle Blanche DuBois, a kind of defeated mirror image of her Scarlett O'Hara. Jessica Tandy had played the role on Broadway—opposite Marlon Brando as the brutishly charismatic Stanley Kowalski, a role that he reprised for the film adaptation. She had been acclaimed for doing so, winning a Tony Award. Leigh was cast in an Olivier-directed production of the play in London in 1949, which was less immediately successful. The fame of the couple involved, and the various changes and edits that the theatrical censor, the Lord Chamberlain, demanded of the "lewd and salacious" play, meant that West End audiences were not seeing the full force of Williams's vision. Still, Leigh was a bigger star than Tandy—and an Oscar winner, no less—and so was cast in Elia Kazan's film adaptation, which was eventually released in September 1951.

Whether or not the award-winning part was the defining role of Leigh's career—one for which she bleached her hair and deliberately made herself look over the hill and unappealing, a contrast to the glamorous roles that she had taken on, most recently Anna Karenina in cinema—it proved to be a grim turning point in her life. A couple of years before, she had casually informed Olivier that she no longer loved him in any romantic sense, and that their relationship would be a professional partnership, nothing more. Now, as she immersed herself in Blanche DuBois, she began the final and tragic act of her life, with her already damaged mental health slowly falling apart. She acknowledged this when she said, "Blanche is a woman with

* As Andrews did for her performance in *Mary Poppins* as the eponymous supernatural nanny.

everything stripped away. She is a tragic figure and I understand her. But playing her tipped me into madness."[14]

It is possible to draw parallels between the fictitious relationship between Henry Higgins and Eliza in *My Fair Lady* and the real-life marriage between Olivier and Leigh. In both circumstances, the older man begins as the superior, better-known partner, seeking to mould the younger woman into a subservient, willing recipient of his wisdom and attention. In both cases, the woman initially acquiesces before rejecting the man's overbearing attitudes and attempts to strike out on her own, finding the interest of a younger man both flattering and rewarding. In the case of *My Fair Lady*, this is the character of Freddy Eynsford-Hill, a young aristocrat who falls in love with Eliza. In Leigh's real-life case, she became besotted with the actor Peter Finch, who Olivier had recruited to star at the Old Vic as part of his nascent National Theatre company.

When the two met, it proved to be deeply auspicious. As Finch's second wife, Yolande, later wrote, "[Peter] had met the greatest actor in the world and he had met the woman who was to be his greatest passion, his mistress and very nearly the death of him."[15] Leigh and Finch had first met in 1949, and had formed a valuable rapport together. When Olivier was working, it was often the younger actor who would spend time with Leigh. The actress Maxine Audley said of their relationship, "Peter was kind of helpless—putty in her hands. He would do anything she wanted. If she rang him up, he would drop everything and go to her . . . he was a fairly weak character . . . she could do anything with him."[16]

When the film *Elephant Walk* was to be made in Ceylon, the producers wanted to cast Olivier and Leigh in the lead roles, but he declined, citing the pressures of theatre work. However, Leigh was keen to take on the part of Ruth Wiley, the wife of a colonial tea planter, and Finch was auspiciously cast as her husband. Olivier saw the two off on filming in February 1953, and his parting words to Finch, laden with portent, were, "Take care of her." The next time he would see his wife, she was engaged in an affair with her co-star; something that Olivier treated with a calm equanimity, as if it took the pressure off him for a time. Leigh was by then on the verge of a full-blown mental collapse, exacerbated by the heat and the constant sex with Finch. The collapse duly occurred, and she had to be shipped back to England under heavy sedation before being admitted to a psychiatric institution, where she underwent electroconvulsive therapy.

After Leigh recovered, she resumed her career, largely as a stage actress, although she did appear in the 1955 film version of her friend and fellow Eaton Square resident Rattigan's adultery drama *The Deep Blue Sea* opposite Kenneth More, who had no rapport with her, unlike the charismatic Finch. Perhaps petulantly, More later dismissed both the film and its star, saying, "The casting of the beautiful Vivien Leigh was absurd. She was supposed to be an outwardly ordinary but secretly highly-sexed woman who meets a young pilot on the golf course and falls for him. . . . When the part is played by a woman generally held to be one of the most beautiful in the world, the whole meaning is lost." He concluded that "we were never in accord. . . . I thought her interpretation was wrong, and so when we played a scene together we had the wrong chemistry between us."[17]

Absence of chemistry aside, the film may have felt uncomfortably close to home for both her and Olivier. They had resumed their professional relationship in another Rattigan play, the heavy-handed 1953 romantic comedy *The Sleeping Prince*—later, notoriously, to be filmed as *The Prince and the Showgirl*, with Marilyn Monroe in the part Leigh created—and had greater success in a trio of Shakespearean plays at Stratford-upon-Avon in 1955, namely *Twelfth Night*, *Macbeth*, and *Titus Andronicus*.

The last, however, attracted a notorious piece of criticism of Leigh by the *Observer*'s ever-acerbic theatre critic Kenneth Tynan, who wrote that, while Olivier's performance was "an unforgettable concerto of grief," Leigh "receives the news that she is about to be ravished on her husband's corpse with little more than the mild annoyance of one who would have preferred foam rubber."[18] It was the culmination of a series of personal attacks by Tynan, who had previously sneered at her "strangely bloodless display" in *The Sleeping Prince*, and shrugged off her Lady Macbeth as "more niminy-piminy than thundery-blundery, more viper than anaconda," although he allowed that the performance was "still quite competent in its small way."[19]

Olivier—who would later recruit Tynan as the National's literary adviser, thereby blunting his considerable claws—took the criticism personally, later writing in his memoirs that the critic was "directly responsible for at least one of Vivien's nervous breakdowns."[20] Even if, when Tynan was faced with Leigh in the flesh, "he became a sort of devoted slave in a way. . . . He fell in love with her when he met her,"[21] there was an essential mismatch between the Oliviers.

The now knighted Laurence was widely held to be the greatest Shakespearean actor in the world, perhaps even simply the greatest actor. Vivien's luminous beauty, however, was offset by her increasing mental instability. When she was in a relatively receptive frame of mind, she took an almost detached interest in her illness, reading F. Scott Fitzgerald's *The Crack-Up* and continuing her relationship with Finch, which Olivier regarded with a mixture of exasperation and suavity.* And when she was in a decline, as she proved to be on the European tour of *Titus Andronicus*, she manically overcompensated for any feelings of inadequacy or guilt with lengthy, emotional outbursts, often directed at her husband, and a succession of parties and drinking sessions. She may have reflected, a decade later, that the hard-living likes of Peter O'Toole, Richard Burton, and Oliver Reed were celebrated, even lionised, for their off-screen behaviour, but she was castigated for it. Yet in the eyes of those around her, she was proving increasingly erratic and unreliable.

Leigh announced that she was pregnant, at the age of forty-two, in the summer of 1956; it remained unclear as to whether the child was Finch's or Olivier's. She miscarried on 12 August, and buried

---

* Hugo Vickers recounts the anecdote of Leigh, Finch, and Olivier all being together in a French villa, and Olivier purring, "Dear boy, I forgot to get you a Christmas present." The two men therefore solemnly exchanged the ties they were wearing.

herself in work and activity, presumably in an attempt to recover from the loss. This activity extended to the purchase of a large flat at 54 Eaton Square in the summer of 1957, which was intended as a London home for both her and Olivier. Her biographer Alexander Walker was able to describe the apartment in minute detail in his later life of her, which also gives us an unparalleled insight into how a wealthy couple of artistic tastes would have furnished an Eaton Square property:

> Olivier's study had blackberry-purple wallpaper contrasting with an acid-green carpet, heavily pleated yellow curtains . . . a purple-and-white *toile de Jouy* sofa and a John Piper painting of Notley. The dining-room—really a deep, pillared alcove off the hall, was in Regency stripes. An Aubusson rug in amethyst, ivy and beige dominated the living-room. . . . The [bedroom] walls were hung with white chintz strewn with large cabbage roses, the carpet lime green like a spring lawn. . . . The bed was a four-poster, quilted and canopied with roses in bud, sprig and full-blown. If the bed looked faintly familiar to visitors, it was not surprising: it was a reproduction of the one at Tara in *Gone with the Wind*.[22]

In addition to the Piper, the apartment had a collection of the Oliviers' art, including a small Churchill painting of rosebuds, a Degas oil of a woman washing, a Cellini drawing, and an unfinished sketch of Leigh by Augustus John. It was uncompleted because Leigh tired of John's habit of continually leaving to top himself up from a whisky decanter, and eventually left the studio, canvas in hand.

While her husband was absent, usually while working or touring in the John Osborne play *The Entertainer* that had been written as a star vehicle for him, Leigh enjoyed a relatively civilised *regime de vivre* in Eaton Square. She would summon her secretary Rosemary Geddes and spend the morning dealing with fan mail, cheques that had to be signed, and deciding which clothes to wear that day, all the while smoking constantly and lying regally in her *Gone with the*

Wind replica bed. She had specific tastes in food and drink: Melba toast and honey for breakfast, orange juice and coffee to drink, smoked salmon salad and gin and tonics for lunch, and early evening cocktails, before disappearing off in Norman Hartnell couture to whichever glamorous party she had been invited to, invariably wearing a mink coat or stole.

In theory, it sounded an enviable, thoroughly enjoyable existence. In practice, moneyed leisure, interspersed with occasional stage work, failed to make Leigh happy. Olivier did not warm to life in Eaton Square with his increasingly estranged wife, and instead made his London base nearby, in a small flat in Walcott Street. Rumours began to proliferate in the newspapers that the two were on the verge of separation, even divorce, and the bland statements that the pair put out—"Larry and I are very much in love," Leigh said, as Olivier excelled himself with the non-committal "I have no comment to make on anything which does not exist"[23]—did nothing to silence the excitable chatter that Britain's most famous thespian couple would soon be parting ways.

Olivier may have reacted to his wife's infidelity with apparent cool, even relief, but it did not stop him from pursuing his own affairs. Armchair psychologists may have been intrigued to see that he engaged in a dalliance with the actress Dorothy Tutin—twenty-three years his junior—when she played his daughter in *The Entertainer*, which Leigh may well have been aware of. When she greeted Tutin backstage at the play's opening night, she said, pointedly, "Dottie! What a performance. Still the perennial virgin!"[24] Yet the Tutin relationship did not last, not least because it was made clear to her that Leigh was likely to kill herself if Olivier left her. The couple seemed to be yoked together in a Strindbergian dance of death, deeply incompatible but unable to live without each other. Which is why it was something of a volte-face that, sitting in Olivier's dressing room at the Palace Theatre in late 1957, Leigh was informed by her husband, without any particular emotion, "I suppose you should know that I am in love with Joan Plowright."

* * *

WHEN LEIGH HAD LEFT *Elephant Walk* a few years earlier, her role in the film was recast with Elizabeth Taylor, who would later go on to act opposite Harrison and Richard Burton in Joseph L. Mankiewicz's notorious 1963 film of *Cleopatra*. Leigh's performance as the Egyptian queen in the rather lower-profile 1945 picture *Caesar and Cleopatra* (opposite Claude Rains as Caesar) caused one of her miscarriages. The apparently never-ending health problems (real and imagined) that beset Taylor on set—never mind her love affair with Richard Burton—made for a challenging experience, even if Harrison subsequently claimed, "I loved working with Elizabeth Taylor on the film because she is in every way the consummate film actress and her professionalism on the set and in front of the camera is quite remarkable to see."*

Harrison is, for a modern viewer, quite the most enjoyable part of *Cleopatra* as a wily, charismatic Julius Caesar, who can still summon up enough of the old *Rake's Progress* charm to make it entirely understandable why Cleopatra-Taylor might fall in love with him. He rose above the largely poor reviews, was Oscar nominated for Best Actor (and won the National Board of Review's accolade), and would soon saunter unscathed into the film of *My Fair Lady*, which finally won him the Oscar. The sixties, at first glance, appeared to be a golden period for Harrison, after a relatively quiet 1950s. As he embraced the life of a character actor, he found many of his greatest and most rewarding parts, and bookended the decade by living on Eaton Square.

Not long after Olivier shocked Leigh by telling her that he was in love with Joan Plowright, Harrison moved into their home at 54 Eaton Square for a short period, while he was playing a run in Chekhov's play *Platonov* at the Royal Court nearby. It was one of

* There have been many in-depth accounts of the sheer chaos of filming *Cleopatra*, but my favourite is to be found in Roger Lewis's *Erotic Vagrancy*, in the section "I.T.A.L.Y."

the dramatist's lesser-known works, but the central role, of a man loved to varying degrees by four separate women, seemed to have been tailor-made for the incomparable Rex, as Kenneth Tynan once dubbed him, who was grateful to be able to escape from the lucrative straitjacket of *My Fair Lady*. He also liked the idea—as Olivier had done with *The Entertainer*—of triumphing in the citadel of the Angry Young Men. Besides, it was only a few moments' walk from Eaton Square. Harrison later commented, "I felt that this young angry brigade despised me and my methods as old-fashioned and reactionary, and affected an attitude of superiority towards me which I found both irritating and amusing. The idea of joining them in their lair, and seeing if I could beat them at their own game, appealed to me a lot."[25]

Harrison was cast opposite the Welsh actress Rachel Roberts, who had made a significant, BAFTA-winning impact in the 1960 kitchen sink drama *Saturday Night and Sunday Morning* opposite Albert Finney. She was recently separated from her husband, Alan Dobie, and was unused to the suave, moneyed glamour that Harrison embodied. As she described it in her diaries, "Rex cut such a dash. There was something Edwardian about him, something silky and ruffled."[26] He, meanwhile, was rebounding from the death of his third wife, Kay Kendall, from leukaemia the previous year. In a complicated and typically Rexian tangle of relationships, he had left his second wife, Lilli Palmer, on the understanding that they would remarry after Kendall's death, but Palmer instead married her own lover, the Argentine actor Carlos Thompson. Harrison was, therefore, single for the first time in decades, and Roberts found herself the beneficiary of his considerable charm and largesse.

Harrison describes his meeting with Roberts with suspicious economy in his memoirs. "She was a very good serious actress . . . [and] much more involved in the angry young movement than I was. As far as temperament and experience is concerned, we couldn't have been more different, Rachel and I, and yet a great sympathy grew up between us and we became very close."[27] As a result of this "great sympathy," the two first enjoyed regular lunch dates at a French restaurant during rehearsals, and then she became a constant visitor to 54 Eaton Square, where she would cook Harrison roast dinners and fry-ups: rather less-refined fare than the salmon salads that Leigh would have picked at delicately a couple of years earlier.

The relationship swiftly turned physical. As Roberts later recalled, "His vitality energised me. I was swept off my feet, felt pampered (wasn't actually), got attention. It was heady." And the appeal of Harrison ("he's everything I want, but maybe not that intelligent") was that of a soigné, wealthy man about town. She summarised him as "that worldly, sophisticated man who drank black velvets, listened to Ray Charles records, lived in Eaton Square, ordered chauffeur-driven cars, consumed her little body, praised her green eyes; loved her very naïveté, her little-girl excitement over cats."[28] *Platonov* was a hit, and Harrison celebrated by taking Roberts to his Italian home in Portofino, announcing to the world that she was now his official paramour. Although Roberts noted that the fifty-two-year-old twice-divorced widower looked "very careworn," she was also aware that the new association was one that could benefit her in every regard. "I began to feel finally not plain, but pretty. Rex was successful. He was acclaimed, looked up to. And he had chosen me."[29]

The honeymoon period of the relationship was intoxicating, but by the time that they returned to Eaton Square in July 1961, something had shifted. Harrison may have liked to give the impression of being a smoothly generous man of means, but he was in fact penny-pinching and fixated on his lack of career progression, which was due to the lack of exposure he had had since his stage success in *My Fair Lady*. *Platonov* had earned him the Royal Court's standard wage of £60 a week, which would not even come close to covering the cleaning bill of Eaton Square, let alone keeping his mistress in lavish holidays and gifts, but his lucrative royalties from the sales of the LP featuring his performance in *My Fair Lady* covered these expenses. What it did not do was to give him the assurance of acclaimed lead roles. A swift return to the Royal Court in Nigel Dennis's play

August for the People was a flop, despite or because it featured both Harrison and Roberts, and she found herself having to act as quasi-maternal comforter. Until, at least, Rex became Caesar. Buoyed by the highest-profile screen role he had enjoyed in over a decade, and with a fee to match, he married Roberts in Italy on 21 March 1962, and thereby gave the international media a brief break from their Burton-Taylor fixation.

His former landlord Olivier, by then divorced from Leigh and newly married to Plowright, publicly expressed pessimism about the union's longevity, suggesting that Roberts had too much in common with Leigh and that Harrison would find the relationship as difficult as he had. (It was with this in mind that discussions for a Harrison-Roberts production of *Much Ado About Nothing*, later in the decade, went nowhere. Olivier, who was to have directed, would happily have worked with Harrison but blanched at the thought of directing someone who was, by then, widely regarded as unreliable at best.) Yet Roberts, aware that she had seen various sides of her new husband over the previous eighteen months, could only hope that sunlit uplands awaited. As she wrote, in retrospect rather sadly, in her diary: "After meeting Rex, all I wanted to be was the best, the most brilliant wife in the world."

LEIGH, MEANWHILE, HAD LONG SINCE passed that point, and her formal separation from Olivier took place in May 1960. Although he had confessed his feelings for Joan Plowright nearly three years before, he was not a heartless or unfeeling man, and he was aware that, if he had handled matters differently, the inevitable result would almost certainly have been a sharp descent into mania, depression, or both, followed by her suicide. Therefore he did what so many wealthy and powerful actors have done before and since to evade domestic responsibilities, and fled to Hollywood, where he made *Spartacus* with Kirk Douglas and Stanley Kubrick. Olivier played the villain, Crassus, who is tormented by an unrequited passion for

Jean Simmons's slave girl Varinia, who becomes Spartacus's wife. That Simmons had played his Ophelia a decade ago, when his *Hamlet* became an Oscar-winning film, only confirmed the sense of his past looming over him mockingly. Socialising with Simmons and her husband, Stewart Granger, he confessed the vagaries of his situation, and said, "It was really seeing you two together, how much you loved each other, that made me decide I wanted that kind of happiness too."[30]*

With Olivier absent, Leigh returned to stage work, appearing in *Duel of Angels,* an adaptation of *Pour Lucrèce,* in 1958, and then following her estranged husband and Harrison's lead to appear at the Royal Court the following year in her friend Noël Coward's *Look After Lulu!,* an adaptation of a Feydeau farce. That nobody was looking after Vivien sufficiently well was a source of guilt to Olivier. He returned from America, having played one Roman general, and headed straight away to Stratford to play another in the form of Coriolanus. Leigh greeted him at the airport and kissed him in front of the waiting reporters, all of whom could not avoid noticing that there was an intrinsic awkwardness between the couple.

Offstage, preparations began for their separation. Eaton Square would now become Leigh's permanent residence, as Notley Abbey would be sold. Olivier joked grimly, "now my baronial period is just about over."[31] When a lengthy, well-sourced article appeared in a German newspaper in November 1959 that suggested that the Oliviers were now permanently estranged, they could barely muster a denial. His relationship with Joan Plowright was common knowledge amongst actors and writers; and he hoped that, in choosing the stable, much younger Plowright over the tempestuous, troubled Leigh, he would be able to regain a degree of autonomy and personal freedom, which he planned to devote to launching the National Theatre that had become his personal crusade.

Coward, seeing Olivier's happiness at the thought of escaping

* Unfortunately, Simmons and Granger divorced the following year.

from his marriage, could also recognise how traumatic it would be for Leigh. He wrote, "She will have to face up to the truth sooner or later and the sooner the better. She will inevitably suffer less as time goes by, but she's still at the stage when she doesn't wish to believe this."[32] It was now Leigh's turn to head to America, where she worked with her Eaton Square neighbour, the actor and dancer Robert Helpmann, on the Broadway production of *Duel of Angels*.

It was while working on this production that she re-encountered the Canadian-British actor John "Jack" Merivale, who had been a supporting actor in the Oliviers' stage production of *Romeo and Juliet* twenty years before, and was now eligible to appear on Broadway by dint of his Canadian birth. Then, the relationship had been briefly stormy; Leigh had accused him of cheating during a game of Chinese checkers, and, when Merivale had appealed to Olivier for moral support, she had shouted, "Don't you try to come between us! We've been together for years. Nobody's coming between us. Don't you try!"[33] Unsurprisingly, they had not stayed in touch, save one fleeting backstage encounter in spring 1945, which was why their reunion was an opportunity to begin a friendship afresh, rather than remind each other of the brief flare-up that had occurred.

Merivale was close in age to Leigh—forty-two to her forty-six—and his residual attraction to her, begun decades before, grew increasingly during rehearsals. Yet he was aware that he was following, literally and figuratively, in the footsteps of Britain's best-known actor, who had left a legacy in Leigh's life that could not be surmounted. He later recounted: "It was obvious things had gone terribly wrong, yet Vivien still seemed obsessively attached to Larry. She had photos of him all around her. And once, at rehearsal, when I was wearing a plaid suit, she reached out and fondled it and said wistfully, 'Larry's got a suit just like that. Oh God, I wish he were here.'"[34] Merivale believed that the relationship would remain platonic, but by March, it was clear that there was a growing attachment between them, and Leigh eventually took the initiative by asking, "When are we going to make love properly?"[35]

It was, as he anticipated, both a thrilling and terrifying experience to, in his words, "have fallen in love with the most famous woman in the world."[36] Merivale, who never became a first-rank actor, knew that he could not compete with Olivier either in terms of reputation or ability, but what he could do was to take the damaged, unhappy Leigh and reassure her of his complete, selfless devotion. It appeared to work. By May 1960, she was buying him expensive presents, referring to him as "my beloved" and announcing "[the gift] is to thank you for all your kindness and goodness to me and it is to tell you that I love you"—but then she received a letter from Olivier on 21 May, asking for a divorce, so that he could marry Plowright. At Helpmann's instigation, Leigh made a press announcement on 22 May 1960 that "Lady Olivier wishes to say that Sir Laurence has asked for a divorce in order to marry Miss Joan Plowright. She will naturally do whatever he wishes."

Olivier had known of her relationship with Merivale, and not only approved of it but hoped that they would marry. He had explicitly asked the younger actor, "Any chance of a union?" and when Merivale had equivocated, there was "a deep sigh across the Atlantic."[37] If Leigh had intended to humiliate Olivier with her public ploy, it succeeded. The actor became the subject of rumour and scuttlebutt in the press, and many of his most famous romantic roles, from Romeo to Heathcliff, were recalled to ironic effect. The *Daily Mail* summed up the mixture of incredulity and sorrow that many felt when it wrote on 23 May 1960, "A legend crumbles. The magic turns to myth."[38]

Leigh may have won what public relations battles there were to be fought, but it came at a great cost. When she realised that her marriage had irreparably broken down, she declined into a manic state, even as an oblivious Harrison, who was passing through New York, congratulated Merivale, saying, "You seem to be doing all right."[39] In fact, Leigh had undergone another course of ECT for her mental health, and when *Duel of Angels* was closed down due to a Broadway strike, she returned to London and Eaton Square, apparently with the intent of seeing if she could, despite everything, reconcile with

Olivier. She even gave an interview in which she expressed her hope of appearing opposite him on-screen in *Macbeth*.

When she was at her flat, she attempted to hold parties and drank heavily, but old friends including Coward counselled her against her behaviour, to her initial rage and frustration.

After she undertook further electric shock therapy, for what was now diagnosed as a "cyclic manic-depressive psychosis," she became much calmer and more amenable. The period of February 1959 to June 1960, during which she had undergone both personal and professional difficulties, was particularly stressful and difficult. The doctor treating her wrote, of this time: "She rapidly loses her natural restraint and normal reserve, talks freely, and during this period loses judgement, reasoning power and insight. She adopts lost causes, will parade in the streets in procession, invade the House of Lords,* and talk freely to the Press."[40] *Quelle horreur*.

To a sympathetic contemporary observer, Leigh's mental health problems were clearly exacerbated by Olivier's essentially abandoning her when she became too difficult for him to deal with any longer. The saintly Merivale had no such qualms about putting her needs (and, by extension, career) ahead of his. When she returned to America, Leigh wrote to him to say, "I am feeling so very very well . . . This has been a most extraordinary week. I think the most extraordinary of my life. Alone and yet so infinitely close to you." She was able to make light of her situation—"there have even been some hilarious moments"—and there seemed, at last, to be a degree of stability, as she concluded, "Sweet dear love, I ache and long to see you."[41]

Olivier not only accepted her new relationship but positively welcomed it, even as he remarked to friends, with an unfortunate double entendre, that "I shall never love anybody as much as Vivien, but it isn't possible to live with her and do my work—I just can't keep it up. She's too exhausting for me."[42] And when Merivale

* As she did on 9 July 1958, in protest against the St James's Theatre being demolished.

re-encountered Leigh, both of them bound for Los Angeles for the revived run of *Duel of Angels* there, he could only hope cautiously that theirs would be a happy, rewarding relationship. He wrote, of their reunion, "it was at that moment that I fell *wholly* in love with her and had *no doubts* at all that we would spend the rest of our lives together."[43] He was right, up to a point.

"IT CANNOT BE SAID THAT the many tensions of making *Doctor Dolittle* was helping the survival of my marriage to Rachel Roberts." So Harrison wrote in his memoirs decades after the event. Strangely, when he began to start work on what should have been his most successful film of the decade, his stock was as high professionally as it had ever been. He had won Best Actor at the Oscars for *My Fair Lady*, had avoided the contaminating effects of *Cleopatra,* and had had a couple of successes since. These included the undemanding, Rattigan-scripted *The Yellow Rolls-Royce* ("one of the most delightful films I've ever made")[44] and a performance as Pope Julius, opposite Charlton Heston's unlikely Michelangelo, in Carol Reed's *The Agony and the Ecstasy*, based on the Irving Stone bestseller. He was widely held to dwarf Heston's grandstanding. Harrison wrote of the former Ben-Hur: "[He was], I felt, altogether too wooden to play this great artist."[45] Most agreed with him.

Still, when Harrison commented that "[Roberts] hated the false glamour of film life, and found it very difficult to hang around waiting for me . . . [She] was so much more at home at the Royal Court Theatre, and the working-class theatre in general,"[46] he may have been both snobbish and patronising, but the actual truth was considerably worse. As Harrison's career resurged, so hers dwindled, with her public standing being nothing more than "Mrs Rex Harrison." The result of this frustration was to push her into ever-heavier drinking sessions. Even the ecstatic reviews—and an Oscar nomination—for her performance in *This Sporting Life* were not enough to give her any confidence in her ability as an actress.

Harrison was soon, by his own account, "bored shitless" by their marriage, declaring, "I vowed never to fit into the life of some woman; she has to fit into mine."[47] He began to take on roles that would keep him away from her, not least because Leigh's return to Eaton Square in the early sixties meant that he was without a London base at this time. Although he was still outwardly loyal to Roberts, calling the composer Lionel Bart "you little homosexual runt" when Bart dared to suggest that she was drunk during rehearsals for his show *Maggie May*, Harrison returned to adultery with the determined air of a man who knew what he was good at. His neglected wife, meanwhile, became more and more outré in public displays, pretending to be a dog and getting down on her knees, barking, and chasing cats. It was unclear whether, like Leigh, she was suffering from a mental disorder, or if the effects of frustration and alcohol overwhelmed her and eroded any remaining restraint that she had.

In any case, by this time Harrison, wishing to cash in the cachet that he had acquired with his Henry Higgins success, accepted the role of Doctor John Dolittle in 20th Century Fox's big-budget adaptation of Hugh Lofting's stories. Harrison demanded a vast fee and creative control, including having all the songs written to his specification; he was by no means a singer and so liked to speak in time to the music. Roberts celebrated the news by taking a huge amount of barbiturates and washing it down with brandy, leading Harrison to believe that she was dying until her stomach was pumped and she was briefly hospitalised.

The animals were hard enough to work with, but Roberts was worse. By the time that she arrived on the film's St Lucia set in the summer of 1966, her behaviour had grown so erratic—including trying to set the trained seals free from their pen—that the producer Arthur Jacobs complained, "We should have taken out an insurance policy against your fucking wife liberating our animals."[48] A defiant Roberts reacted to being thus castigated by performing a striptease, "the Dance of the Forty Pussies" at a reception at the British embassy. As Harrison's son Carey described it, "To my amazement, his expression was almost one of gratification. For someone who had always had a public reputation of being a 'bad lad,' to have a wife who outdid him in public misbehaviour now seemed to overjoy him."[49]

Still, his usual response to her bad behaviour was to drink heavily and then offer similar outrage himself, such as performing a rewritten version of the song that inspired the title *My Fair Lady*, "London Bridge is Falling Down," in front of an audience of the Hollywood elite, which, with typical wit and class, Harrison now titled "My Big Cock." Catastrophically, after the *Dolittle* debacle, Roberts and Harrison made a picture together in Paris, *A Flea in Her Ear*, an adaptation of the Feydeau farce. Like a thespian version of the couple in Albee's *Who's Afraid of Virginia Woolf?*, they would stage tempestuous, ornate arguments both on- and off-set. This eventually climaxed in a drunk Roberts gatecrashing a dinner party that had been held in Harrison's honour and announcing, in sloppy but adequate French, "*Excusez moi, je suis très tard. Mais j'ai fucké le chauffeur de mon mari.*"[50] Harrison's response to this particular revelation was not recorded.

She had written in her diary, understandably, that "Rex grew more and more stiff and distant from me, and I suppose I drank more and more."[51] *Doctor Dolittle* flopped, taking Harrison's resurgent career down with it. He returned to Eaton Square, this time to number 75, and Roberts lived separately, at nearby Lowndes Square. The separate residences were hardly conducive to a happy and fulfilled marriage; and soon enough Harrison began another long-term affair with Richard Harris's wife, Elizabeth, who would, eventually, become his fifth spouse. Roberts, distraught, drunk, and deserted, moved to Los Angeles in a vain attempt to keep her career going. She eventually died of a deliberate overdose of barbiturates and weedkiller, washed down with alcohol, on 26 November 1980.

Harrison made no reference to her death in his memoir; and his only recorded comment, to a *Daily Express* journalist, was to say, "It's a tragedy. Suicide is always a tragedy."[52] He opened in a new production of *My Fair Lady* the next night in Los Angeles, and seemed every bit the committed show business veteran. Still, he was not entirely heartless. The show's director, Patrick Garland, was watching from the wings and said, "When he came to the 'Grown accustomed to her face' number at the end of the show, I'm as sure as anything that he was singing it with the memory of Rachel in mind. I was standing in the wings, quite close to him, and I saw a tear well over and trickle down his cheek."[53]

Two decades before that, Leigh made a concerted effort to change her life after her separation from Olivier, aided by Merivale. She drank less and returned to Tennessee Williams for her first film in six years, an adaptation of his novel *The Roman Spring of Mrs. Stone*. She starred opposite a young Warren Beatty in the tale of a middle-aged American woman and her doomed love affair with a young gigolo. The film was not a success, but Williams was delighted with it, writing, "I think that film is a poem. It was the last important work of both Miss Leigh and of the director, José Quintero, a man who is as dear to my heart as Miss Leigh is."[54]

Merivale was a positive influence on her life, but he was less impressive as a leading man. By the time that *Duel of Angels* had opened in Australia in July 1962, he ruefully said of himself, "I wasn't Laurence Olivier. I was not star quality."[55] It did not help that Olivier was now married to Plowright, with their son Richard being born on 3 December 1961. Although Olivier and Leigh maintained as amicable a relationship as they could, her mental health was still erratic, and there could be unpleasant, protracted flare-ups. When she appeared in the Broadway musical *Tovarich* in 1963, she had a breakdown on-stage and walked off, requiring heavy sedation before she returned to England. Just before the tranquilisers kicked in and had their necessary effect, she had a pressing question for her lover. "Does Larry know?"[56] The irony was that she was sufficiently professional—and more than sufficiently competent—to win a Tony for Best Actress in a Musical, demonstrating that, despite her personal demons, she was still able to pull off a show.

There would be one final film, Stanley Kramer's 1965 ensemble drama *Ship of Fools*, in which Leigh, as befitting her star status, was given top billing for her performance as Mary Treadwell, a faded divorcée who comments, of her former husband, "I made life hell for him." Audiences may have enjoyed the gleam in her eye as she delivered the line, but it would be the French actress Simone Signoret who would receive a greater share of the acclaim, and the award nominations. It was extraordinary that Leigh was able to make the film at all, given that her far from robust mental health had again declined, although many might agree with Coward's despairing comment, "Why does Vivien keep choosing roles that cast her as a rejected, fading beauty?"[57]

At the beginning of 1967, her professional life seemed all but over, despite a well-received run in John Gielgud's production of Chekhov's *Ivanov*, opposite Gielgud himself, on Broadway the previous autumn. Yet her issues with mental health were now about to be outweighed by a collapse in her physical well-being. She believed that she was suffering from an attack of influenza at the end of May that year, but when she went to a Harley Street clinic to be X-rayed, it became clear that she was suffering a recurrent bout of tuberculosis, which she had previously suffered in North Africa, shortly after making *Gone with the Wind*. Leigh was confined to her Eaton Square home, where she was visited by many friends. These did not include Olivier, who had recently been diagnosed with prostate cancer and was receiving treatment at the nearby St Thomas's Hospital.

Leigh seemed to know that her illness was terminal, and made black-humoured jokes about it, commenting, "Why can't I have a nice respectable illness like cancer?"[58] Her lung was covered in what Merivale described as a "great black hole." Although she agreed to three months of bed rest in an attempt to combat the disease, she was too weakened to be able to survive it and finally died in the night of 8 July 1967 of a pulmonary attack brought on by tuberculosis. She was fifty-three, the same age as Roberts was when she died thirteen years later.

A distraught Merivale telephoned her family, friends, and inevitably

Olivier, who discharged himself from hospital the following day and headed to Eaton Square. There, as he wrote in his memoirs: "I stood and prayed for forgiveness for all the evils that had sprung up between us."[59] He and Merivale briefly exchanged condolences, before Leigh's body was removed, and she passed into the immortality of legend. As for her former lover, there could be one small consolation, passed on to him by none other than Harrison. "You have at least a tiny compensation," the older and rather sadder actor wrote. "Yours was a guardianship of great worth in the Eliot sense."[60] Blanche DuBois, after her final mental collapse in *A Streetcar Named Desire*, famously remarks, "I have always depended on the kindness of strangers." Vivien Leigh could at least depend on the kindness of her friends at the last, for all the event and tragedy of her brilliant, brief life.

UNKNOWN ARTIST, C. 1920 (CUBITTS COMPANY/PUBLIC DOMAIN)

Thomas Cubitt (1788–1855). The man responsible for building Eaton Square was able to combine business acumen and aesthetic ability, and wound up a favourite of Queen Victoria in the process.

EDWIN LANDSEER, C. 1834 (PUBLIC DOMAIN)

William Arden, 2nd Baron Alvanley (1789–1849). The dissipated Lord Alvanley may once have been a bosom companion to Lord Byron and the Prince Regent, but by the time he arrived in Eaton Square, he was a diminished figure.

THE TICHBORNE TRIAL, FREDERICK SARGENT, C. 1875 (HAMPSHIRE COUNTY COUNCIL MUSEUMS SERVICE, WINCHESTER/PUBLIC DOMAIN)

Matthew James Higgins, aka "Jacob Omnium" (1810–1868), was a satirist and crusading journalist, but perhaps his most notable public involvement was in the trial of the fraudulent "Tichborne claimant," Sir Arthur Orton.

HERBERT ROSE BARRAUD, LATE 1880S (BONHAMS/PUBLIC DOMAIN)

Sir W. S. Gilbert (1836–1911) was the "Gilbert" half of Gilbert and Sullivan, and was one of the wittiest men who ever lived in Eaton Square, satirising the high society that welcomed him into its upper echelons.

ANONYMOUS PHOTOGRAPHER FOR BASSANO, 27 JANUARY 1932 (BASSANO/PUBLIC DOMAIN)

Diana Mitford (1910–2003). Infamy and notoriety surrounded Diana, the most beautiful and celebrated of the Mitford sisters, after she embarked on a scandalous affair with British fascist Oswald Mosley.

ANONYMOUS PHOTOGRAPHER FOR BASSANO, 27 JANUARY 1932 (BASSANO/PUBLIC DOMAIN)

LIBRARY OF CONGRESS, 1923 (NATIONAL PHOTO COMPANY COLLECTION/ PUBLIC DOMAIN)

Stanley Baldwin (1867–1947). One of the many prime ministers or politicians to have inhabited Eaton Square was Stanley Baldwin, whom even the newspaper publisher Lord Beaverbrook saluted as "the toughest and most unscrupulous politician you could find."

ANONYMOUS PHOTOGRAPHER FOR BASSANO, FEBRUARY-MARCH 1936 (BASSANO/PUBLIC DOMAIN)

Neville Chamberlain (1869–1940) has been unfortunate enough to be regarded as one of Britain's most unsuccessful prime ministers, but he did lease his Eaton Square home to none other than Joachim von Ribbentrop, the German ambassador to the United Kingdom.

ALLAN WARREN, 1976 (ALLAN WARREN/GNU FREE DOCUMENTATION LICENCE)

Rex Harrison (1908–1990). This suave playboy actor and occasional habitué of furnished flats in Eaton Square belied his nonchalant public image with a mixture of heavy drinking and a frustration that others failed to appreciate his talents.

ANONYMOUS PHOTOGRAPHER, 10 JUNE 1957 (ANONYMOUS/PD-OLD-70)

Vivien Leigh (1913–1967) was fortunate enough to be a double Oscar-winning icon of screen and stage alike, and married to Laurence Olivier, but she was unfortunately beset by both physical and mental ill health during her time in Eaton Square.

UNKNOWN PHOTOGRAPHER, 1958 (ANONYMOUS/PUBLIC DOMAIN).

Raymond Chandler (1888–1959), the great crime and detective novelist, was briefly a resident of Eaton Square, where he befriended Ian Fleming, but his grief at the death of his wife saw him spending his time there in an alcoholic stupor.

Sir Terence Rattigan (1911–1977). The consummate playwright of the repressed human heart, Sir Terence Rattigan was one of Eaton Square's most stylish—and also unhappy—inhabitants, pouring out his sorrow into his peerless dramas.

ALLAN WARREN, 1975 (ALLAN WARREN/GNU FREE DOCUMENTATION LICENCE)

Lord Boothby (1900–1986) consorted with both high and low society alike from his Eaton Square flat, but when he formed a friendship of sorts with the notorious gangster Ronnie Kray, the repercussions were nearly disastrous.

8

Raymond Chandler, Ian Fleming, and Terence Rattigan: 29 and 116 Eaton Square

"Put more feeling into my typewriter"

One of the many challenges while writing *The Secrets of Eaton Square* has been the careful separation of documented fact from speculative fiction. In some cases, this has been as simple as ignoring some of the more bizarre stories associated with the residents of the square. I remain unconvinced that Diana Mitford and Oswald Mosley held black masses at 2 Eaton Square at Hitler's instigation, having not found a shred of evidence for such a supposition, save some hysterical rumours that I heard from people who perhaps should have known better. In others, however, it has been difficult to prove who did, and didn't, live in one of the houses or apartments for a certain amount of time.

I thought it unlikely, for instance, that Bee Gee Barry Gibb was a resident of Eaton Square. However, photographs exist that show him in his hirsute glory in the bathtub of number 68 in June 1968, enjoying the fruits of the success of such singles as "To Love Somebody" and "Spicks and Specks"; his relaxation anticipated the greater triumph that would occur when the band's album *Idea* would be released later that year, including the songs "I've Gotta Get a Message to You" and "I Started a Joke." Gibb would live at the square until at least 1970, enjoying the luxurious lifestyle that his musical talents offered. The 1968 photo shoot by Tony Gale suggests that Gibb's substantial apartment boasted all the modern conveniences that any self-respecting musician would demand as their right, including—naturally—a large blue rug, a prominently displayed television set, and copious quantities of leather furniture. All that is missing from the sixties idyll is a trouser press, but no doubt Gibb possessed such a then-aspirational item, as otherwise his immaculate white trousers would surely have struggled to retain their elegant crease.

Bee Gees, yes; black masses, no. But what of some of the square's other purported residents? Someone who knew a great deal about the darker side of the world—in fictitious form, at least—was the actor Christopher Lee, and several articles and biographies confidently state that he was a resident of Eaton Square. However, exhaustive research suggests that this may be a mixture of geographical error and wishful thinking. Instead, he lived on Cadogan Square nearby.

I was also intrigued by the suggestion that the Poet Laureate Alfred, Lord Tennyson, was a resident of the square, but in fact he lived briefly at 9 Upper Belgrave Street, between 1880 and 1881. Thereafter, he lived at Farringford House on the Isle of Wight and in Sussex at Aldworth House. Chopin did indeed play his first London concert in the summer of 1848, but at 99 Eaton Place rather than 99 Eaton Square. And did the actress Kate Winslet and musician Elton John live there separately? There exists no proof that either of them ever did, despite their being rumoured to have done so. It's another example of biography's near desperation to imbue the square with as many glamorous and successful figures as possible, to bolster its reputation and sustain house prices alike. Living next door to an Oscar-winning actress or a legendary rock star is, after all, a more appealing idea than your neighbour being a wealthy overseas-dwelling hedge fund owner. Until, that is, the parties begin.

Yet by far the most discussed resident of Eaton Square is one of the most famous British men who, strictly speaking, never actually existed at all. Commander James Bond, CMG, RNVR, first found public recognition in his creator Ian Fleming's novel *Casino Royale* in 1953, and went on to appear in twelve of Fleming's novels and two short story collections, as well as near-innumerable spin-off books by other hands and, at the time of writing, twenty-seven film adaptations. The spy has passed into public consciousness; and many of his catchphrases—"Bond . . . James Bond," "shaken not stirred,"* and the rest—have been repeated so many times that their greatest appeal now lies in their subversion rather than their self-conscious use. Yet amidst the globe-trotting shenanigans, the larger-than-life villains and their plots to achieve financial or world domination, and naturally the many women who the world's most priapic civil servant encounters on his glamorous way, there is a consistent discussion as to whether James Bond actually lived in Eaton Square.

Fleming's original novels don't offer a great deal of clarity. In *Moonraker*, the third book in the series, Bond is said to live on "a small but comfortable flat off the King's Road," and that the spy leaves his car under "the plane trees in the little square." The substantial plane trees that can be found in the centre of each lawn at Eaton Square, itself not far from the King's Road, might seem to be the giveaway here, to say nothing of the preponderance of "comfortable flats" in one of London's most expensive locations. Yet others, including William Boyd, the author of the later Bond continuation novel *Solo*, have seized upon the further detail in 1961's *Thunderball* that Bond "swerved out of the little Chelsea square and into the King's Road. . . . Bond pushed the car fast up Sloane Street and into the park."

The brief commute from Eaton Square up to Regent's Park, where the MI6 headquarters are said to be located, could *theoretically* be accomplished thus, but it would make little sense for 007 to reverse his Aston Martin DB5 down this particular end of the

* There remains considerable and lively debate as to whether a martini should be served shaken or stirred; friends in the know assure me that stirring is preferable, but *chacun à son gout.*

King's Road and thereby extend his journey unnecessarily. Likewise, Eaton Square—London's largest square—could hardly be described as "little." Boyd and others have suggested that it's more likely that Bond would have been resident at Wellington Square, a good half-mile away from Eaton Square. Boyd believes that he lived at number 25, the real-life home of the *Sunday Times* literary critic Desmond MacCarthy, where Fleming may (or may not) have attended the odd soirée and therefore had an idea of the layout. The biographer John Pearson, who also places Bond's home at Wellington Square, confidently states that the secret agent lived at number 30, although Boyd dismisses this as Pearson's private in-joke with a university friend who was a resident of that address.

The evidence, such as it is, for Bond living on a thinly disguised Eaton Square is circumstantial at best, as well as appearing to contradict the (admittedly slim) geographical details that Fleming teases the reader with in *Thunderball.* While the rumour continues to be an amusing one, it remains impossible to claim, as confidently as some estate agents and feature writers do, that 007 spent his London days in Eaton Square. Still, Boyd and Pearson's similarly self-assured statements smack of a desire to solve a mystery that generations of readers (and, indeed, viewers) have not seen as in urgent need of resolution.

However, Fleming himself was intimately acquainted with Eaton Square. It is a source of amusing serendipity that one of his own London residences was 22b Ebury Street. It was not only round the corner from the square, but, when Fleming took over its lease in October 1936, he inherited the property from none other than Oswald Mosley, who gave it up when he married Diana Mitford in Berlin. While Fleming lived on Ebury Street, he was initially an unsuccessful stockbroker, who amused himself out of working hours with a fast-living, hard-drinking set of young men and occasionally women, whom he christened "Le Cercle gastronomique." Their licentious, studiedly carefree ways would inspire many of the characteristics of his most famous creation. In any case, he pronounced the apartment, which was located in a converted Greek Revival building, suitable for his daily needs: "far enough away from Fitzrovia, close enough to Bohemia and within reasonable distance of the City."[1]

Fleming remained in Ebury Street until 1941, when, irritated by the demands of blackouts that compromised his dark blue–tinted skylight, he moved out to various hotels and members' clubs for the duration of the war and beyond. He finally made his London home at the more substantial address of 16 Victoria Square in 1953, where he would live for the final eleven years of his life. He pronounced it "frequently . . . festooned with effeminate intellectuals,"[2] and liked to escape further afield, to his Jamaica home of Goldeneye and on "business trips" to Las Vegas and New York, where he could socialise with hard-living expatriates.

In London, he was compelled to dine with his wife, Ann's, friend Lucian Freud, whom he loathed and who despised him in return. Fleming would later complain, in true philistine mode, that "Annie is always surrounding herself with bloody intellectuals, and intellectuals always make me feel inferior. I always felt inferior with my brother [Peter] because he was an intellectual, and I simply detest having to relive the same pattern with my wife."[3] His own preference, he claimed, would be to watch half-naked German Rhine maidens wrestle in mud in a Hamburg strip club. It was, after all, what James Bond would probably have preferred to do.

Some rare relief, at least, came in the arrival of the thriller writer Raymond Chandler to an apartment at 116 Eaton Square in the summer of 1955. The sixty-six-year-old Chandler was one of the best-known crime writers in the United States, responsible for such hard-boiled classics as *Farewell, My Lovely*; *The Big Sleep*; and *The Long Goodbye*, as well as creating perhaps the ultimate cynical, philosophical private detective in the inimitable form of Philip Marlowe. Yet Chandler was a strange mixture of heavy-drinking cynical American and British public schoolboy. He had studied at Dulwich College, where he had been a contemporary of none other than P. G.

Wodehouse* and had then gone on to be alternately a civil servant, a reporter for the *Daily Express*, and a writer of half-assed romantic poetry. Chandler knew that "I was distinctly not a clever young man. Nor was I at all a happy young man."[4] In his mid-twenties, he left for his parents' home country of the United States, where he devoted himself to his new existence and profession.

By the time that he returned to London forty years later, he was heartbroken at the recent death of his wife, Cissy.** Chandler was also in the superficially attractive but personally compromising position that he was an international celebrity, lionised the English-speaking world over after the success of the film adaptations of his work. "I am not happy," he complained to his American publisher in April, shortly after he arrived. "The racket here is just too intense."[5] He initially sequestered himself from the madding crowd at the Ritz, but, realising that he wished to have a more permanent base, agreed to take out a short lease on the Eaton Square apartment.

He described the acquisition of his temporary home with typical wit to his friend Louise Loughner, which also incidentally gives some insight into how any of Eaton Square's well-known tenants took up residence there. "The interview was very formal and by appointment. I was so bloody polite that I began to sicken myself. So I suddenly said to the man: 'I'm naturally a very polite person but I do think I'm overdoing it a little at the moment.' He laughed and stood up and held his hand out and thanked me for coming in. I said 'What about the lease?' He said, 'Well, usually we do like some sort of document, but in practise we rather tend to overlook the necessity.' That's the way they work over here. And that's why for generations they were the bankers of the world."[6]

---

* Who I expected to feature more heavily in this book than he has. A fleeting reference to "St Jude's the Resilient, Eaton Square"—a disguised St Peter's—in *Cocktail Time* is one of the very few allusions in Wodehouse's fiction.

** Fleming commented in his *London Magazine* article that "When the police arrived they found Raymond Chandler in the sitting room firing his revolver through the ceiling."

Chandler was photographed and interviewed by the press about his plans, in which he airily announced that he would write a West End play and remain in Britain for the foreseeable future. He gave good copy—"I've never made a pass at a woman unless I was sure she wanted me to"[7]—and was pleased to be treated with respect. He was less delighted by the photographs of him looking shrunken and reduced, which he likened to images of "a dope smuggler" or "Grandma Moses." There were, however, compensations, not least the knowledge that every literary soirée and grand dining table in the capital would invite him, which provided a useful distraction after Cissy's demise. Most notably, he was introduced to Fleming at a party thrown by the *Sunday Times*, before the two met again at a dinner given by the poet Stephen Spender and his wife, Natasha.

Fleming's first impression of Chandler was a mixture of respect and faint surprise. As he wrote in a 1959 article for the *London Magazine* after the older writer's death: "He must have been a very good-looking man but the good, square face was puffy and unkempt with drink. In talking, he never ceased making ugly, Hapsburg lip grimaces while his head stretched away from you, looking along his right or left shoulder as if you had bad breath. When he did look at you he saw everything and remembered days later to criticize the tie or the shirt you had been wearing. Everything he said had authority and a strongly individual slant based on what one might describe as a Socialistic humanitarian view of the world."* Still, the acquaintance began promisingly. "We took to each other and I said that I would send him a copy of my latest book and that we must meet again."[8]

While *Casino Royale* and its follow-up, *Live and Let Die*, had both been modestly successful, Fleming was also aware that he was not close to the big time, or even the medium time. (At one point, he considered killing off Bond altogether and starting afresh.) He

* Fleming's own politics—like Bond's—might best be described as conservative with both a large and small *c* alike.

believed that the endorsement of an A-list author would be vital for the continued existence of his books, let alone greater sales. He had failed to attract the patronage of either Graham Greene or W. Somerset Maugham, much to his frustration, but he was buoyed that Chandler had praised *Casino Royale*, not least because he had wished Bond to be similar to a Chandler protagonist.

Both writers were united in having created characters who represented idealised, heightened versions of what the authors saw themselves as. Chandler admitted this to Fleming, saying, "Well, yes, one puts a certain amount of oneself into one's hero because one knew more about him than anyone else,"[9] even as he suggested that Marlowe contained Chandler's less appealing habits, too. And this cut both ways. Fleming's biographer John Pearson wrote that "Ian detected very much an ally, a fellow spirit, in Chandler, who, as he was trying to do with Bond, had created something out of the ordinary with his character of Philip Marlowe . . . This was literature, it wasn't just thriller writing. This was very much what Ian wanted."[10]

When Fleming sent his third book, *Moonraker*, to Chandler at his Eaton Square home, Fleming was buoyed that Chandler swiftly telephoned him to say how much he had enjoyed the book, "and asked if I would like him to say so for the benefit of my publishers." Then as now, endorsements by well-known authors are eagerly sought by editors, and the association between Chandler and Fleming would be invaluable for the latter. Therefore, "rather unattractively," Fleming wrote to him to say, "I wouldn't think of asking you to write to me about *Moonraker* but if you happen to feel in a mood of quixotic generosity, a word from you which I could pass on to my publishers would make me the fortune which has so far eluded me." Amidst other literary flattery, he also observed that "the impact you are having on London is that of Father Christmas in Springtime."[11]

The blurb that Chandler gave Fleming was a magnificent one. He wrote: "You are probably the most forceful and driving writer of what I suppose must still be called 'thrillers' in England." His private praise was no less effusive. "In spite of the fact that you have been everywhere and seen everything, I cannot help admiring your courage in tackling the American scene." He concluded: "If this is any good to you would you like me to have it engraved on a gold slab?"

Fleming was delighted and replied to Chandler in similar mock-heroic tones. "These are words of such gold that no supporting slab is needed and I am passing the first sentence on to Macmillan's in New York and Cape's here, and will write my appreciation in caviar when the extra royalties come in. Seriously, it was extraordinarily kind of you to have written as you did and you have managed to make me feel thoroughly ashamed of my next book which is also set in America, but in an America of much more fantasy than I allowed myself in *Live and Let Die*." He concluded with an invitation to dinner at a refurbished Victoria Square, writing: "I hope you will be one of the first to darken our now gleaming doorway."[12]

Unfortunately, when Chandler did come to what Fleming called a "gabfest," the event was a disappointment. Ann Fleming pronounced it a "disaster" on the grounds that "Raymond Chandler was either drunk or so permanently drunk that the difference was difficult to say."[13] Fleming was informed that he must never bring any of his literary friends to the house again, and he reluctantly agreed. His own description of the event was more tactful and made no allusion to drink. "The luncheon was not a success. The Spenders were there and Rupert Hart-Davis and Duff Dunbar, a lawyer friend of mine and a great Chandler fan. Our small dining room was overcrowded. Chandler was a man who was shy of houses and 'entertaining' and our conversation was noisy and about people he did not know. His own diffident and rather halting manner of speech made no impact. He was not made a fuss of and I am pretty sure he hated the whole affair."[14]

Yet this did nothing to dampen the friendship between the two men, who continued to correspond regularly throughout the summer of 1955. While Chandler was no admirer of Ann, who he described as "one of those bitchy women who are all 'darling, darling, darling' when they meet you but have an assortment of little knives for your back,"[15] he saw in Ian something of the same hard-drinking machismo, undercut by the decidedly lily-livered profession of writer, that he aspired to. They referred to each other by the mock-military titles of "Private Fleming" and "Field Marshal Chandler"—the disparity in their respective success acknowledged in the difference in their ranks—and Chandler, who was mainly spending his days in London moping about his late wife and engaging in unsuccessful flirtations with various new women, would be driven to refer to Fleming as "one of the few friends I know well enough to care about."[16]

Fleming was emboldened by his friendship with Chandler to write to his publisher Jonathan Cape and name-drop hideously, saying, "By the way and sucks to you, I had a drink with Raymond Chandler last night and he said that the best bit of *Live and Let Die* was the conversation between the two Negroes in Harlem, which he said was dead accurate. Perhaps you remember that you nearly sneered me into cutting it out on the grounds that 'Negroes don't talk like that.'"[17] The pair called themselves "Slacking Shakespeares"; and Fleming was a regular visitor to Eaton Square, although Chandler's excessive alcohol consumption—he remarked in August that "I have a blood count at the edge of nothing"[18]—had to be tempered and he went through a lengthy teetotal spell, during which, British visa expired, he miserably returned to America, being compelled to give up his flat in the process.

The good relationship between the two men even survived a decidedly mixed review that Chandler gave Fleming's fourth James Bond novel, *Diamonds Are Forever*, for the *Sunday Times* in March 1956.* By this time Chandler was living in St John's Wood, drinking heavily, and becoming prone to alcohol-induced delusions, such as believing that Stephen Spender's wife, Natasha, was prepared to leave her husband and marry him instead.

* Ironically, the novel was published three years to the day before Chandler died.

Yet his criticism of one of Fleming's weaker novels was firm-minded and accurate. Chandler wrote in his review: "These are pages in which James Bond thinks. I don't like James Bond thinking. His thoughts are superfluous. I like him when he is in the dangerous card game; I like him when he is exposing himself unarmed to half a dozen thin-lipped killers, and neatly dumping them into a heap of fractured bones; I like him when he finally takes the beautiful girl in his arms, and teaches her about one-tenth of the facts of life she knew already . . . But let me plead with Mr Fleming not to allow himself to become a stunt writer, or he will end up no better than the rest of us."

Although he included a few more flattering comments that would be used by the publishers—"[this is] about the nicest piece of book-making in this type of literature which I have seen for a long time . . . Mr Fleming writes a journalistic style, neat, clean, spare and never pretentious," it also contained a complaint that could equally have been applied to the Marlowe novels: "Of course Mr Bond finally has his way with the beautiful girl. Sadly enough his beautiful girls have no future because it is the curse of the 'series character' that he always has to go back to where he began."[19] (It was not for nothing that, when asked by the *Daily Express* who would win in a fight between Philip Marlowe and James Bond, Chandler said, "I'd back Marlowe, I think. More subtle.")[20]

Fleming thanked him for the piece, saying, "Personally I loved your review and thought it was excellent as did my publishers, and as I say it was really wonderful of you to have taken the trouble." An unapologetic Chandler replied, "I thought my review was no more than you deserved and I tried to write in such a way that the good part could be quoted and the bad parts left out. After all, old boy, there had to be some bad parts. I think you will have to make up your mind what kind of writer you are going to be. You could be almost anything except that I think you are a bit of a sadist!"[21]

After Fleming acknowledged the flaws of the Bond novels—"Probably the fault of my books is that I don't take them seriously enough and meekly accept having my head ragged off about them in the family circle . . . You after all write 'novels of suspense'—if not sociological studies—whereas my books are straight pillow fantasies of the bang-bang, kiss-kiss variety. But I have taken your advice to heart and will see if I can't order my life so as to put more feeling into my typewriter"—Chandler continued to give him robust, fair-minded advice.

He stated on 1 May 1956: "I don't think you do yourself justice about James Bond and I did not think that I quite did you justice in my review of your book, because anyone who writes as dashingly as you do, ought, I think, to try for a little higher grade. I have just re-read *Casino Royale* and it seems to me that you have dis-improved with each book." He was even more blunt on 4 July, saying, "Of course I liked *Diamonds Are Forever* and I enjoyed reading it, but I simply don't think it is worthy of your talents."[22] Yet Fleming, far from being offended or hurt by Chandler's straightforwardness, took the slug as manfully as Bond or Marlowe would have done. He replied, "My talents are extended to their absolute limits in writing books like *Diamonds Are Forever*. I am not short-weighting anybody and I have absolutely nothing more up my sleeve. The way you talk, anybody would think I was a lazy Shakespeare or Raymond Chandler. Not so."[23]

Fleming attempted to coerce Chandler into writing more novels, but subsequently commented that "the truth of the matter was that it had nearly all gone out of him and that he simply could not be bothered." He continued to hold him in high esteem, and the two men continued their friendship until Chandler's death on 26 March 1959, caused, predictably enough, by alcohol, or "pneumonial peripheral vascular shock and prerenal uremia," as his death certificate put it. At the end of Fleming's heartfelt tribute to him in the *London Magazine*, he wrote, "The long and perceptive obituary in *The Times* would have given him real pleasure. I wish I had been the author so that I could have repaid him for the wonderful tribute he had written out of the kindness of his heart for me and my publishers.

How pleased he and his publishers would have been with the final sentence in *The Times*: 'His name will certainly go down among the dozen or so mystery writers who were also innovators and stylists; who, working the common vein of crime fiction, mined the gold of literature.'"[24] It is hard to disagree with this summation of one of Eaton Square's shorter-lived but more colourful inhabitants.

Even if Fleming never lived there and if it remains doubtful whether James Bond was intended to, there is an amusing irony that two actors who played 007 were purported to own property in Eaton Square. Sean Connery—who was the first and, for those of a certain age and inclination, greatest James Bond—was the possessor of flats in 6 and 7 Eaton Square, although it is doubtful that he ever lived in either of them. The last property that he inhabited in London was a Victorian mansion in Putney Heath that he eventually left because he was sick of the desperate attentions of autograph hunters, and he instead lived most of his later life in the Bahamas.

His successor but one as Bond, Roger Moore, was also believed to own an apartment in 22 Eaton Square, although, again, he had long since made his primary residence outside the United Kingdom, skipping merrily between Switzerland, the South of France, and Monte Carlo with the same élan as the secret agent he so enjoyably played. Amusing though it is to imagine Connery and Moore popping round to each other's homes to compare notes on how they played the most famous spy in British popular culture, to say nothing of pouring martinis for each other, such an idea is best restricted to the pages of rather less distinguished fiction than the Fleming novels.

We shall revisit 22 Eaton Square in chapter 10, but whether Connery ever did inhabit the apartment he was supposed to own, there is a diverting connection between him and another one of the square's literary residents. In 1961, just before he took on the role that would define the rest of his career, Connery played Alexander the Great in the television adaptation of Terence Rattigan's play *Adventure Story*, an ironic account of Alexander's many triumphs and gradual disillusionment with his conquests. Not only did the star-making role land Connery on the front cover of the *Radio Times*, but *The Times* itself was driven to say, "certain inflexions and swift deliberations of gesture at times made one feel that the part had found the young Olivier it needs."[25] Connery's biographer Christopher Bray, meanwhile, writes, "Rattigan's Alexander is a moon-ruled, mood-swinging myth of a man, and Connery rises to the challenge with a performance full of variety and invention," even if he allows that "his Alexander is just a little too gesticulatory, just a little too theatrical for the confines of the TV screen."[26]

Rattigan's original play was written in 1948, and opened the following year. At that point in his life, the thirty-seven-year-old playwright had already enjoyed outstanding success with several of the dramas that would establish him, for a time, as the most sought-after dramatist and screenwriter in Britain. Before *Adventure Story* was first performed in London on 17 March 1949,* starring Paul Scofield as Alexander, Rattigan had had a steady stream of hits, from his West End debut, the 1936 comedy *French Without Tears*,** to a plethora of plays that contained tears in abundance, including 1942's wartime melodrama *Flare Path*; 1946's true-life drama *The Winslow Boy*; and, just before *Adventure Story* opened, the one-act *The Browning Version*, an emotional account of a repressed schoolmaster realising how he has wasted his life.

Rattigan commented presciently that it was the play that he would most like to have been remembered for. Although he continued to write masterpieces—most notably 1952's *The Deep Blue Sea*—he had peaked as a dramatist before the end of the forties, shortly before the trappings of wealth and audience regard turned

---

* Appropriately enough, at the St James's Theatre, which his friend Vivien Leigh had tried so hard to defend.

** Which the former Eaton Square resident Ribbentrop had seen eight times while he was in London. "Why not? He paid for his seat, like Michael Foot," Rattigan said, shrugging, to the *Times* theatre critic Irving Wardle.

him into the most renowned of contemporary playwrights. Yet there was, as the plays suggested, another, unhappier side to Rattigan. Homosexual at a time when offences were punishable by imprisonment and commensurate disgrace, his various relationships, which included the politician Chips Channon and the actor Peter Osborn, were conducted in a clandestine and near-shamefaced fashion. The guilt that Rattigan felt—at the necessity of concealing his affairs, rather than his homosexuality itself—became utterly central to the DNA of his drama.

A particularly significant lover of his was Kenneth "Kenny" Morgan, aged twenty when Rattigan, by then already a successful writer, met him in 1939. The two began a relationship, which was stymied first by the outbreak of war and second by Morgan's lack of career success compared with his older, worldlier lover. Although Rattigan did his best to cast his boyfriend in his plays (one friend described how "Kenneth was ambitious, and Terry wanted him to succeed desperately"[27]) Morgan was intimidated by his lover's fame and first insisted on an open relationship before leaving him for another actor, the "unreliable and bisexual" Alec Ross in late 1948, shortly before *The Browning Version* opened.

Rattigan was devastated by what he saw as the younger man's betrayal. He also failed to grasp why Morgan had turned his back on a glamorous, comfortable life with him—as well as moving in circles where homosexuality was not only tolerated but practically de rigeur—in favour of the precarious, often lonely existence of a closeted gay man. It proved to be too much for Morgan, too, who committed suicide on 28 February 1949, while *Adventure Story*—coincidentally enough, about a figure who has often been described by historians as either bisexual or homosexual—was on a provincial tour before its London opening.

Rattigan, who had hoped that Morgan would return to him, was horrified by the circumstances of his lover's death. He had taken an overdose of sleeping pills, and, when they had failed to take effect, he had gassed himself. It was a personal blow like the playwright—who came from a comfortable, upper-middle-class background—had never suffered before; not least because he was terrified that the press would discover a connection between him and Morgan and thereby not only expose his sexuality but suggest an element of culpability in his death. Yet amidst his fear and paranoia, the shard of ice in the heart still lingered. Rattigan remarked to his friend Peter Glenville, on the day that he heard of the death, "The new play will open with the body discovered dead in front of the gas fire."

In the event, although *The Deep Blue Sea* begins with its heroine, the middle-aged and lovelorn Hester Collyer, passed out insensible in such a way, she does not die,* and much of the remainder of the play is taken up with a penetrating and acute examination of grief and the aftermath of the relationship between Hester, who became a version of Morgan mixed with Rattigan himself, and her selfish younger lover Freddie, who also incarnated Morgan's more frivolous side. The character of Hester's abandoned husband, a judge named Sir William, represented Rattigan, too, but also Channon, who had desperately attempted to keep the younger man in his life by showering him with ever more elaborate gifts and desperate protestations of affection.

It was, in other words, the most purely autobiographical play that he had written until then, although subsequent rumours that it was originally conceived as a play about a homosexual relationship, starring "Henry Collyer" and then changed in order to avoid any scandal or disapproval from the theatrical censor, the Lord Chamberlain, have been denied by those involved in its production.

Its director, Frith Banbury, commented that "it's always said that Terry wrote a homosexual play and then re-wrote it because it was banned, which was absolute rubbish. . . . But he would never have written a homosexual play *per se*, knowing that it would be lucky to

* In a splendidly Rattigan touch, this is not because she sees sense or is rescued by a deus ex machina, but because the money in the gas meter has run out before she can asphyxiate herself.

get two or three weeks at a club theatre.* He was very commercially minded and he wanted his plays to make money. Never for one moment did he refer in any of his conversations with me at that time to a homosexual version."[28] In fact, the character of the doctor Mr Miller—based on Rattigan's psychiatrist Keith Newman—is himself homosexual, and disgraced as a result, although such is the tact and euphemism with which his "sin" is dealt with that many audiences would have believed that he was a back-street abortionist instead.

The play eventually opened, to enormous acclaim and success, on 6 March 1952, starring Peggy Ashcroft as Hester. The year would prove to be a crucial one for Rattigan. Not only did his father, Frank—a stern, emotionally repressed figure who nonetheless engaged in flagrant acts of adultery, and would be immortalised by his son as the philandering protagonist of his 1950 play *Who Is Sylvia?*—die of a stroke three days after the play opened, without having seen it, but his brother, Brian, died of cancer in September that year. Rattigan wrote a heartfelt, even anguished letter to him on 19 August when he discovered the news, acknowledging, "It's been my profession all my life to use words dishonestly and now I need them to record, rather than induce, an emotion most honestly and deeply felt, they seem to be taking their revenge on me." He then expressed his "simple truth," with the underwhelming sentiment that "if ever and whenever my time comes to receive news as grave as the news you have received, I can only hope and pray I receive it as well as you have—but I deeply doubt it."[29]

Professional triumph and personal trauma led Rattigan to take the same step that many outwardly successful men and women had followed over the previous century, and he took a lease on the penthouse apartment of 29 Eaton Square, leaving his previous home in nearby Chester Square. (Perhaps coincidentally, the character of Sir William Collyer is said to live in Eaton Square, as does the wealthy

* A small, privately licensed members-only theatre that was not subject to theatrical censorship.

novelist Mark Walters in Rattigan's late play *In Praise of Love.*) Naturally, he also maintained a substantial country residence, Little Court in Windlesham, Surrey as befitted his wealth and fame. His now widowed mother, Vera, lived nearby, in Stanhope Gardens in Kensington, and Rattigan ensured that she had all the comforts and company that she could have wished for. Yet his own existence in Eaton Square was altogether more grandiose. His drawing room was sixty feet long, with balconies stocked with window boxes and facing the square's gardens, and its walls decorated with a substantial photographic mural of a French forest scene. In the dining room, meanwhile, he had another mural, this time an engraving of scenes of old London.

Rattigan was interviewed at his new home for *John Bull* magazine, a glossy lifestyle title that attracted many of the country's best-known writers both as contributors and as subjects for profiles. The now forty-one-year-old playwright was photographed in his dining room, holding a whisky glass and clad in an impeccable tailored suit. He was, to the casual observer, the definition of a successful writer, deservedly enjoying his success and acclaim. Yet there is a far-away look in Rattigan's eyes that suggests the trauma and heartbreak that he had felt over the past few months. He may have been wealthy, powerful, and acclaimed, but happiness appeared to elude him, as it had done for most of his life.

His private torments were concealed from all but his intimate friends, and he now took on a new role, that of the dressing gown–clad Belgravia poseur. Whether in conscious imitation or homage to his friend and occasional rival Noël Coward, Rattigan adopted a louche existence where he would sprawl on a sofa while writing his plays—and increasingly the well-paid screenplays that would occupy his time—in longhand and with a fountain pen, which would then be taken away by his secretary, Mary Herring, and typed up.

He rose relatively late and began work at ten thirty, writing until three in the afternoon, with only a light lunch, prepared by his housekeeper, to keep him occupied. (Food did not play a large role in Rattigan's life. When asked by the housekeeper what she should serve at a party, he replied, "some of those nice little savoury things you made the other day,"[30] leaving her barely the wiser.) He would take a break for a couple of hours for a walk round Belgravia, return to work by five, be finished for the day by eight, and then head to dinner or to a club with friends. Rattigan prided himself, while adopting this routine, of being able to write a play in eight weeks, and a film script in even less time, which gave him an annual income, since the early forties, of at least £30,000 a year, the equivalent of well over a million pounds today.

Rattigan took his life as a public figure seriously, calling himself, with only mild exaggeration, "the prettiest playwright in London."[31] The suits were always immaculate, and he was proud that the fashion magazine *Tailor & Cutter* featured him in its selection of Best Dressed Men, although he must also have been aware that there were inevitable overtones of Bertie Wooster's article "What The Well-Dressed Man is Wearing" from the (fictitious) title *Milady's Boudoir*. Rattigan was also an expert in presenting a smiling, pleasant front to the world and concealing the misery and anger that he felt. On one occasion, he was contacted by an opportunistic blackmailer, who threatened to reveal Rattigan's homosexuality and its overtones in his drama to a no doubt interested world. Many would either have ignored the man or earnestly enquired as to how he might (legally or otherwise) be dissuaded from spreading his poison further. Rattigan dealt with it differently. He invited the stranger out to lunch, where he offered him wine, good food, and civilised conversation. Just before the meal ended, he paused and said, "Oh, by the way, what an extraordinary letter you sent me. I hope you won't send me another one, because if you do I shall send it to my solicitor. Would you like some more brandy?"[32] The cognac, delicious though it undoubtedly was, would have stuck in the opportunist's throat. Rattigan remained free of his entreaties thereafter.

For all the poise and charm, Rattigan was as prone to pettiness, lust, and jealousy as any of his characters. After Morgan left him, he embarked upon a long-lasting relationship with the failed designer Michael Franklin, another much younger man. It was soon based around a transactional understanding that Rattigan provided a luxurious lifestyle and Franklin would pay for it in kind. The playwright's friends saw him as opportunistic and little better than a paid companion, disparagingly nicknaming him "the Midget," but he fulfilled his purpose. Rattigan said of him, with appropriate disparagement: "He was a service as it were."[33]

In any case, the playwright knew that he was the subject of innuendo and rumour as a bachelor about town. His homosexuality was a sufficiently open secret for the *Sunday People* to run an article in late 1950, ostensibly to promote *Who Is Sylvia?*, which featured Rattigan, the couturier Norman Hartnell, and the musician Ivor Novello and was headlined "Britain's Three Most Eligible Bachelors." The piece may have sighed, "Why can't they find the right girl," but only the most horrendously naïve would have read it at face value.

It was therefore unsurprising that, even while Rattigan was entwined with Franklin and others, he made a public show of squiring some of London's most beautiful women to parties and first nights, including the model Jean Dawnay—with whom he embarked upon what amounted to a committed but wholly platonic relationship—and the actress Margaret Leighton. She suggested that she would happily have married the playwright if he had asked, but such a request never came.

Nevertheless, when at home in Eaton Square, the pretence dropped. Rattigan was instinctively most comfortable around London's gay and theatrical crew, who included such figures as John Gielgud; the impresario and producer Binkie Beaumont; and Franklin, if he could be trusted to behave himself. However, the dominance of good-looking boys at the Eaton Square soirées baffled his mother, Vera, who once remarked, apparently innocently, "Why are there always so many young men and so few girls at Terence's parties?"[34]

For all the grand parties and ostentatious first nights, there was a hollow core at the centre of Rattigan's life and career. As someone who wrote about loneliness and pain better than any other English playwright, it was as if he needed private misery in order to be able to write more clearly, or at least more honestly, about his characters' suffering. His relationship with Franklin soon went in a similar direction to that of Morgan, as Eaton Square's walls frequently reverberated to the sound of raised voices and hysterical threats of self-slaughter, followed by quieter, more soothing noises of reconciliation. Yet there was never equality between the two, and that wholly suited the older man.

Rattigan may have regarded the exploits of his friends and colleagues with distaste, and society may have proved his discretion correct. When Gielgud* was arrested on 22 October 1953 for "persistently importuning male persons for immoral purposes," he was fined £10 and told to see a doctor, shortly before the press found out about his misdeeds and briefly turned it into a career-threatening cause célèbre. Rattigan may have offered public and private support, saying, of Gielgud's return to the stage, "He had enough courage to go on and the audience had enough grace and sympathy to accept him purely as an actor. . . . The acceptance by these very ordinary people of something about which they had little understanding was very moving,"[35] but the inherent condescension in his implicit belittling of the unsophisticated audience was matched by his ruthlessness in turning life into art. The central character in his one-act play *Table Number Seven*, the bluff but fraudulent "Major" Pollock, was initially arrested for a similar offence to Gielgud's, until Rattigan took fright and changed his offence to that of making improper advances to young women in the cinema. Many years later, the original, richer version was discovered, and has now been performed instead.

Still, after the golden decade that began with *Flare Path* and

* For whom *The Browning Version* had originally been written.

concluded with *The Deep Blue Sea*, Rattigan seemed to be marooned in Eaton Square–based ennui. Trifles like the Laurence Olivier commission *The Sleeping Prince*—later adapted by him into the plodding Monroe–Olivier vehicle *The Prince and the Showgirl*, an off-screen story vastly more interesting because of the clash of personalities involved than anything seen on-screen—were beneath his considerable talent. His increasing interest in well-paid, undemanding screenplays smacked of a man cashing in on his fame and ability alike. Then two separate but oddly complementary things occurred that would jeopardise Rattigan's peerless standing and begin a decline in his reputation that would last until his death and beyond.

The first was his own fault. When he was putting together the second volume of his collected plays for his publisher, Hamish Hamilton, in the autumn of 1953, he was prevailed upon to write a preface. They may have expected only a couple of thousand urbane words, but Rattigan took it upon himself to offer a justification of his work and attitudes. Unfortunately, he did so in a manner that became notorious. He confessed that he aimed his plays towards a fictitious busybody, of whom he wrote, "Let us invent a character, a nice, respectable, middle-class, middle-aged, maiden lady, with time on her hands and the money to help her pass it. She enjoys pictures, books, music, and the theatre and though to none of these arts . . . does she bring much knowledge or discernment, at least, as she is apt to tell her cronies, she 'does know what she likes.' Let us call her Aunt Edna."

Keeping Aunt Edna happy was all-important for Rattigan. Even though he ridiculed her as a "hopeless lowbrow" who scorned the work of Kafka, Picasso, and Walton, he admitted that "should he displease Aunt Edna, he is utterly lost," although he also suggested that "She will be listened to. Aunt Edna always is. The playwright who has been unfortunate or unwise enough to incur her displeasure, will soon pay a dreadful price. His play, the child of his brain, will wither and die before his eyes." Yet this did not mean that she had to be wholly pandered to, as Rattigan explained:

"Although Aunt Edna must never be made mock of, or bored, or befuddled, she must equally not be wooed, or pandered to, or cosseted. I even made a rather startling discovery; that the old dear rather enjoys a little teasing and even, at times, bullying." He concluded, rather dramatically, that he was Aunt Edna himself, or at least a version of her. "Aunt Edna, or at least her juvenile counterpart, was inside my creative brain and in pleasing her I was only pleasing myself." She and he would, Rattigan declared, "be joined in a friendship that I trust will never be broken."[36]

If he had wished to offer his enemies and the critics—far from mutually exclusive entities—ammunition forever after, Rattigan could not have given them a greater arsenal. Tynan called him "the bathtub baritone of the drama," pulling back on his statement that *The Deep Blue Sea* was "the most striking new English play I had seen for a decade," and Rattigan became unfashionable almost immediately. Nobody in his circle suggested to him that anything in his preface was de trop, either because they believed that he was exaggerating for comic effect or simply because they did not wish to offend a man who, underneath his urbane surface, could be prickly and defensive, qualities borne of long battles against critics both theatrical and personal. There is only so much pain and abuse that a human being can stand before they retreat into a shell of their own creation, and Rattigan's Savile Row–clad, epigram-spouting, cigar-toting carapace was simply a more upmarket version of the armour that his characters invariably wore.

The reviews for *The Sleeping Prince* were inevitably—some would say deservedly—dire. Olivier was compelled after reading them to say to Rattigan, at the opening night party at Eaton Square, "On behalf of my wife and myself as actors, and personally as your director, I would like to apologise, dear Terry, for mucking up your play." Not to be outdone in humility, Rattigan announced, "Darlings, both, on my behalf, as an author, please forgive me having written such a mucky trivial little play."[37] This self-deprecation, even self-flagellation, may have been ritualistic, but it was also founded on Rattigan's belief that, at the age of forty-two, his greatest days as a writer were already behind him.

The second occurrence that led to Rattigan's reputational downfall was the opening of John Osborne's *Look Back in Anger* at the Royal Court on 8 May 1956. By chance, Rattigan attended the first night with his friends Beaumont and Leighton. A photograph of Rattigan from that evening shows him looking grim-faced and tense; unsurprisingly, given that Osborne's play was a furious, full-frontal attack on the comfortable English middle-class society that Rattigan had made his name and fortune chronicling. Its protagonist, the so-called angry young man Jimmy Porter, rails articulately against the traditions of his country and its inhabitants, which include, by implication, its playwrights.

Beaumont, who had made his money pandering to the types Porter was attacking, left, horrified, at the interval. Rattigan was tempted to do the same, but was advised by his critic friend Cuthbert Worsley that to do so would show a lack of appreciation for contemporary theatre. Nonetheless, when a dazed-looking Rattigan was approached at the play's conclusion by the *Daily Express*, looking for a comment by the grand middle-aged man of theatre, he was unable to come up with anything more original than the disparaging sneer that Osborne was saying, "Look, Ma, I'm not Terence Rattigan." The implicit hauteur in his remark,* and the implication that he was the only figure in English drama who Osborne wished to contend with, would not serve him well in public estimation.

Rattigan was, all the same, too big to fail. *Table Number Seven* and its companion piece, *Table by the Window*, were presented as the combined play *Separate Tables*, which had conspicuous success on Broadway—never a given for Rattigan's extremely English

* Coward did rather better when he wrote in his diary on 17 February 1957, "I wish I knew why the hero is so dreadfully cross and what about? I should also like to know how, where and why he and his friend run a sweet-stall and if, considering the hero's unparalleled capacity for invective, they ever manage to sell any sweets?"

drama—and was subsequently filmed in 1958, with a script co-written by Rattigan along with the American screenwriters John Gay and John Michael Hayes. His earnings mounted inexorably, and his Eaton Square and Sunningdale life—counterpointed by regular trips to Europe and America—was a glamorous and apparently happy one. Yet as he ruefully observed, "There I was in 1956, a reasonably successful playwright . . . and suddenly the whole Royal Court thing exploded, and Coward and [J. B.] Priestley and I were all dismissed, sacked by the critics."

Some of Rattigan's friends adapted to the new order. Olivier, Leigh, and Gielgud—as well, of course as Rex Harrison—all acted at the Royal Court, embracing the contemporary tradition of theatre. Coward headed to Las Vegas, where he made a fortune as a cabaret performer, before taking well-paid and inconsequential cameo roles in big-budget films. And even Beaumont pivoted away from straight drama to the last remaining conservative art form, musicals, and had huge success presenting the first British stagings of *West Side Story* and *My Fair Lady.* What all this gallingly suggested was that success in the entertainment industry lay less in talent than in versatility. Rattigan, who was peerlessly skilled at what he did but lacked the ability or inclination to be anything other than a playwright and screenwriter, was bound for a precipitous decline. He ruefully recalled how Somerset Maugham, another washed-up figure, had once counselled him that no playwright had more than twenty years' success in them. Come 1956, two decades after the first production of *French Without Tears*, and Rattigan seemed to have reached his sell-by date.

No resident of Eaton Square has ever successfully been able to play the common-man card. (One thinks of the politician Julian Amery's much-ridiculed 1971 remark in the Houses of Parliament, of his Eaton Square home: "I have not lived on a council estate, although I have lived in a terraced house since I was born.") This is why the likes of Barry Gibb, whose reputation lay in providing a universal, relatable appeal to his wide audience, moved swiftly into other, less historied residences. Rattigan, though, had nothing to gain by moving to a more socially acceptable part of London. His world was that of Mayfair, Kensington, and Belgravia, not the bomb-blighted East End or the immigrant hotspots of Notting Hill and Kilburn. And ironically enough, his homosexuality—which had been regarded as no more significant a part of his life and character than the colour of his hair by his inner circle—now became a professional issue, too.

George Devine, the powerful and charismatic artistic director of the Royal Court, may have stood on the barricades and fought the cause for most oppressed minorities, but middle-aged gay men were not amongst them. Devine detested homosexuality. In Osborne's words, Devine believed that "the blight of buggery, which then dominated the theatre in all its frivolity, could be kept down decently by direct appeal to seriousness and good intentions from his own crack corps of heterosexual writers, directors and actors."[38] Never mind that many of these, such as Osborne, treated their partners and wives appallingly (in the playwright's own words, his behaviour was "grotesquely indefensible");[39] they were rough, tough straight men, and this was vastly preferable to the feminised camp that Devine saw implicitly in Rattigan's plays and explicitly in his person.

The rest of the fifties saw Rattigan produce only one significant theatrical work, *Ross*, a play about T. E. Lawrence that was adapted from an unproduced screenplay he had written. It was intended to star Dirk Bogarde, until the announcement of the David Lean–Peter O'Toole epic crushed it. (Rattigan may also have been irritated by the knowledge that *Lawrence of Arabia*'s screenplay was written by Robert Bolt, another younger, left-wing figure whose 1960 play, *A Man for All Seasons,* was a significant hit.)

In its depiction of Lawrence's repressed homosexuality and the way in which his heroism and exalted reputation gradually curdled into social contempt and eventual anonymity—Lawrence adopted the pseudonym "John Hume Ross" in order to enlist in the RAF in 1922, long after he had become a figure of international renown—Rattigan came as close as he dared to offering an unflattering autobiographical portrayal. He related to Lawrence's own statements: "I long for people to look down upon me and despise me, [but] I'm too shy to take the filthy steps which would publicly shame me and put me into their contempt. I want to dirty myself outwardly, so that my person may properly reflect the dirt which it conceals."[40]

Ross, which starred Alec Guinness—who would later take a leading role in *Lawrence of Arabia* as the Arab leader Prince Faisal—was performed in the West End, opening on 12 May 1960. Rattigan was suffering from pneumonia at the time, the latest installment of what would become a series of attacks of ill health. The reviews were modestly complimentary without being adulatory, but an attempt at a lighter play, a musical adaptation of *French Without Tears* titled *Joie de Vivre*, was a notorious, humiliating failure when it opened two months later.

Amidst the debris of the opening night party in Eaton Square, Rattigan could only describe the disaster from the audience's perspective, of their having suffered through "a trivial, meretricious little piece, hopelessly dated." It closed after three days, and Rattigan did himself no favours by engaging in an epistolary spat with Tynan, who had savaged the play. In response to Rattigan's attacks of boorishness and abuse, in which he called Tynan "dull and ill-tempered and ideological," Tynan faux-innocently responded, "I really don't know why you put up with me. There must be moments when you wonder whether it's all worthwhile."[41] The clear implication was that the old lion of theatre should retire and cede his place to younger, more *relevant* playwrights.

Rattigan did not quit, and continued to write until the end of his life. Yet the sixties brought on well-paid disillusionment rather than bracing reappraisal of his work. Even as Coward became part of the repertoire of Olivier's new National Theatre with a much-praised revival of *Hay Fever* in 1964, directed by the playwright himself—"Dad's Renaissance," a pleased Coward called it—Rattigan seemed an increasingly detached and irrelevant figure. He gave up the Eaton Square flat in April 1965, and the last photo shoot that exists of him taken there, from May the previous year, shows a man, now in his early fifties, who had clearly aged significantly from the relaxed figure of just over a decade before. Instead, there was now a tightness and furtiveness to Rattigan's fixed smile that barely concealed the unhappiness beneath. The play that he had hoped would be regarded as his late masterpiece and restore his reputation, the 1963 family saga *Man and Boy*, flopped, and took his self-esteem down with no hope of recovery.

Superficially, the last dozen years of Rattigan's life represented a lucrative Indian summer. There was a much-welcomed knighthood in 1971, revivals of *The Winslow Boy* and *Separate Tables*, and new screenplays—most interestingly for a musical version of James Hilton's evergreen classic *Goodbye, Mr Chips*, with Peter O'Toole as the singing pedagogue—as well as a series of plays, written from Rattigan's new home in Bermuda. All of them were greeted with mild curiosity, but it was now the era of Pinter, Stoppard, and Beckett, not of Rattigan and Coward. Even his support for a young, brilliant, and doomed gay playwright, Joe Orton, had to be done almost surreptitiously. Rattigan remarked, "In a way, I wasn't Orton's best sponsor. I'm a very unfashionable figure still, and I was then wildly unfashionable critically. My sponsorship rather put critics off, I think."[42]

When Rattigan died from bone cancer on 30 November 1977 at the age of sixty-six, he was dutifully hailed as a great British playwright, albeit with a surprising, even disappointing degree of reticence. Most of the obituaries and tributes took it as read that he was the undisputed master of the well-made play but hesitated to make any more claims for his excellence. The *Times*'s judgement that he was "one of the leaders of the twentieth-century stage in what has come to be known as the Theatre of Entertainment,"[43] with comparisons to Pinero and, of all people, the long-forgotten Henry Arthur Jones,* was typical. Only Michael Billington of *The Guardian* dared to make a greater claim for Rattigan's likelihood to be remembered by posterity, stating that, rather than being the playwright of the bourgeoisie par excellence, he took his audience's conditioning and expectations and turned them back upon them. "His whole work is a sustained assault on English middle-class values: fear of emotional commitment, terror in the face of passion, apprehension about sex. In fact few dramatists this century have written with more understanding about the human heart than Terence Rattigan."[44]

His reputation first enjoyed a rehabilitation with a 1993 revival of *The Deep Blue Sea*, with Penelope Wilton, and since then it has barely ceased to flourish. Three recent British revivals of work major and minor alike—a double bill of *Table Number 7* and *The Browning Version*, under the title *Summer 1954*; *The Deep Blue Sea*; and *In Praise of Love*, all in 2024 and 2025—continued to display Rattigan's virtuosity and versatility alike. This particular Eaton Square resident knew both triumph and disaster, and was unable to heed Kipling's advice to "treat those two imposters just the same." Yet nearly forty years after his death, this greatest of twentieth-century British playwrights is in an untouchable position of respect, adulation, and love for his great work. He is beloved by actors, directors, and other playwrights alike; and as I write this, there is a campaign to see a West End theatre named after him, as the likes of Pinter and Coward have been similarly recognised.

Few would argue that Rattigan was a modern playwright. When, later in his career, he tried to become slightly edgier—*In Praise of Love* includes jokes about pretentious televised drama, which would have been unthinkable twenty years before—he seemed uncertain, even shaky. Yet it is this classicism and dedication to three-dimensional characterisation and compelling yet comprehensible plotting that

* A prolific, conservative writer of the Victorian and early Edwardian eras, who inspired Wilde to quip, "There are three rules for writing plays. The first rule is not to write like Henry Arthur Jones; the second and third rules are the same."

makes his work so enduring. You might even compare him to Thomas Cubitt, doughtily working away on his foundations in the hope that something of lasting value would be constructed in the process. In both cases, the peerless legacy—both of Eaton Square, and beyond—that they created seems inarguable.

9

Lord Boothby: 165 Eaton Place and 1 Eaton Square

"A bounder but not a cad"

Eaton Square has not been presented as often as we might imagine in television or film. Samantha Bond's Lady Rosamund character from *Downton Abbey* lives there, and the great ITV series *Upstairs, Downstairs* is set at the fictitious 165 Eaton Place, which brought the square, and its environs, to perhaps the greatest attention that it received internationally. The show might have been called *That House in Eaton Square*, *The Servants' Hall*, or the inappropriately Mikado-esque *Two Little Maids in Town*, and although it superficially focused on the lives and loves of the aristocratic, often scandal-riddled, Bellamy family, it was actually far more concerned with events "downstairs," and treated its characters with both empathy and psychological nuance. It was the first British television show to delve into the lives of servants in the pre-war era, and tore away any idea that theirs would have been easy or enjoyable existences.

It was created by the actresses Jean Marsh and Eileen Atkins, themselves both from working-class backgrounds, but everything was against the show from the outset. Marsh, who played the character of head parlourmaid, Rose Buck, and Atkins were convinced that they had created a show that would not only find an audience but that that audience would respond to its unusual and penetrating examination of class politics—initially broadcast in 1971, when Britain seemed to be in a state of national chaos—with enthusiasm. Yet costume drama was regarded as old hat and television schedulers initially sidelined the show by placing it in a graveyard slot, where it was left to expire.

However, it not only attracted stellar word of mouth, but the first season won a BAFTA for Best Drama Series, ensuring that it would be recommissioned and given the attention that it deserved. It was a high-end, high-class show that was watched by eighteen million viewers in Britain, and, by the time that it sold overseas, would eventually be shown in eighty countries to as many as a billion people.

Unsurprisingly, it was especially popular in the United States,* where it won a total of seven Emmys, including three separate awards for Best Drama Series in 1974, 1975, and 1977. Marsh—who observed that, as the apparently attainable Rose, she got more lascivious fan mail than the actresses playing the aristocrats—described its success frankly when she said of the reaction, "I am not being naïve or disingenuous when I say it was beyond our wildest dreams." Speaking in 2010, she remarked: "We still seem to want it, because if you rose out of your class, you knew you had done well. And we like it because the past is not as worrying as the news."[1]

A SIMILAR, IF RATHER MORE violent, examination of Eaton Square–based class duality came in Brian Helgeland's 2015 crime picture *Legend*, featuring Tom Hardy as both Kray brothers Ronald and Reggie. About halfway through the film, Ronnie Kray and his acolytes, Taron Egerton's Mad Teddy Smith and Charley Palmer Rothwell's Leslie Holt, visit John Sessions's dyspeptic Lord Boothby at his home—wrongly shown as number 35 Eaton Square, rather than

---

* The unsuccessful 1975 American spin-off show *Beacon Hill* was an attempt to take a very British series and transpose it to the Boston Brahmin milieu of the eponymous setting.

Boothby's true address at number 1—in order to interest him in a scheme that might involve building a quasi-utopian city in Nigeria.

Boothby, described in the film's hackneyed voice-over simply as "a distinguished member of the House of Lords," is initially reluctant to help, but once his attention, and intentions, are captured by the handsome Smith ("Ice and a slice please, Teddy bear, and don't spare the horses"), the innuendos flow as fast as the gin and tonics that they are drinking. "Down the hatch. Do you like it down the hatch, Teddy?" In the next scene, the action moves from the salubrious settings of Eaton Square to a fancifully depicted party in Ronnie's flat in Cedra Court in North London, in which the "perverted peer" Boothby is shown wandering around drunk, exchanging greetings with the various dignitaries present ("Tom,* not in the House of Commons tonight?"), while Ronnie spanks half-naked young men with a carpet beater.

Despite its starry cast, and Hardy's manful efforts, the clichéd *Legend* could not be described as a good film. Yet the late Sessions excels in his tiny role. Although only on-screen for a couple of minutes, he mixes camp lechery with a Machiavellian charm that makes his brief scenes stand out from the dross that surrounds him. I once interviewed Sessions, and he mentioned that he had improvised his dialogue (which shows—it's better than anything else in the film).

He was disappointed that Helgeland had deleted one of his scenes, in which Boothby recounts meeting Hitler. Pleasingly enough, the politician includes the story in his appropriately titled 1978 memoir, *Boothby: Recollections of a Rebel*, in which he recounts: "It is true that when I walked across the long room to a corner in which he was sitting writing, in a brown shirt with a swastika on his arm, he waited without looking up until I had reached his side, then sprang to his feet, lifted his right arm, and shouted 'Hitler!'; and that I responded by clicking my heels together together, raising my right arm, and shouting back: 'Boothby!'"[2] The story may have no greater credence

* A depiction of the politician Tom Driberg, although he is barely glimpsed.

there, but at least it has consistency, which is more than can be said for its teller.

Amidst the many colourful residents of Eaton Square throughout the twentieth century, Robert Boothby stands out. It has been my great wish to write about him for years, so perfectly does he summon up a very British combination of malfeasance, good living, personal impropriety, and an absence of hypocrisy that meant that he could be described, as the Queen Mother supposedly did to her confidant Woodrow Wyatt, as "a bounder but not a cad." Boothby's own doctor was once driven to write to him to say, "You have a great heart . . . spiritually and anatomically. If you ever give a postgraduate course in *living*, may I enrol?"[3]

Boothby's enormous social circle included everyone from Maurice Bowra, warden of Wadham, and the conductor Malcolm Sargent to the film director John Huston and the musician Yehudi Menuhin. Boothby was a popular, well-known figure despite having no notable political achievements. In *Boothby: Recollections of a Rebel*, he wrote: "All the major causes I have espoused—for a good monetary policy, against appeasement, for rearmament, and for a united Europe—were lost."[4] Yet his once-stellar public image has received considerable and justified criticism since his death in 1986. Thanks to a cache of previously unseen letters and other documents, recently purchased by the National Library of Scotland, I can now tell the full, sordid story with the detail that it merits.

Many Eaton Square inhabitants lived there for only a relatively short time, but Boothby lived in his flat at number 1 for forty years, between 1946 and 1986. During those decades, he was able to watch politics and society change beyond recognition, from post-war asperity to the rather different stringency of the Thatcher regime. He became a celebrity, author of three memoirs and countless newspaper articles, and even had the honour of being a guest on the popular television show *This Is Your Life** on 17 October 1963. Yet he

* A British version of a popular US show, which stopped airing in 1961.

may still be best known for being photographed, smirking, next to Ronnie Kray and Holt in 1 Eaton Square: a compromising picture that sent the establishment, already in a febrile state, into turmoil. And the Boothbyian irony was that he sent it out into the public domain himself.

By that point in his life, Boothby was not a well man. He had declared in 1962 with what his *Daily Telegraph* obituary euphemistically described as "cheerful frankness" that "I drink a great deal of alcohol. I have had cardiac trouble and very nearly thrombosis. I have had bronchitis every year for four years. I am overweight. I fear the doctor because I know exactly what he is going to tell me and that it is true."[5] He still managed to live for another twenty-four years, which included a somewhat unlikely late marriage. The obituaries concentrated on his life in politics and his enormous bonhomie, and nearly all of them used the word "flamboyant."

Although his long-running adulterous affair with Harold Macmillan's wife, Dorothy, was tactfully referred to—*The Times* called it "a grave personal wrong" that had been visited upon the former Conservative PM—there was little or no mention of his entanglement with the Kray brothers, nor the legal, political, or journalistic shenanigans that ensued. Instead, most newspapers respectfully reprinted Michael Foot's tribute that Boothby was, "too intelligent, too humane, too warm-hearted to be a real Tory." Most tributes saluted his longevity—entering the Commons at the age of twenty-four, he served as an MP for nearly thirty-four years, before taking up a peerage in 1958—and his status as a celebrity, well known for his appearances on television and radio.

Notably, the then Conservative prime minister Margaret Thatcher offered no public encomium to Boothby when he died,* and what

---

* She did write a note of condolence to Lady Boothby in which she said, "All my political life the name Bob Boothby and that wonderful voice have been known to almost everyone. His life and service spanned so many decades. His speeches were always penetrating and interesting. Now he has gone, it seems as if a whole era has passed with him." It is tempting to wonder, judging by the kind but somewhat stiff

correspondence she had with him during his lifetime was formal and stilted. Her letter of 17 June 1982 thanks him for a note about the government's recent performance: "I feel simply that we have reflected the basic strengths of this nation."[6] When Boothby wrote, "as the personal attacks upon you mount, I feel that I must send you another line to congratulate you on your dauntless courage,"[7] she replied simply that "it was very good of you to have written as you did, and I appreciate, enormously, your encouragement and support."[8] Most of her notes to Boothby are a few lines at most and boilerplate in the extreme; the words "great encouragement" are used frequently, and it is difficult not to feel that the departure of this particular lifelong rebel was not mourned too deeply.

Boothby enjoyed the status of a great English eccentric. His preferred subject of discussion in the House of Commons was herrings. After his death, the journalist W. F. Deedes wrote in the *Daily Telegraph* that "the first question I heard him ask in the House of Commons was about herrings. The second I heard was about—herrings. The third . . . with that rich, throaty voice, he made herrings sound thrilling." In a BBC interview with John Freeman and others on the show *Frankly Speaking* on 11 December 1958, in which Boothby made a number of admissions of varying degrees of candour, he declared, "I adore herrings; I could eat half a dozen a day and be perfectly happy, and never want anything else—and in any form, salt, raw, broiled—anything you like."

He once suggested that his epigraph should be: "He was a man who loved life—and lived it."[9] During his *Frankly Speaking* conversation, he confessed, "I would much rather die than give up food and drink," and, when contemplating the infinite, said, "I thought to myself at one moment, when I thought I might be on the way out, 'Well, thank God, I've had as good a time as I had. And when nobody can take it from me, I've had a good life, and I've had a

---

letter ("You will be so lonely for a time") whether Thatcher saw the passing of that era as altogether regrettable.

full life, and I've seen the hell of a lot, and I'm delighted.'" Others around him may have regarded it differently.

This "good life" began with his birth on 12 February 1900 in Edinburgh, after which he went through the usual rituals of an upper-class education, attending Eton and Magdalen College, Oxford, then briefly spending some time in the army, namely the Brigade of Guards. However, Boothby's greater ambitions lay in politics; and so, at the age of twenty-four, he was elected as the Conservative and Unionist candidate for the Scottish seat of Aberdeen and Kincardine East, which he would hold without serious challenge until 1950. He was even re-elected with a virtually unchanged vote share in the massacre of 1945, a testament to his personal popularity. Boothby was a charming and ambitious young man, and these qualities went neither unnoticed nor unrewarded. His most notable achievement was to become parliamentary private secretary to Winston Churchill in 1926, only a couple of years after he first entered Parliament, and remain in this post until 1929.

Even after he left Churchill's side, the two continued to enjoy a close relationship, only briefly interrupted when Boothby lost his temper at what he saw as Churchill's vacillations and inconsistencies during the abdication crisis of 1936, which, in his view, cost Edward VIII the throne. Boothby, in what would become a pattern throughout his life, sent Churchill an intemperate letter in which he roared, "You have delivered a blow to the King, both in the House and in the country, far harder than any that Baldwin ever conceived of . . . *and you have done it without any consultation with your best friends and supporters* . . . What happened this afternoon makes me feel that it is almost impossible for those who are most devoted to you personally to follow you blindly . . . because they cannot be sure where the hell they are going to be landed next."[10] A subsequent epistle contained suitably grovelling apologies, but the rashness and impetuosity were noticed.

Although the American novelist Paul Gallico once remarked that "if they would only let me have a vote, I would cast one big, juicy one, for Boothby as Prime Minister,"[11] it was perhaps just as well for Britain that Boothby never had any serious inclination towards high office. The closest he came was to be parliamentary secretary for the Ministry of Food for a few months in 1940, when Churchill took over from Neville Chamberlain as prime minister. However, in what would be his first serious brush with notoriety, Boothby was compelled to resign for asking a question in Parliament that benefitted his friend the Czech-Austrian businessman Richard Weininger, without declaring any interest in the financial bonus that he stood to receive if Weininger's assets were unfrozen.

It was an embarrassing misstep that derailed his career at any senior level,* although Boothby protested his innocence. He was fortunate to have an influential supporter in the form of the newspaper magnate and Minister of Aircraft Production Lord Beaverbrook. The tycoon offered Boothby apparently unequivocal support during the 1940 scandal that nearly ended his career—"I will not believe you are guilty until I see the evidence of it"[12]—but theirs was a complex and shifting relationship that was based on a combination of the transactional and the intemperate.

It had once been warm. Beaverbrook sent Boothby encouraging letters early in his parliamentary career praising him and saying, "you are making a good and great name for yourself,"[13] but this soured after the press magnate believed, erroneously, that Boothby had stood against Edward VIII, and therefore him, during the abdication crisis. After that, the relationship switched from friendship to a businesslike accord, in which rote regards were exchanged and the two men watched each other warily. "We do not meet as often as I would like," Beaverbrook growled in May 1949, even as he went on to deliver elegant threats masked as compliments. "I

---

* When Boothby, sacked by Churchill, desperately asked what he should do, the prime minister angrily retorted, "Get yourself a job with a bomb-disposal unit."

hope you will not think me patronising in saying words of admiration. But I supported you then with good reason and I back you now."[14]

The implication—that Boothby owed Beaverbrook a favour because of the career-saving support that he was offered at a time of crisis—was clear; and Boothby replied, "I know what you did on my behalf in 1940; and shall be for ever grateful."[15] The knowledge that their relationship could never be one of equals remained. When Boothby, who had been hosted for dinner by Beaverbrook on a trip to Jamaica in January 1953, offered his gratitude, it was not without equivocation. "You have given me some hard knocks in the course of my somewhat erratic political career—most of them, I do not doubt, well deserved. But I never forget that whenever the sea became so rough that it looked like drowning me, you were the first to throw a life-belt; and the consciousness of your friendship, at the deepest level, has been one of my most treasured possessions through nearly 30 years of stormy political life."[16]

A pattern developed. Beaverbrook, through his newspapers, attacked Boothby, and his party, and an aggrieved Boothby fought back. Beaverbrook would then airily profess ignorance of any personal grievance and claim that it was all fair sport and that none of it was intended to offend. Even as Boothby observed in June 1954 that "you have supported, kicked, praised, cursed and stimulated me throughout my political career"[17] and claimed to be grateful for this most vexed relationship, there was no doubt who the senior partner was.

Eventually, it all became too much, and Boothby snapped. On 14 January 1958, he wrote, "I don't know whether you have instructed the editors of the *Daily Express* to humiliate and insult me; but that is what they have been doing, in a very big way." Boothby acknowledged their once-great mutual regard, but now stated, "I cannot believe that you want to push me about at a time when I have been very ill, and am still pretty ill," and concluded, "I can't go on in public life as a Member of Parliament." In exchange, Boothby asked that "you should now call the boys off,"[18] talking of his severe cardiac trouble.

Beaverbrook's response was typically lordly. Acknowledging that "the opening paragraph of your letter is most offensive to me [but] I have learnt since to regard your utterances on a different basis to everybody else's," he continued to make not-so-veiled threats. "Don't make up your mind to retire from public life. It is better to do like Churchill, or, as in the song of our countryman Harry Lauder, 'keep right on to the end of the road.' And when you reach it you will find me waiting at the gate along with Lloyd George and the other old boys who were such fun."[19]

A semi-apologetic Boothby, conscious of the enemy that he might have made, replied, "Whenever I have dealings with those who exercise great power, something seems to go wrong; and I do, say or write things which cause offence . . . I think there must be a muddy and rebellious imp in my subconscious who wants to squirt ink at great—and successful—men of action." Yet he also stood his ground, concluding, "You tell me not to retire, and I am sure you mean it. But it is not so long ago that my constituents were being exhorted almost every week, in the columns of the *Sunday Express*, to hound me out of public life!"[20]

Boothby would indeed stand down as a Conservative MP on 18 August 1958, but this was done so he could take up a life peerage. His correspondence with Beaverbrook continued its previous pattern, one moment complaining about his treatment at the hands of the proprietor's newspapers and the next praising him for some kindness or speech. And Beaverbrook's responses remained noncommittal—"the newspapers with which I am connected will always give you a square deal . . . Your many years of service in the House of Commons have given you a prestige that has not often been excelled in the history of the House," even as he remarked, "I have always deplored your being involved in European affairs."[21] When Boothby overstepped the mark, Beaverbrook let him know. "Surely I have shown you my friendship for you over and over . . . and with me, of course, as you know, friendship is a continuing process,"[22] he snarled in November 1960, when Boothby remarked in an interview with the *Sunday Dispatch* that he was unsure whether Beaverbrook was "a fan" of his.

Yet the ultimate break in relations came on 23 March 1962, when Boothby appeared on the five hundredth edition of the radio show *Any Questions?* and, after what he called "a very good dinner" in a "light-hearted and gay" atmosphere, made some carelessly ill-judged comments that insulted both Canadians and the "squalid stooges" of the *Daily Express*,* which he referred to as "a bloody awful newspaper, packed with lies." A furious Beaverbrook wrote to Hugh Greene, the director-general of the BBC, to threaten legal action, saying, "the attack made upon me in your service was of such a character that the transmission should have been cut off, and of course in the circumstances, I hold you responsible."[23] Beaverbrook now sprang into action. Not only did he ask for another investigation of Boothby's "strange conduct" in 1940, but he also asked for a copy of a 1959 interview with Boothby's "friend" Robert Bevan, a seventeen-year-old petty criminal who was given a year's probation for stealing a watch and chain from "Bob."

Bevan's account of his crime, and how he knew Boothby, was riddled with oddities and strange lacunae. He claimed that he was hired to work at Boothby's Eaton Square flat when the newly ennobled politician was suffering from a heart condition, and that the two men hit it off, visiting the cinema together and dining at expensive restaurants. In his interview, Bevan gave a brief cameo of Boothby's life on the town away from publicity. "I had been drinking in his flat in the afternoon and we dined at the Quo Vadis restaurant. We had French wines with dinner but it was the liqueurs that finished me. Then I introduced him to a little club called The Pelican in the West End. The owner was very pleased to see us and he set up drinks on

---

* The comments were made in response to Prince Philip's reported statement that the *Daily Express* was "a bloody awful newspaper, packed with lies," and Boothby was asked whether he agreed with it, rather than this being his freely expressed opinion.

the house." After Bevan stayed at Boothby's home, he claimed that he was too "stone drunk" to realise he had stolen the watch, and pleaded his continued respect and affection for Boothby, who he called "not only generous but . . . a great character," and concluded "I'll always be grateful for his kindness to me."[24]

At the time, Beaverbrook chose to publish the story as a relatively low-key one in the *Daily Express*, under the headline "Thief Lets Down Boothby," and included a blasé quote from the politician in which he said, sorrowfully, "He is very young—I think the temptation was too great."[25] It was a rap across the knuckles, but now Beaverbrook's fury with his former protégé meant that he was looking for further ways to expose and humiliate him. Even as Boothby, in receipt of a solicitor's letter ("writs were descending on my bloody but unbowed head like snow") apologized, saying, "I very much regret what I said on that programme . . . You know well enough *how* it is when I am in a merry mood, and I can only say that I am sorry,"[26] Beaverbrook sneered that "you have taken a long time to write that letter [of apology]." In Boothby's defence, this was because he was concerned about the legal ramifications of any communication. The publisher remained resolute in his determination to take action against the BBC, which eventually resulted in their paying £2,000 damages to Beaverbrook,* which it then attempted to extract from the errant politician.

Magnanimously, and pointedly, Beaverbrook halted this. He informed Boothby that he had made it a condition of the settlement that the peer was not liable for payment of any costs, "provided of course that I get an apology from you in open court which has my approval."[27]

The implication was clear. Beaverbrook's true adversary was the BBC; Boothby was a minnow (or herring) in comparison. He let Boothby know how generous he had been, telling him that "the

* He had initially requested £5,000; in either case, the money was not important, but the principle was.

writs that I directed against you represented no expenditure on your part. I absolved you from all damages even though the BBC lawyer suggested that you should pay half."[28] A relieved Boothby was, naturally, grovellingly grateful. Yet Beaverbrook believed that a far greater scandal would soon overtake him in any case.

This can be seen by a letter from his friend George A. Drew, Canadian high commissioner to Britain, in which Drew first bemoaned Boothby's "extraordinary statement" as being "consistent with the statements he has been making both publicly and privately," before suggesting that his comeuppance was imminent. "I do not know whether there is any background of personal experience which makes him so bitterly anti-Canadian. Perhaps there is another explanation. His own background suggests that possibility.* I still find it difficult to understand why both the BBC and ITV give him the opportunity to reach such a large audience with his destructive propaganda . . . We shall have an opportunity to discuss that when I see you personally."[29] Boothby had made his reputation and media career on skating on thin ice, while charming onlookers with his antics, but now it seemed if the cracks were starting to form.

In May 1963, the *Daily Express* published another story about Boothby's associations, rich in innuendo and menace. Under the headline "Riddle of Cheque Lost by Peer," the piece was thick with faux naïveté about why James Buckley, a seventeen-year-old cloakroom attendant at the fashionable nightclub Esmeralda's Barn in Belgravia, should have come into possession of Boothby's chequebook. The paper took delight in noting that the prosecutor of the

* Canada was notoriously homophobic at this point. Homosexuals were described as "criminal sexual psychopaths" and "dangerous sexual offenders" and could be imprisoned indefinitely for their offences. Those wishing to enter public service were made to participate in a kind of aversion therapy known as "the fruit machine test" in which their responses to homoerotic imagery and "homosexual words" were tested by a primitive form of lie detectors. If subjects were judged to respond too enthusiastically, they would be barred from employment in anything but the most menial jobs.

case had remarked, "Buckley has since refused to say how he got hold of the cheque so the mystery remains still unsolved."[30]

If these were repeated warnings, then Boothby chose to ignore them. He decided that he was now sufficiently popular, even beloved, to be untouchable by the press. In a spectacular display of self-destruction, he wrote a letter to the editor of the *Sunday Express*, following Beaverbrook's (admittedly self-serving) encomium to the ailing Winston Churchill, and declared, "Lord Beaverbrook's tribute to Sir Winston Churchill is moving. He has reason to be grateful to Churchill, who did him well. But who was the greatest champion and supporter of Neville Chamberlain before the war? Beaverbrook. Who supported the shameful Munich Agreement—against Churchill? Beaverbrook. Who supported the filthy Nazi regime? Beaverbrook. Who wrote, day after day, 'THERE WILL BE NO WAR'? Beaverbrook. So the tribute is not only moving. It is also nauseating."[31]

It was, appropriately, a declaration of war. When it was suggested by Beaverbrook's solicitors that it was so outrageous in its statements that it must have been either forged or sent under the influence of intoxicants, Boothby announced unrepentantly, "Of course I never, for one moment, expected [the letter] to be published . . . I must therefore make it plain that I have regarded Lord Beaverbrook's direction of the policies of his newspapers during the fateful years between 1935 and 1939 as only slightly less deplorable than that of the late Lord Rothermere [etc.] . . . If he wishes to argue the case with me in the House of Lords, I am very willing to do so . . . but I would be reluctant to have a public dispute with one whom I have known so long, and who proved to be a staunch friend at a critical moment in my life."[32]

Beaverbrook's solicitor described Boothby as being "filled with hatred and malice," and, no doubt leant on by his employer, wrote, "it might well be wise to treat him with the contempt he deserves although perhaps one can never say when dealing with a person of this nature—a gentle threat not followed by action might only serve to whet his appetite and the next occasion might result in further publication."[33] And Beaverbrook himself was furious, sending a memo to his subordinate A. G. Millar that read, "The sentence that I object to is 'who supported this filthy Nazi regime—Beaverbrook.' Of course it is not remotely true, and I think it is libellous." The old era of amused tolerance was past. "I think it might be quite interesting to go after this fellow again and this time to bankrupt him if I can. I would like you to consider it."[34] In another, undated memo, Beaverbrook growled, "I think as I get old and . . . get very near the end of my life, it is stupid of me to accept all these insults."*

There were two ways of taking revenge. The first, and most orthodox, would be to sue Boothby for libel, which had the intrinsic difficulty of having to prove that Beaverbrook had been maligned by an unpublished letter to his newspaper's editor, and also exposing him to the humiliation of the greater exposure of Boothby's remarks about Beaverbrook's putative Nazi sympathies.** The second was to remove any protection from Boothby, meaning that any unflattering stories about him might be published with impunity. In the end, Beaverbrook's ill health meant that the matter was not pursued to its conclusion in the courts, but instead he took the second means of redress, a tacit nod to other newspaper proprietors that it was now open season on his tormentor. Beaverbrook did not live to see Boothby's moment of greatest peril—Beaverbrook died of cancer a few weeks before the stories about Boothby's extracurricular activities made it into the press. Had Beaverbrook been alive, it is impossible to know how he would have directed his newspapers to act, but it was no coincidence that, without his protection, Boothby's baroque private life would now come under scrutiny as never before.

* The only extant biography of Boothby, by his friend Robert Rhodes James, is filled with inaccuracies and lacunae, but one of the most jaw-dropping is its statement that "cordial relations were resumed, which lasted until Beaverbrook's death."

** Even if, of course, British libel law places the burden of proof on the defendant rather than the plaintiff, meaning that Boothby would have had to prove the accuracy of his statements.

Describing Boothby as homosexual would be a little like calling Sir Edmund Hillary a keen hill walker. Boothby rejoiced in the nickname "the Palladium" as an undergraduate—so called because, like the London theatre, he was said to be "twice nightly." Although he was said not to have had heterosexual relations until his mid-twenties, thereafter he enjoyed buccaneering exploits with women and men alike. These notoriously included a lengthy affair with Harold Macmillan's wife, Dorothy, which may or may not have resulted in Sarah Macmillan being Boothby's illegitimate child. He remarked to his cousin Ludovic Kennedy, "Dorothy has thighs like hams and hands like a stevedore, but I adore her," but also said to a fellow parliamentarian more coldly, "to tell the truth, she reminds me of a caddie I once seduced on the golf course at St Andrews."[35]

Boothby was a man of no sexual morals whatsoever. A brief and ill-fated marriage to Dorothy's younger cousin Diana Cavendish between 1935 and 1937 only proved that his buccaneering ways and marital fidelity were wholly incompatible. He moved in circles where homosexuality and bisexuality were regarded as marks of honour, rather than causes of shame. In this, at least, pre- and post-war political society might have been regarded as being ahead of its time, but Boothby's antics did not go unnoticed by the less easily impressed employees of MI5. They began keeping a file on him in 1936, because of what they termed "certain dubious business associates and [because] he was also at that time a supporter of the Friends of the Soviet Union." His friendship with Oswald Mosley was also a cause for suspicion—"Mosley has known him for some time and thinks very highly of him"[36]*—but it was decided in 1951 that nothing Boothby had done warranted further investigation by the director general of MI5. This remained the case until a young civil servant

* Their friendship, which continued long after Mosley's disgrace and downfall, may be epitomised by a letter that Boothby wrote Mosley on 18 May 1930, after his friend left Labour. Boothby, in advice he should have taken himself, suggested, "This country is old—obsolete—and tradition-ridden, & no-one—not even you—can break all the rules at once. And do take care of the company you keep. Real shits are apt to trip you up when you aren't looking."

named John Vassall was arrested under suspicion of espionage on 12 September 1962.

Vassall was also homosexual, and had been blackmailed by the Russians into working for them in 1954, which he had done with diligence and efficiency. When he was eventually caught, he was equally thorough in his confession, although this did not stop him from being sentenced to eighteen years' imprisonment, serving ten. While incarcerated at Wormwood Scrubs prison in London, he made the acquaintance of Colin Jordan, a neo-Nazi, who produced a document titled *Behind the Democratic Curtain: Homosexual Network Endangers National Security* in August 1963. In this, he wrote that Vassall had informed him that "there exists in Britain today a network of homosexual politicians, high civil servants and others of power and prominence, gravely endangering our security."

Jordan was not treated as trustworthy—an MI5 document noted, "[he] must be regarded as a tainted source," and suggested that he had embroidered what he had heard from Vassall—but with hindsight, the account was more useful than how it was initially regarded. Particular interest came in Jordan's description of how "an acquaintance of Vassall who kept an establishment catering for perversions at an address in London W8 numbered among his distinguished clients one of our most televised peers, who used to go there to procure 'chickens' (the homosexual term for boys)."[37] This would prove to be an accurate description of some of Boothby's peccadilloes, although had they known the full extent of them, they would have been disgusted. One biographer wrote, "one of Boothby's particular pleasures was to watch boys excrete above him as he lay beneath a glass-topped table."[38] But what Jordan and Vassall were unaware of was the extent of the televised peer's acquaintance, which encompassed some decidedly dangerous characters.

Chief amongst these, naturally, was none other than Ronnie Kray, who co-owned Esmeralda's Barn with his twin brother, Reggie. The Krays had established themselves as two of London's most vicious "faces," as organised gangsters were known; but by the early sixties, both men were attempting to transition from the unavoidably messy lives of crime that they had both pursued since their teenage years into new careers as respectable businessmen. The legalisation of gambling in 1960 had helped them immensely in this regard, as new opportunities to make considerable amounts of money now came to them, as well as the chance to socialise with many of London's best-known celebrities. Given Ronnie's own homosexuality—although if you disrespected him by alluding to it too obviously, you ran the risk of being beaten, or worse—it was inevitable that he would meet Boothby, and that the results would be unorthodox.

An MI5 source, "believed to be reliable," gave a lengthy and detailed account of how Boothby and Ronnie Kray came to be photographed sitting next to each other in Boothby's Eaton Square flat. By early 1964, Boothby was involved with a young man, Leslie Holt, whom he employed as a part-time chauffeur. The source, with an element of disbelief, recounted how, "Boothby has been using him a long time. He has given him expensive cars and they have even been to the opera together a couple of times, which is rather bold. They are genuinely attached; this is no fly-by-night affair." Yet as the source described, "Leslie is not a well-known villain, though he's had a couple of convictions. Still, he does turn up occasionally with much money . . . and he runs an E-type Jaguar given to him by Boothby. Leslie's cash may come from Ronnie Kray, who runs a gambling club, Esmeralda's Barn, up in Knightsbridge."[39]

Holt had been introduced to Boothby after the incident of the missing cheque. MI5 described how "one of the cheques stolen from Lord Boothby was 'passed' [at Esmeralda's]. Boothby himself is said to have related the story that shortly after that incident he was visited at his house fairly early one morning by two smooth-looking characters who announced themselves as the Kray brothers. Their alleged reason for their call was to apologise to Lord Boothby for any inconvenience caused to him over his cheque. They explained that one of their men had been responsible, but that he was no longer with them and was unlikely to do that sort of thing again."[40]

Boothby, who was about to head overseas, thanked the Krays for their attention but expressed his desire to return to work, which is when he was introduced to the "pleasant, fair-haired" Holt, who was offered up as a form of compensation for his trouble.

The MI5 source went on to stress that Ronnie Kray, who had been released from prison in 1961 after serving an eighteen-month sentence for running a protection racket, was the owner of a legitimate business—albeit one acquired with a strong arm*—and was using this as a means of meeting people. As he described it, "Boothby is a kinky fellow and likes to meet odd people, and Ronnie obviously wants to meet people of good social standing, he having the odd background he's got; and of course, both are queers. Leslie never suggested that there was any villainous association between the two and they are not likely to be linked by a queer attraction for each other; both are hunters (of young men)."[41]

MI5's greatest interest in Boothby was derived less from his homosexuality and more from the possibility of his being blackmailed by Russian agents, as Vassall had been. There was enormous paranoia in the country after the John Profumo and Christine Keeler scandal of 1963, to say nothing of the unmasking of the Cambridge spy ring in the previous decade, and the possibility of a politician combining both facets was dangerous indeed. However, although an MI5 agent named Courtenay Young commented, "this might blow up into a minor Profumo affair,"[42] there was no serious danger of an intelligence breach. Boothby had never been regarded as trustworthy or reliable enough to be allowed near any significant state secrets. Instead, he was better suited to praising herrings, red or otherwise, from the House of Lords.

In one of the innumerable biographies that one or both of the Krays was involved in, 1988's *Our Story*, they alluded as to their involvement with Boothby. In this instance, Ronnie wished, as part

* The source observed that "almost at once, the other partners in the business sold out to him because they didn't want to be associated with a man of his reputation . . . Still, he gave them a fair price for their shares."

of his attempts to become a legitimate businessman, to invest in a building project in Enugu, Nigeria. Fearing that the £25,000 that he and his brother had put into the initiative would end up wasted, Ronnie tried to solicit a meeting with Boothby, "who had expressed some interest, but he wanted to discuss the project with someone else who was investing money to compare notes."[43] Therefore, in this version of events, the meeting that took place at Eaton Square between Ronnie, Boothby, and Holt was wholly innocent, and wilfully misinterpreted by the press, not least the *Sunday Mirror*, as part of a "get the Krays" strategy, with Boothby as an innocent victim in the whole affair.

This is not remotely true. The Krays' biographer John Pearson* described Boothby in 2010 as "a drunk, a liar, a reckless gambler and a bisexual with a taste for rough-trade sex and teenage boys."[44] This was a considerable volte-face from a letter that Pearson wrote to Boothby on 2 December 1968 in which he described the contretemps as "obviously one of the century's supreme examples of a story that never was," although, faux innocently, he also wrote, "all I have to do is to explain the answer to your question of why they stuck to crime instead of simply picking up the fairly honest thousands that were there for the asking. This, however, is not quite so simple and is really one of the most fascinating conundrums in their whole tortuous career."[45]

Many years later, Pearson, and others, were able to answer what he called "the sixty-thousand-dollar question," albeit with explicit reference to the entanglement that soon arose between Boothby, the Krays, and the Labour politician and journalist Tom Driberg. Amusingly, Driberg, whose homosexual inclinations rivalled Boothby's for their indiscriminate and heroic application, was a writer on the *Daily Express* and accordingly a favourite of Beaverbrook's, who not only paid him lavishly but saw to it that no breath of scandal could attach itself to his (rather tarnished) golden boy, even if he

* And, coincidentally, Ian Fleming's, too.

would sigh, after getting him off from yet another homosexual scandal, "Tom, how many times do I have to save you from arrest?"[46] Driberg, unsurprisingly, was an intimate of the Krays as well, and was able to tip them off as to the likely chemistry that would ensue between Boothby and Holt. He was not to be disappointed, even as he himself took up with the more mercurial figure of "Mad" Teddy Smith.

For a couple of years in the early sixties, Boothby was leading a strange double life. By day, he was a much-loved public figure, always on hand for an appearance on *Any Questions?* or to make a diligently reported speech on fishing in the House of Lords. By night, he, Driberg, and other minor celebrities were feted by the Krays, whether as honoured guests at Esmeralda's Barn or participants in the sex parties organised at Cedra Court. Even as Boothby, nicknamed "the Queen Mother" by those around the Krays—although never by Ronnie—conducted himself with cheery indiscretion, presumably in the belief that nobody would dare to provoke his criminal chums, he seemed unaware that he and his friends were the subjects of simultaneous Scotland Yard and *Sunday Mirror* investigations. Whichever one got there first would destroy Boothby, Driberg, and the Krays in one fell swoop. Unless, of course, they got something dramatically wrong.

IN 1959, THE AMERICAN MUSICIAN and show business personality Liberace sued the *Daily Mirror* for libel. Their columnist William Connor, under the pseudonym "Cassandra," had described the piano-playing wonder in 1956 as "the summit of sex—the pinnacle of masculine, feminine, and neuter. Everything that he, she, and it can ever want . . . a deadly, winking, sniggering, snuggling, chromium-plated, scent-impregnated, luminous, quivering, giggling, fruit-flavoured, mincing, ice-covered heap of mother love."[47] Its implications were clear, and after a trial in which it was debated whether "fruit-flavoured" would have been known to Connor as an allusion to homosexuality,* the jury found in favour of Liberace and he was awarded £8,000, then the largest ever sum recorded for libel. The musician famously quipped—not for the first or last time—that he "cried all the way to the bank."

Five years later, it was to be the turn of the *Mirror*'s Sunday publication to find itself in similar territory. Yet, just as Liberace had managed to turn the strictures of Britain's libel laws to his advantage—the *Mirror* could not provide proof of his homosexuality, so Connor's accurate statement became a hugely expensive embarrassment for his newspaper—so it would prove when the *Sunday Mirror*'s chief crime reporter Norman Lucas, tipped off by his closely (and expensively) nurtured contacts at Scotland Yard in July 1964 that the Krays would be arrested in due course for racketeering and for their involvement in a homosexual vice ring, decided that he would put the newspaper's reputation on the line and write a story that would expose both the Krays and Boothby.

It helped that the proprietor of the *Mirror* newspapers, Cecil King, had decided to transfer his support from the increasingly enfeebled Conservative administration, rocketed and buffeted by the Profumo case, and lend it to Harold Wilson and Labour. Therefore, Lucas was allowed to write and run a story on 12 July in the *Sunday Mirror*, entitled "Peer and a Gangster: Yard Enquiry," which declared that "the Police Commissioner, Sir Joseph Simpson, has ordered a top-level investigation into the alleged homosexual relationship between a peer who is a household name and a leading thug in the London underworld, involved in West End protection rackets."[48] For good measure, with the sub-heading "Public men at seaside parties," the story suggested that a number of clergymen were also involved, and that there had been many weekend visits to Brighton.

The story would have been read by as many as five million people, most of whom could have guessed who the "household name"

* "Fruit" was American slang for a gay man.

peer was,* even if the "leading thug" was a harder character to recognise. And the following week, the paper ran another installment, which was, if anything, even more damning. Under the headline "The Picture We Must Not Print," Lucas wrote that the paper possessed a photograph of "a well-known member of the House of Lords seated on a sofa with a gangster who leads the biggest protection racket London has ever known." In thunderingly moralistic tones, Lucas declared that "this situation cannot be tolerated" and that "the *Sunday Mirror* will continue to build up its dossier on the frightening growth of lawlessness, extortion, blackmail and intimidation in London."[49]

A few days after the story broke, Boothby returned from a holiday in France, whereupon he was visited at Eaton Square by a delegation of "men in dark suits" from the Conservative party, including the Home Secretary Henry Brooke, to ask what his reaction was to the allegations in the *Sunday Mirror*. Boothby, bluffing, denied that there was any truth to them, but when they left, promising that there would be a thorough investigation, he was reduced to near-suicidal despair and began drinking heavily. Perhaps under other circumstances he might have contacted Kray, but even a top-flight London gangster would be unable to brave the combined forces of the Conservative party (and government), Scotland Yard, and Fleet Street. When the German newspaper *Stern* not only ran with the story on 22 July but named Boothby in the process, commenting that "his position in society helps the gangsters towards more lucrative customers who prefer gambling halls and other 'queer amusements'" and that he would become "the central figure of a scandal that will overshadow the Profumo affair,"[50] the politician seemed finally to have run out of luck.

How Boothby managed, Houdini-like, not only to escape the

* Amusingly, the only other candidate for such a description, Viscount Montgomery of Alamein, panicked similarly, although he was a rampantly homophobic figure who once said that "this sort of thing may be tolerated by the French, but we're British—thank God."

censure—or worse—that his actions may have begotten but also managed to take revenge against his tormentors at the *Sunday Mirror* is an extraordinary reversal of fortune that was the doing of the lawyer Arnold Goodman. He was a man who was known to his friends and admirers—not least Wilson—as "Mr Fixit," a skilled and canny advocate who was able to discern weaknesses in an opponent's case that few others could have begun to detect. To his enemies—who were equally numerous—"Two Dinners' Goodman" was a Rabelaisian, unprincipled figure who used his considerable legal knowledge to manipulate and even exploit the law in order to ensure that his client, whatever their level of guilt or innocence, would emerge triumphant. How Goodman ended up working for Boothby—a man who was on the other side of the political fence and, in the wider details of what the *Sunday Mirror* had accused him of, guilty as sin—is one of the most fascinating, and opaque, stories in the whole bizarre saga.

It is commonly believed that "the little man," as Boothby referred to Wilson, saw that the Kray scandal was a plague on both Labour and the Conservatives and that Driberg was as likely to be pulled into it as Boothby had been. Therefore, it was in Wilson's interests not to jeopardise his anticipated premiership and so he licensed Goodman to make the whole thing go away, even if it would result in the embarrassment of a Labour-supporting paper in the form of the *Sunday Mirror*. This, however, may be broadly accurate, but it ignores the detail that Boothby was seriously considering defecting to the Labour party, whether out of political principle or self-preservation. When Boothby was ennobled, Wilson had written to him meaningfully to congratulate him and to say, "It is curious but true that I think we have always agreed in politics. I hope you will believe me when I say how glad I am to have your good wishes."[51]

Boothby was avowedly to the left of the Conservative party, and his support for the 1957 Wolfenden report into homosexuality—which would eventually be decriminalised during the Wilson administration—was dictated as much by clear-sighted principle as it was self-interest.

Boothby was close friends with leading Labour politicians such as Michael Foot—as well, inevitably, as Driberg—and felt instinctively more at home amongst their company than he did around the likes of the cuckolded Macmillan and the Benzedrine-popping Anthony Eden.* Had Boothby defected to the other party, Wilson would have seen perhaps the most popular politician in the country give an endorsement to his new administration. It would have been an undeniable coup, but to achieve this, Boothby would have to be cleared of any wrongdoing. Enter Goodman.

For "Two Dinners'"** to act on Boothby's behalf, however, Goodman had to be assured that no embarrassment would attach itself to him or, more particularly, to Wilson. With this in mind, Goodman and the barrister Sir Gerald Gardiner—who knew Boothby of old, having shared rooms with him at Magdalen in his "Palladium" days—went through a rigorous interrogation of the *Sunday Mirror*'s story, concentrating on whether any of it was not only true but provably so. Gardiner would subsequently apologise to Boothby, saying, "I do realise that you must have had an awful 6 days and felt that we were all being very tough with you, but that sort of thing requires a great deal of thought and some very careful handling."[52]

Gardiner knew of Boothby's homosexual past, and so there could be no question of accepting that the story was a fabrication. Therefore both Goodman and Gardiner carefully asked whether Boothby had had relations with men in the last ten years, which Boothby denied. Had either lawyer been minded to mount their own investigation into his activities, they would swiftly have found proof that this was a lie; but for the sake of harmony and Harold Wilson alike, the falsehood—or "Boothby's word as a gentleman"—was allowed to stand. Goodman then arrived at a solution which was ruthlessly elegant as well as daring. Boothby would write a letter to *The Times*

* Interestingly, and perhaps revealingly, there is no surviving correspondence of any note between Boothby and the great Liberal roué Jeremy Thorpe.

** *Private Eye* gave him the kinder—although still pointed—description of "the Blessed Arnold."

in which he would assert his identity as the anonymous peer in the *Sunday Mirror*'s story, testify to its untruthfulness, and thereby either push the newspaper into fighting a libel suit substantiating their story or backing down and retracting it.

The single detail that saved Boothby from disgrace, or worse, was that Lucas's reporting was uncharacteristically sloppy. Whoever his source was, Lucas had embroidered or simply imagined details, meaning there were obvious mistakes in the story as published. Boothby and Kray had never been involved in a homosexual relationship with each other—as MI5 knew—and their activities were concentrated on the gay brothels and clubs in London, rather than some fanciful mélange of Brighton and clergymen. Therefore, Boothby's letter, suffused with righteous if put-on anger, declared, "I have never been to all-male parties in Mayfair. I have met the man alleged to be the King of the Underworld only three times, on business matters, and then by appointment at my flat, at his request, and in the presence of other people. The police deny having made any report to Scotland Yard or the Home Secretary in connection with any matters that affect me. Lastly I am not, and have never been, a homosexual. In short, the *Sunday Mirror* allegations are a tissue of atrocious lies."[53]

This letter, which Boothby hand-delivered to the *Times* editor Sir William Haley, was itself a tissue of atrocious lies, and Boothby fled to Cambridge afterwards to lie low for a few days. Yet when it was reported the day after its publication that he intended to sue and had retained Gardiner for that purpose—Goodman went unnamed—Boothby blustered, "All I now want to say is that I have not made any firm or final decision of any kind; that I shall be guided entirely by legal advice, which will be given to me on my return to London." MI5 noted on 4 August that, while the *Mirror* was sufficiently unnerved by Boothby's robust response to let the story lie, "they doubt whether Boothby will dare sue, because he has too much to hide," and that "they are continuing to collect all available 'dirt' about people in high places, for use as and when appropriate in the future."[54]

They were soon proved wrong when the next, greater flourish took place the same day. Ronnie Kray gave the *Daily Express* the most flattering example of "the picture we must not print" of him and Boothby at the latter's Eaton Square flat, for which they paid the gangster £100 and then splashed it over the front page. During the course of an interview, the much-photographed peer not only happily admitted to having received Kray but even took a telephone call from him, confirming that the picture was in his copyright. Ronnie, meanwhile, backed up the story, saying of Boothby, "I found him to be a frank and outspoken man. He was everything I expected of an English gentleman."[55]

The battle lines were now drawn. Boothby not only had *The Times* and, ironically given his previous dealings with Beaverbrook, *Daily Express* implicitly on his side, but both Ronnie Kray and Arnold Goodman, two East End lads who took remarkably different, and remarkably effective, paths to achieve what they wanted. And the hapless editor of the *Sunday Mirror*, Reg Payne—a marginal figure who had been assured by Lucas and the paper's editorial director Hugh Cudlipp that the now-rickety story would stand up to investigation—was increasingly isolated. The only figure of any stature who was nominally on his side was Cecil King, the newspaper's chairman.

Yet when Goodman telephoned King to discuss reparations, he found him remarkably prepared, even grateful, to discuss terms that would avoid a long, expensive, and embarrassing court case. A sum of compensation was agreed upon—Goodman suggested £50,000, King countered with £30,000, and £40,000 was the compromise—and a full apology on the front page of the *Sunday Mirror* asked for and accepted. There would be a further piece of humiliation, too. King wrote Boothby a terse note on 10 August, a week and a half after the *Times* letter was published, to say, "Thank you for your kind words. The *Sunday Mirror* editor is to be relieved of his job tomorrow." The blameless Payne ended up editor of *Tit-Bits*, a dumbed-down weekly news digest magazine.

The gamble had succeeded spectacularly even, as it were, peerlessly. Not only was Boothby now richer to the tune of £40,000—over a million pounds in today's money—but the *Sunday Mirror's* high-profile climb-down and settlement had meant that no other newspaper would ever dare investigate any of his peccadilloes. As a by-product of his success, it also meant that the Krays themselves were out of bounds; and for several years newspapers had to be contented with calling them "the well-known sporting brothers," rather than even hinting at their crimes.

Boothby, naturally, was delighted with the outcome. Showily donating £5,000 to the King Edward VII hospital,* which had previously treated him for heart trouble, he would have enjoyed *The New Statesman* and *Economist* praising him for his actions. The *Statesman* saluted him by saying, "Boothby has demonstrated for all the world to see that the right way to tackle a newspaper smear is to hit back hard and openly. Not all have his courage. Perhaps more will in the future as a result of his action."[56] And his friends lauded him for his victory over the gutter press. Gardiner, enjoying a victorious holiday at the Cipriani in Venice, praised Goodman as "one of the shrewdest bargainers in the business" and called it "the fastest and largest settlement of the kind ever made. So it should have been."[57] And Foot, perhaps with a view to Boothby joining his team in due course, wrote to say, "You displayed great nerve & courage. But who would have expected otherwise . . . I must add this one cautionary word. A non-playing captain who gets £40,000 in one slap runs a grave risk of losing his amateur status."[58]

The captain may have scored, but there was one outstanding difficulty. The Krays had helped Boothby in his hour of need and would expect repayment in kind. Of course, they could count on his gratitude, but Ronnie also possessed numerous pieces of correspondence

* Alice Saxby, matron to the hospital, wrote to Boothby on 6 August to thank him for the donation and to say, "we have all been so sad and utterly depressed this last week for you—in your hour of persecution—but today we are enchanted and happy to know that it was all the most ghastly mistake—as I *believed* all along."

testifying to a far lengthier acquaintanceship between the two than the *Times* letter would have had anyone believe. As an immediate thank-you, Ronnie received £5,000, thereby placing his needs in the same category as the Edward VII hospital, but both men knew that this would not be the conclusion of the affair.

Boothby continued his relationship with Leslie Holt until later that year, when, tiring of him, the peer sent him a letter dispensing with his services as his "chauffeur," and offering him a pay-off of £2,000 as well as the Jaguar and Ferrari that Holt had already received. The angered young man made noises about going to the press with his story, which would not do. He was sent on a fortnight's holiday to Spain, courtesy of Boothby, and then accepted a reduced pay-off of £200, courtesy of Ronnie. In the words of an MI5 source, "[Boothby] had got Ronnie Kray to threaten him that it would not be a good thing for him to do anything or say anything against Boothby."[59]

The peer was in receipt of Ronnie Kray's "protection," and such luxuries did not come cheaply. Kray declared disingenuously in *Our Story*, "Boothby was a good man, an honest man. Some time later, when I was charged by the police with demanding money with menaces from a West End club owner, Lord Boothby asked a question in the House of Lords about why the police had held me in custody for five weeks without trial."[60] This was not done out of simple kindness. It was not the first time that Boothby had asked a question in Parliament without revealing his motives in doing so; but in this case, he was being held on the tightest of reins by Kray, who had previously furiously insisted that Boothby intervene with *The Times* and home secretary alike in order to obtain an American visa on his behalf, without success.*

Therefore, Boothby, who knew that the case was still sub judice and therefore liable to be prejudiced by his involvement, stood up on behalf of both Ronnie and Reggie, only to be silenced by shouts

* Ronnie's previous convictions having barred him from obtaining such a thing.

of "Order, order" by his fellow peers as soon as he launched into his peroration. The House knew what he was asking was unconstitutional, verging on the criminal. Ironically, the Lord High Chancellor was none other than his old Magdalen contemporary and subsequent advocate, Gerald Gardiner, who could have chosen to issue a stinging reprimand to this particular member of the House of Lords, but did not. Yet even if Boothby escaped punishment on this occasion, he was still a puppet on a string as far as the sporting gentlemen were concerned. A substantial proportion of the remaining £40,000 went on paying for the Krays' defence when the trial eventually came to court on 7 March 1965. Helped by various prosecution witnesses miraculously going over to the defence instead, the brothers grim were acquitted. They would finally be convicted and sentenced to life imprisonment four years later, meaning that Boothby spent a troubled time worrying that he might be called upon again at any moment.

Goodman may have seen to it that the *Sunday Mirror* story went away, but there was also another strange coda. Years before, Wilson had been discreetly sounding Boothby out about joining the Labour party, but now that Wilson was prime minister and Boothby had been through the biggest scandal in public life since the Profumo affair, the idea of this colourful character adding to the gaiety of his party's benches in the House of Lords seemed less beguiling.

Boothby, however, now wrote to Wilson on 12 November 1964, shortly after Labour's much-anticipated election victory, and made it clear that he was willing to serve. He informed the new prime minister that "if it is not an impertinence for me to say so, after forty years of unbroken public service in parliament I have not got what I ought to have. This, I know, means little or nothing to the public. But if, at any time, you could see your way to put it right, it would give very great satisfaction to me."[61]

Boothby was after a lucrative and respected ambassadorship, probably to Paris, although it is tempting to wonder whether a more colourful city may have been more his line: Bob Boothby, ambassador to Rio, has a certain ring to it. In any case, Wilson, who had observed the farrago at close quarters earlier that year, declined to offer him that or any other post, or to welcome him into the Labour party. Instead, a member of his staff wrote on the letter, "Can these [questions] be regarded as having answered themselves do you think?" And with that, Lord Boothby's hopes of political advancement ended.

The next two decades were hardly uneventful. On 30 July 1967, Boothby married a much younger Italian woman, Wanda Sanna, who he had known for more than a decade and had continued a largely epistolary relationship with while engaging in more forthright antics with Holt. Perhaps unfathomably, Sanna agreed to become Lady Boothby, and gave faintly surreal press interviews in which she often struggled to explain why the thought of marrying an over-the-hill, disreputable bisexual of pensionable age appealed to her. She once declared that "I suppose he thought I was his child and wife and everything,"[62] which did little to suggest that his motives in proposing the marriage were anything other than the quasi-pederastic acquisition of a helpmeet and a convenient means of dispelling the rumours about his homosexuality.*

As he would not be given any significant office, Boothby instead capitalised on his media profile. A glance through the archives that he and Sanna kept reveal many oddities, whether it's Boothby talking about his drug use in his late sixties—"A friend gave me the marijuana cigarettes and said, 'Try these. See if they do anything for you.' They didn't . . . so I am now looking out for some heroin"[63]—or his wholehearted support for an Israeli state, a subject that he knew rather less about than he did herring. And as he aged, he took a certain perverse pleasure in his weary body's decrepitude. Boothby

* Shortly before his marriage, one friend, the financier Bill Wasserman, wrote to him wearily to say, "I have learned that—according to your usual form—you have succeeded to make yourself notorious by getting drunk, and falling down the stairs, and requiring seven stitches. I wonder if you will grow up before you die."

once advocated euthanasia for everybody at the age of eighty, but at eighty-one said he was glad that the bill did not get anywhere as he was "enjoying being an old man."[64]

Boothby's death in his Eaton Square home on 16 July 1986 was greeted with respect and even reverence. The *Daily Telegraph*'s obituary hailed him as a "charmer with a brilliant touch." His peccadilloes were either ignored altogether or dealt with euphemistically, as in his "uncontrollable passion for adventure" that "sometimes led him into trouble," although the obituarist also concluded that "there was the core of a lovable human being and the world is the poorer for the loss of any man of whom that can be said."[65] In his late memoir *Recollections of a Rebel*, Boothby—who does not mention anything to do with the Krays or the *Sunday Mirror* in the book—writes in the epilogue that "I think I have managed to do something practical to help the fishermen, the farmers, the cancer-sufferers, the Czech refugees, the buggers and the osteopaths. It is not precisely the programme I planned for myself when I first entered public life. But it is something."[66]

Over the four decades since his demise, and the steady drip feed of scandalous revelations into the public domain, Boothby has become an increasingly notorious figure, with the avuncular, bow-tie sporting household name replaced by a sinister and exploitative abuser of young boys. A great deal of his infamy is deserved, and many will rightly wonder how someone so obviously drawn to dining with panthers managed to escape exposure, indecent or otherwise, during his lifetime. Yet he also possessed something that many of the other Eaton Square denizens featured in this book did, and that was charm in abundance, which enabled him to wriggle out of compromising situations with his status, if not always his integrity,* intact. Perhaps the archetypal Boothby

* Inevitably, on at least one occasion—this time when he was preparing to give an after-dinner address—Boothby had to be informed by one of his fellow peers, Lord Birkenhead, that "your trouser buttons are undone." He did not record what activity he had undertaken for this semi-debagged state to exist.

story is one of the best-known. When Ludovic Kennedy called him, with a mixture of censure and amazement, "a shit of the highest order," Boothby laughed, literally rubbed his hands together in merriment, and replied,"Well, a bit. Not entirely." Some might even concur with him.

10

Lord Lucan: 22 Eaton Square and 46 Lower Belgrave Street

"Help me! Help me! I've just escaped from being murdered!"

Eaton Square is associated with many things, but violent fatalities have thankfully played a relatively small role in its eventful and chequered history. Before the events of the night of 7 November 1974, the only truly horrendous event that took place in the vicinity of the square—excluding World War II bombings—was the murder of Field Marshal Sir Henry Wilson on 22 June 1922 outside his home at 36 Eaton Place. Wilson, the former chief of the Imperial General Staff, was killed by two Irish republicans, Reginald Dunne and Joseph O'Sullivan, who were implacably opposed to his anti-nationalism views.

They knew that by assassinating such a high-profile figure, they would make themselves martyrs for their cause. They also precipitated the subsequent Irish Civil War, which began a few days later and lasted until 24 May the following year. Dunne even stated at his trial that "if, as I surmise, you will find me guilty, although some of you may have been my comrades in the late war, I trust that a higher court, the only court that matters will judge me by my actions in this world and consider the purity of my intentions."

Just over half a century later, another bloody and rash act took place in a house on the corner of Eaton Square and Lower Belgrave

Street. It was not precipitated by any kind of greater moral or social cause—unless you believe that the acquisition of custody of one's children occasioned by the brutal murder of one's spouse can somehow justify such a deed—but because of the aristocratic standing of those involved, the botched killing itself, and most notoriously of all the question of what happened to the supposed perpetrator of the crime, it has remained one of the most talked-about and grimly fascinating events to have taken place in London in the past half century. Numerous books have been written about what precisely happened on that November evening, and whatever became of Lucan afterwards.

As with all mysteries and riddles, when the simple facts of the case are analysed calmly and rationally—with numerous pieces of new evidence that have come to light during recent years, thanks to a major BBC investigation—then an altogether different, and far more fascinating, story emerges than the prurient and excitable fabrications beloved by tabloid newspapers and sensational true-crime writers. It is no exaggeration to call Lucan, as the historian and writer Alex von Tunzelmann does, "the world's most famous missing person,"[1] but our understanding of what happened, and why, is only now beginning to reach any kind of explanation.

Richard John Bingham, a man described by his biographer Laura Thompson as "part Dracula, part Scarlet Pimpernel,"[2] may not have been born on Eaton Square—his birthplace was 19 Bentinck Street in Marylebone, where he arrived on 18 December 1934—but the area had vital associations for him and his family. John, as he was known, came from wealthy lineage; his father, George, was an Anglo-Irish peer who had been educated at Eton and Sandhurst before embarking on a military career that would involve service in both the First and Second World Wars.

Even from a young age, Bingham was still faced with a mixture of privilege and privation. His mother, Kaitlin, was an invalid who suffered from blood clots on her lung and so he and his younger siblings, Sally and Hugh, barely saw their parents until the end of the war. They were sent first to Wales, then to Toronto, and finally to wealthy Mount Kisco in New York State, where they were fostered by the millionaire Marcia Brady Tucker. Although there was a war raging on the other side of the world, Bingham knew little about privation or want but instead enjoyed an affluent, even cossetted existence that would give him a lifelong appetite for good living and the casual expenditure of money.

This paradisical existence ended when the three children returned to Britain in the aftermath of war. By now, the family had moved from their Cheyne Walk residence, which had suffered bomb damage during the war, to 22 Eaton Square, but this had not escaped privation either. Like much of the rest of the square, the house's windows had been blown out during the blasts and had to be crudely boarded up. Bingham, by now approaching his eleventh birthday, lived in a grim, straitened country, and his existence was an unhappy one. Nonetheless, even this was to switch in a couple of years. He was sent to Eton aged thirteen, and, during his early education there, his grandfather George Bingham died, meaning not only that his father became the 6th Earl of Lucan but that Richard would now be known as Lord Bingham.

At any other school, this might have marked him out as exceptional, and not in a good way, but he was amongst his literal peers. Bingham was regarded, if he was thought of at all, as an undistinguished character. He was described as "a pretty quiet type, not what you would call brilliant, a sort of good average in form and not frightfully keen on the playing fields."[3] Instead, it was a different kind of turf that appealed to Bingham, namely acting informally as the school bookmaker. The combination of moneyed pupils and proximity to several of the country's largest racecourses was one begging for exploitation, and Bingham was able to operate a sophisticated syndicate, helped by his own flair for backing the right horses. It led him to believe that he was one of life's born gamblers and that the odds would remain forever in his favour.

He followed his National Service with a brief career in the

Coldstream Guards, where he was stationed in West Germany but was more interested in developing his poker playing than in demonstrating any kind of military prowess. Still, he was widely believed to be his regiment's most talented poker player. Drawing on a mixture of his family's money and his salary, Bingham would take stoic pleasure in betting far larger sums than his fellow soldiers would ever have considered wise, as well as, more often than not, winning his gamble. When he returned to Britain in 1955, he began a career in merchant banking, where he worked at William Brandt's Sons and Co. on a salary of £500 a year. By night, he wagered increasingly vast sums in the city's casinos. If he won, all was well, but if he did not, disgrace or bankruptcy beckoned.

It was around this time that Bingham met John "Aspers" Aspinall, a bookmaker who had not only won a case in court brought against him by the government, but whose victory, given the name "Aspinall's Law," led to the invention of private casinos and clubs in Britain, which had previously been illegal. Aspinall celebrated his success by opening a Mayfair establishment, the Clermont Club, in 1963, which catered to an exclusive and moneyed clientele. He used the profits that he made from his club to subsidise the zoos that he was obsessed by. He was also briefly resident in Eaton Square, where he kept a leopard, a Himalayan bear, and a Capuchin monkey; the leopard would have to be walked at 3 a.m., so as not to disturb the other inhabitants of the square. There was once an unfortunate incident when the leopard encountered a German shepherd being taken out for a nocturnal call of nature, leading to an extra meal for the no doubt delighted feline.

By the time that Bingham encountered Aspinall, their own relationship bore similarities to the predatory big cat and the smaller, more vulnerable canine, although Bingham himself was a large, handsome man whose Etonian-bestowed charm, apparent wealth, and ease around London's best tables—dining and roulette alike—saw him attract a string of girlfriends. Yet as the early sixties wore on, Bingham pursued two objectives: to give up the world of banking, in which he never felt comfortable, in order to pursue an enjoyable and lucrative career as a professional gambler, and to find a wife.

Had he married for money, then he might have found someone willing to stake his losses, but instead he met the publican's step-daughter Veronica Duncan in the summer of 1963. Veronica was charming, petite, and appeared to be complaisant with her new boyfriend's belief that she should be entirely subservient to him; never expressing her own opinions or thoughts in any meaningful fashion; and, above all, understanding that his penchant for gambling was not to be questioned under any circumstances. With these conditions accepted, Bingham could airily say of Veronica that "she's an ash-blonde, she's very short . . . and she hasn't got any money!"[4] She, meanwhile, was enraptured enough to gush, "I had been looking for a god and he was a dream figure."[5]

By the time that they had met, Bingham had weathered embarrassingly horrendous losses—£8,000 or £10,000 a night was not unheard of, which necessitated loans from family members in order to pay them off—but he had also won £26,000 over two nights: more money than he would have made had he worked at Brandt's for another half century. He therefore announced, "Here I am working for so much a year less tax and I can win £26,000 in two nights! I'm going to quit and gamble."[6] That this decision was contingent on his continuing to win similarly vast sums—and that even the most successful of gamblers would invariably find that their luck could change—did not affect his decision to embrace this novel, riskier way of life, complete with newly acquired wife.

There were clear signs that Bingham was not simply the dashing but gentlemanly man about town that he appeared to present himself as. One of his many expensive leisure occupations was racing powerboats; and he called one of these boats *White Migrant*, which hinted at his right-wing and racist views. These would only become more explicit with time. Yet he also presented himself as a loving husband; and his first child, Frances, was born less than a year after Bingham and Veronica were married on 20 November 1963, necessitating a move from his bachelor accommodation at Park Crescent to a family home at 46 Lower Belgrave Square. His father had died in January 1964, and Bingham inherited the title of Lord Lucan, as well as a fortune that some estimated in the region of £250,000.* It was more than enough for a temperate man to pay off his gambling debts and to live a decent, even lavish existence.

Yet Lucan's instinct to keep on betting on everything—including, it appeared, his own future—would never disappear. At first, Veronica seemed besotted by both her aristocratic spouse and his lifestyle. When a friend asked her, "Don't you mind marrying a man who doesn't go to work, who gambles for a living?," she replied loyally, "I don't care. He can do what he likes."[7] Lucan himself said of his occupation, "I think you must understand that this is a profession. I go out and *work* every afternoon. We all have a job of work in life, they all happen to be different, and this is mine. And I work as hard at that as you do at your job."[8]

What his friends were too tactful—or self-interested—to mention was that their jobs, unglamorous and taxing though they sometimes were, did at least come with a guaranteed rate of return. Lucan's lengthy stints at the Clermont, where he earned the nickname "The Old Fossil" because of his constant presence there, may have allowed him free food and wine during his time at the tables, but the ever-mounting bills that he accumulated from his losses were a reminder that this largesse was not dished out because of his personal charm. He briefly considered an acting career as a diversion from gambling—the James Bond producer Albert "Cubby" Broccoli was said to have remarked, "He had it all—the looks, the breeding, the pride. I seriously wanted to test him for Bond but all he'd say to that was 'Good heavens!'"[9]—but Lucan had no screen presence, his natural charm and charisma disappearing as soon as he felt awkward and self-conscious before a camera.

* Recently discovered probate papers suggest that the sum was closer to £50,000, or around £1 million in today's money.

Lucan and Veronica's second child, a son named George, was born in September 1967, and all should have been domestic bliss. However, not only did Veronica begin to suffer from increasingly strong bouts of postnatal depression, but Lucan's political views drifted ever further into the unacceptable realms of near fascism. He called one of his greyhounds "Sambo's Hangover" and spoke vehemently about the need for a strong right-wing government that would bring about mass repatriation and the apparent indiscriminate application of corporal and capital punishment alike.* He was not a voracious reader, but there was one book that he was keen to be seen reading: It was, inevitably, *Mein Kampf.*

It was a source of grave disappointment to Lucan when the death penalty was abolished in November 1965, and he often spoke darkly about how Britain faced its own version of the Russian Revolution when what he termed "the undesirables"—in other words, anyone who wasn't a white, upper-class conservative man—were allowed free rein. His preferred listening at home was not the Beatles or the Stones but recordings of Hitler's speeches from Nuremberg.

Even the most robust of women would have found such a husband challenging to be around. Veronica became increasingly anxious and querulous, worried that Lucan was either going to lose all his money and throw his family into jeopardy, or alternatively that he would tire of her and take up with another, more pliable woman. After their third and last child, Camilla, was born in June 1970, Veronica was unable to be left alone with her children, being reduced to a state of perpetual nerves about every aspect of her life.

Lucan, in a classic example of cold pragmatism, attempted to institutionalise her in a psychiatric clinic in Hampstead, but she refused to stay there, fearing that she—like Vivien Leigh—would have to undergo a gruelling course of ECT. She was instead prescribed

---

* It was rumoured that Lucan subjected Veronica to regular and vigorous canings while she was attired in a special tight-fitting rubber outfit, although the author James Fox, who interviewed her, suggested that these were conducted "more in sexual passion than in anger."

strong antidepressants and tranquilisers which made her virtually catatonic. When she was not taking them, she would be argumentative and even violent; like her husband, she drank heavily, at a level that might have led to her being labelled an alcoholic. On one occasion, while drinking at the Clermont with another "gambling widow," she was sufficiently enraged by the other woman's conversation to throw a glass of wine over her, causing Lucan embarrassment and fury in equal measure. When he was drunk, which was frequently, he would speak almost wistfully about what his life would be like if his wife were to die.

After a series of tumultuous arguments over Christmas 1972, Lucan left the family home, with no intention of returning. He moved into a flat on nearby Elizabeth Street and tried and failed to obtain sole custody of the children on the grounds of Veronica's mental incapacity. He was shocked to discover that various nannies were prepared to testify that he had been violent towards her, and the result of the hearing was that he was limited to seeing his children every other weekend. It was further proof, if he had wanted it, that his once-beloved country had gone to the dogs and that the lordly likes of him were now discriminated against.

Lucan concocted ever-more grandiose plans to pay Veronica vast sums of money in exchange for her returning his children to him and abandoning any claims on their upbringing. He also employed private detectives to watch the Lower Belgrave Street house in the hope that they would observe some flagrant piece of illegality taking place that could be used against his now-estranged wife. Money was uppermost in his mind. He complained about the ever-shifting rota of nannies and their costs, at one point writing, "am I obliged to bribe someone to live in 46 Lower Belgrave Street so that my wife may comply with the Court Order?"[10] When he was not brooding on the downside of this particular gamble, he drank heavily at the Clermont, or made lonely vigils outside his former home in his blue Mercedes. It was inevitable that the increasingly desperate psychological and personal states of both Lucan and Veronica would have to reach some kind of resolution. On 7 November, that fatal occurrence duly took place.

When Veronica desperately ran into the nearby Plumbers Arms on 14 Lower Belgrave Street, at about ten to ten, the barman, Arthur Whitehouse, was horrified at what he saw. He would later testify in court: "She was head to toe in blood, but it was crusted. She was quite all right for a few minutes. Then she started shouting: 'Help me, help me, help me! I've just escaped from being murdered! My children, my children! He's murdered my nanny! He's murdered my nanny!" Whitehouse suggested that Veronica was "just in a delirious state. . . . I could not get much sense out of her and she was in such a state of shock that eventually she went completely silent. Her head injuries were quite severe. She had been hit four or five times."[11] Whitehouse duly telephoned the police; and the duty log stated, with remarkable brevity, "Person assaulted. Ambulance called. 10.07 p.m. Distressed female."

The question of what happened between around eight o'clock that evening, when Lucan parted from a friend he had been drinking with, and just under two hours later, has preoccupied millions for the past half century. Various facts are indisputable. The Lucan children's latest nanny, Sandra Rivett, was at 46 Lower Belgrave Street, having changed her day off so that she could see her boyfriend the previous day. Veronica and the children were all in the house, watching television, and there were no apparent signs of forced entry into the building, meaning that the only people present either lived there or would have known how to enter without causing any disturbance. Sandra was murdered, bludgeoned to death with a length of lead piping in the basement; and Veronica was similarly attacked, but she managed to escape and head into the Plumbers Arms with her anguished account of what had happened.

The abiding question, then, is what happened to Lucan on the night of Sandra's murder and Veronica's attempted murder, and then thereafter? He was said to have driven past the Clermont, at around quarter to nine, and asked if anyone was in yet; however, this is one of many only semi-corroborated stories of his actions that evening. The only movements of his that are certain are that, in the hours after the killing, he telephoned his mother in a state of panic before heading to his friend Ian Maxwell-Scott's house Grants Hill in Uckfield, Sussex. Here, he was greeted by Maxwell-Scott's wife, Susan, before he wrote two letters to his brother-in-law Bill Shand Kydd, whose half-brother Peter was Princess Diana's stepfather and who was married to Veronica's sister Christina. In these, Lucan offered what both those who defend him—and those who condemn him—have used as evidence for either the prosecution or the defence:

> Dear Bill,
>
> The most ghastly circumstances arose tonight which I briefly described to my mother. When I interrupted the fight at Lower Belgrave St. and the man left Veronica accused me of having hired him. I took her upstairs and sent Frances up to bed and tried to clean her up. She lay doggo for a bit and when I was in the bathroom left the house. The circumstantial evidence against mc is strong in that V. will say it was all my doing. I will also lie doggo for a bit but I am only concerned for the children If you can manage it I want them to live with you—Coutts (Trustees) St Martins Lane (Mr Wall) will handle school fees. V. has demonstrated her hatred for me in the past and would do anything to see me accused. For George and Frances to go through life knowing their father had stood in the dock for attempted murder would be too much. When they are old enough to understand, explain to them the dream of paranoia, and look after them.
>
> Yours ever
>
> John[12]

He also wrote a similar letter to his gambling friend Michael Stoop, which reiterated several of the same points and arguments: that he was the victim of appallingly bad luck; that he was fleeing in order to protect his children; and that, if he did not, he would end up framed, either for murder or attempted murder:

> My Dear Michael,
>
> I have had a traumatic night of unbelievable coincidence. However I won't bore you with anything or involve you except to say that when you come across my children, which I hope you will, please tell them that you knew me and that all I cared about was them. The fact that a crooked solicitor and a rotten psychiatrist destroyed me between them will be of no importance to the children. I gave Bill Shand Kydd an account of what actually happened but judging by my last effort in court no-one, let alone a sixty-seven-year-old judge—would believe—and I no longer care except that my children should be protected.
>
> Yours ever,
> John[13]

After Lucan left Grants Hill early on 8 November, there is no further authenticated sighting of him. He did not have his passport or his own car. The Ford Corsair, a "dirty old banger," that he was seen driving had been borrowed from Stoop a few weeks before, perhaps in an attempt to provide himself with an alibi. Even before the murder and attempted murder at Lower Belgrave Street, Lucan was in a disturbed state of mind. He had been drinking heavily; held a vindictive and poisonous obsession with his estranged wife, who he blamed for taking his children from him and consequently ruining his life; and was facing bankruptcy because of his considerable debts, which were believed to run to around £45,000, around twice the amount that he held in assets.

If he had visited his former home to remonstrate with Veronica, had accidentally murdered Sandra, and then attacked his wife in the process, it is not difficult to see why he would wish to commit suicide rather than face the additional shame of his children seeing their father convicted for murder and sentenced to life imprisonment. Although no body has ever been found—and it certainly has not been for want of effort on the part of the police, both at the time and subsequently—Lucan's powerboat racing experience would have allowed him to have a clear idea of which parts of the sea were the most treacherous, and, in turn, where a body could simply disappear.

This is the simplest (if far from the most straightforward) explanation to the mystery; that Lucan, not drunk but emboldened by a couple of glasses, headed to Lower Belgrave Street either to argue with Veronica or to murder her, and had accidentally bludgeoned Sandra to death before attacking his wife. After Veronica prevailed upon him to stop, then fled, Lucan left the house in a state of shock and the dawning realisation that he would, in all likelihood, be imprisoned for the rest of his life for having killed the wrong person. Therefore, in a state of appalled contrition, he committed suicide, presumably after having either thrown himself off the notorious Sussex hot spot Beachy Head—around twenty miles from the Maxwell-Scotts' home—or, having somehow smuggled himself onto a ferry or boat of some kind leaving from nearby Newhaven, by drowning himself a safe distance from Britain.

Lucan was officially declared dead on 27 October 1999, after his death was privately assumed from about seven years earlier. His son, George, took up the family title on 3 February 2016, after many more years of legal wrangling about whether a death certificate can be issued without a body. Veronica committed suicide by an overdose of barbiturates and alcohol on 26 September 2017,* after having spent decades offering contradictory and often confused

* Always a victim of erratic mental health, she convinced herself that she was suffering from Parkinson's disease.

testimony to journalists, biographers, and policemen alike as to what happened on the night of 7 November. She even suggested, albeit many years later, that the events had not been particularly traumatic for her, saying variously, "I don't have a very high opinion of human life"[14] and that "it might have been better for our family if he had succeeded in killing me."[15]

There were two major developments after Lucan's disappearance, one of which has been minutely documented in the press, at the time and since, and one of which has been shrouded in rumour and mystery. The first was the final inquest into Sandra's death, which was held from 16 June until 19 June 1975, and resulted in Lucan being convicted of the murder without being there to defend himself. The jury took a mere thirty-one minutes to offer a guilty verdict.

But the second was altogether more interesting, and took the form of a lunch on 8 November that Aspinall convened for a group of Lucan's gambling cronies—"friends" might be putting it too strongly—which included Shand Kydd; the racing tipster Charles Benson; and the artist Dominic Elwes, who had painted a portrait of Lucan shortly before his disappearance. "Aspers" always claimed that the lunch was nothing more than a group of concerned chums coming together to discuss how they might help a friend in need if he should reach out and ask for assistance. Yet given that Lucan owed him and the Clermont thousands of pounds in gambling debts, it is hard not to wonder whether the assistance that Lucan may—or may not—have been offered smacked more of a return on investment.

When the inquest took place, it was more than eight months since there had been any sighting of Lucan, although press speculation and rumour had persisted every day since his disappearance. The appearance of Veronica in the witness box, therefore, inevitably sent the media into near-apoplectic frenzy on the grounds that this was the first time that she would publicly discuss the events of 7 November. She suggested that Sandra had been the same height as her, of slightly fuller build, and murdered in the darkness in the basement by Lucan, who had mistaken her for Veronica. She then recounted a vicious fight that she had with him, in which he thrust three gloved fingers into her mouth and attempted to bludgeon her with the same length of lead piping that he had killed Sandra with a few moments before. There was sensational detail by the score—"during the course of it, he attempted to strangle me from in front and to gouge out my eye. . . . I was hit with an object. It appeared to be slightly curved and hard."[16]

According to her testimony, Veronica grabbed Lucan's testicles as they fought, which stopped him in the midst of his fury. Then the two went back upstairs to her bedroom, and Lucan went into an adjoining bathroom to fetch a towel and face cloth to tend to the wounds that had been inflicted on her a matter of a couple of minutes before. Sensing a chance to escape, Veronica "heard the taps running and I jumped to my feet and ran out of the room and down the stairs" to the Plumbers Arms. She was subsequently admitted to St George's Hospital, where she would remain for a week. It seemed a straightforward, if dramatic, piece of evidence, so the question as to whether Veronica's injuries might have been self-inflicted seemed an almost irrelevant question, not least because the doctor who had tended them at St George's, Hugh Scott, replied, "yes but it is very unlikely." Still, this did not stop Veronica from years later saying to the *News of the World*, "It was only then I realised that I myself was suspected of murdering Sandra."[17]

If she had killed Sandra, it would have been an act of motiveless malignity. Sandra was, by all accounts, a cheerful and friendly woman whose chequered romantic history—she had two illegitimate children, one who had been put up for adoption and the other who was being raised by her parents—meant that there were a number of boyfriends of varying degrees of commitment and seriousness in her past. Police investigation into the movements of these various paramours swiftly revealed that all the men had alibis.

Therefore, there were only three people who could have realistically killed her: Veronica, Lucan, or an interloper, presumably the man who Lucan referred to in his letter to Shand Kydd. Neither

Veronica nor Lucan would have had any motive to murder Sandra—there has never been any convincing explanation put forward for why Lucan would want her dead, let alone going to the trouble and expense of hiring a hit man to kill her—which means that it is reasonable to assume that the murder of Sandra Rivett was indeed a case of mistaken identity and that the intended victim was Veronica Lucan.*

Lucan would not have had very long at the house if he had been seen at the Clermont an hour before Veronica staggered into the Plumbers. Although Berkeley Square, where the Clermont was located, was no more than a mile and a half from his former home, London traffic, on a normal Thursday evening, meant that it would realistically have taken as much as half an hour to get from Mayfair to Belgravia, meaning that Lucan would potentially have had no more than thirty minutes to reach the house, surreptitiously enter it, murder Sandra, stuff her body into a mail sack that he had procured for that purpose, fight Veronica, agree to an unlikely peace with her, and then attempt to somehow ameliorate matters, all with the children in their bedrooms and a corpse in the basement.

It sounds fanciful, even ridiculous, but the alternative explanation is no more convincing. By this rationale, Lucan, driven to desperate hatred of the spouse who he believed had taken his children from him, borrowed the sum of £3,000 at extortionate interest rates from his gambling buddies, ostensibly to settle his debts but in reality to hire a hit man, who would have staged Veronica's death as a break-in gone wrong and therefore allowed Lucan to regain custody of his children and to move back into the family home.

However, once this assassin was hired, Lucan was overcome by either guilt or fear of being caught—depending on how much credit one gives him for a conscience—and rushed back to the house to

---

* I suppose it is just within the bounds of possibility that Veronica had murdered Sandra and inflicted the wounds on herself in order to frame her husband, but there was no immediate benefit to her to see him wrongfully convicted of murder, either from a custodial or financial basis.

frustrate the murder, only to find that the killer had already murdered Sandra and that Veronica was convinced, understandably enough, that he had hired someone to kill her. The mysterious and anonymous hit man then departed, never to be seen or heard from again; and Lucan chose to disappear rather than offer any rational or satisfactory explanation as to what happened.

Lucan was, by his own admission, at Lower Belgrave Street on the night of the murder. There was no necessity for him to be at his estranged wife's home, and the only truly satisfactory explanation was that he expected Veronica to be killed that evening, either at the hands of someone he was paying to do so or by himself. While there is no clear motivation for her proposed death, save that it was to be done out of loathing for her—hence the comment in his letter about "V. has demonstrated her hatred for me in the past and would do anything to see me accused"—there is also the logical flaw that, unless one believes that it really was a case of Lucan coincidentally driving or walking past the darkened lower ground floor of his former home and observing a struggle between a woman and an unknown man, he either went there to kill her himself or to make sure that someone else had done his bidding instead.

Those who would seek to depict Lucan as the innocent victim of a series of bizarre circumstances—and to place the blame, directly or otherwise, on Veronica or person or persons unknown—are scrabbling around to ignore the clear evidence that puts him at the centre of the scene and, in his wife's testimony, as the aggressor and would-be murderer. There are undeniably details that do not fit or add up—such as Lucan's much-discussed aversion to the sight of blood—but this can be said of virtually any crime scene several months after the fact. In the absence of anyone coming forward to claim culpability or guilt for Sandra's murder, we must assume the veracity of the most logical explanation. Lucan, having established an alibi, returned to his family home, killed a woman he did not know in a frenzy of pent-up frustration and violence by mistake, attempted to do the same to his wife before being struck by both exhaustion and, perhaps some form of remorse, and then, after she fled to the pub, attempted to extricate himself from the situation and almost certainly the country as well.

And this is where the more intriguing saga truly begins.

WHEN JOHN ASPINALL DIED ON 29 June 2000, at the age of seventy-four, he received what might have been kindly described as "a mixed press" in the obituary notices. *The Guardian*—admittedly, not a paper that the thoroughly right-wing Aspers would have ever taken in his home or club—described how he "was perceived as either a magnificently over-lifesized English gentleman, animal lover, gambler and eccentric, or as a distinctly more sinister individual, who would have been quite content to feed his fellow human beings to his preferred species—the ferocious tigers with which he spent his life trying to 'bond.'"[18]

The Telegraph, a newspaper more attuned to his inimitable brand of anti-European politics, wrote: "In his mind there had once been a golden age in which animals and humans had been equal. Mankind, though, had launched a vicious campaign against the beasts and Aspinall saw it as a duty to fight for the victims. He castigated the human race as a species of vermin, and positively welcomed natural disasters as a means of reducing the plague of *Homo sapiens*. He would gladly end his own life, he declared, if he could take another 250 million with him. There was something to be said, he felt, for Hitler's ideas about eugenics. 'Broadly speaking,' he said, 'the high income groups tend to have a better genetic inheritance.' Aspinall's special antipathy was clever women of Left-wing views; they made him fume." The anonymous obituarist sighed that, for all his genuine and deep-rooted love of animals, "his quasi-fascist views earned him obloquy."[19]

Aspinall had sold the Clermont for £500,000 in 1972 to the Playboy Enterprises executive Victor Lownes. Aspinall loudly proclaimed that he would plough the money back into animal welfare, not least at his private zoo, Howletts, in Kent. Here, he operated an unorthodox regime that was intended to break down the barriers between animals and their keepers by allowing them to socialise without the usual cages and restrictions and thereby build trust and affection between one another. The steady litany of deaths and maimings at Howletts and its sister institution, Port Lympne, suggested that this was a misguided and excessively utopian idea that misunderstood animal nature. But it did, at least, give him a private stable of carnivorous animals, to be deployed in whatever fashion or purpose he so wished.

When it comes to Lucan biographers, those who believe that the missing earl was an innocent victim of circumstance mention Aspinall and his circle as little as they reasonably can. Those who contend that Lucan was a guilty man, who either killed himself or fled to a distant country in order to avoid punishment, are only too eager to devote great detail and energy to exploring the machinations of "the just men,"* as the half-dozen who gathered for lunch at Aspinall's Lyall Street home the day after the murder were dubbed by the press.

The assembly—which did not include the entrepreneur James Goldsmith, despite an erroneous and therefore costly story in *Private Eye* suggesting that he was present—claimed that they were not meeting with any nefarious intent in mind but with the aim of discussing how they would help their friend and fellow clubman if he asked them for aid. Benson later informed Roy Ranson, the detective in charge of the Lucan investigation, that the lunch had been a "perfectly normal reaction to a horrifying situation, in which none of us knew very much about what had happened . . . It was a rather sombre occasion. There was a little hock—but not much—some cold meat and some cheese."[20]

Dominic Elwes went to visit Veronica, but Benson was keen to clear this up, too, in case it was believed there might be any

* A reference to Edgar Wallace's 1905 novel *The Four Just Men,* about wealthy vigilantes who take it upon themselves to punish those who they believe have not received their due judicial comeuppance.

intimidation or coercion. "Dominic did go to see her, but it was entirely off his own bat. He went to be sympathetic, and he was pretty shattered by seeing Veronica lying back and battered and not in very good shape."[21] That one of his gambling friends may well have been responsible did not stop Elwes from suggesting that, if Lucan should reappear, that he should be helped to get on, in Benson's description, "a banana boat to South America," which was not taken seriously by the group.

Whatever the outcome of this lunch, Lucan was charged with murder in absentia five days afterwards, and a warrant for his arrest issued. Aspinall chose to mark this development by giving an interview to ITV News, in which he talked emotively of how much it had hurt Lucan when Veronica had been granted custody of the children—"like the person that he was, he took this internally. There was no sign of outward bleeding—he kept up appearances—but those who knew him best knew it had caused internal haemorrhage." Then, in response to the news that a telegram had been sent to Lucan's flat at Elizabeth Street, apparently offering him asylum in Haiti if he wished for it, Aspinall offered a strangely equivocal comment. "I know of few people less fitted to being a fugitive in Haiti or Brazil. I don't think he has the capacity to adapt. He is a man of enormous virtue and honour. He could rely on many friends to help him with advice."[22] Many might have expected that a public statement of this nature would have implored Lucan to hand himself into the police and allow British justice to take its course. After all, if he was innocent, surely the courts would find this to be the case?

Lucan never took the opportunity to appear. In 1990, Aspinall mused to the journalist Lynn Barber while at Howletts that his friend and fellow gambler had done the honourable thing and killed himself. "He was very skilled at motor-boat racing, and I think he had a boat there at Newhaven, where his car was found, and I think he jumped into one of his little motor boats, went out to sea, put a big weight round his body, and jumped overboard. And scuttled the boat. That's what happened."

Barber, however, pressed him, and an irritated Aspinall, who had just been knocked down and nearly trampled on by one of his elephants, replied, "Well, I always think that if someone who has been a great friend is then in a terrible position, you rather feel more warmly towards him because that's when you're needed. A friend is needed when things are going badly. Anyone can be a friend of a successful man, who's done nothing wrong and is in the New Year Honours. But somebody who's in trouble, who's snapped and done something silly, that's when you need your friends."

He then made what Barber believed to be a rare, even careless admission. "I'm more of a friend of his after that than I was—though I haven't seen him—because if he wanted me to do something, I'd do it for him. Because he needs one and, like everyone else in life, I like to be needed. What's the use of a friend who, because you make one mistake, suddenly . . . I don't believe in that."[23] Certainly, there are many who believe that, long before Aspinall gave semi-incriminating interviews to journalists, he had been involved in Lucan's disappearance and that, quite literally, he knew where the bodies had been buried.

Kray biographer John Pearson, in his 2005 book, *The Gamblers*, suggested that Lucan had been killed at Aspinall's behest after having been sheltered for several months after his disappearance—which was also the conclusion of the 2013 drama *Lucan*—but there remains the persistent and admittedly lurid rumour that Lucan died at Howletts, whether by his own hand (whisky, revolver) or at the instigation of one of the "just men," who convinced the fugitive that his family would be better off without having to go through the embarrassment of a trial. Or alternatively, there may be something in the story, much beloved and recycled by the tabloids, that Lucky Lucan had finally run out of good fortune in the tiger enclosure at Aspinall's zoo, and that the disgraced peer made for an unusually flavoursome—if alcohol-soaked—meal for Aspers's pets.

Whatever the truth behind the end of Lucan—and there are still occasional news stories suggesting that he has been sighted in some far-flung part of the globe,* even though, at the time of writing, he would be well over ninety—it is fascinating to see how the coverage of his disappearance has played out in various publications. The author Sally Moore, for instance, was convinced that he was innocent, and writes explicitly in her 1987 book *Lucan*, which painstakingly offered several theories explaining why it was impossible for him to have committed the murder, that "I believe that the inquest verdict condemning Lord Lucan should now be quashed without delay, and that the police should launch a new investigation to find the real killer. I hope this book will help to correct the distorted picture of Lord Lucan which has been presented for so long. And that it will encourage him—if he is still alive—to come forward and clear his name."[24]

Quite another kind of hope was expressed at the end of the Javert-like Ranson's account of his investigation into Lucan's disappearance, published nearly a decade later. The detective suggested that he had no doubt of his quarry's guilt and concluded: "I believe that Lord Lucan has been able to live in relative comfort in the warmth of southern Africa. Probably with a little help from, as yet, unidentified friends he has built a reasonable life; conceivably even a more useful life than his wastrel twilight existence as a gambler in the London he left so abruptly behind." Ranson ended his book with an invitation, or threat. Although he sighed that "there has been no single response that has led me further towards my goal of finding Richard John Bingham," he implored his readers, "Take a look now at the man sitting next to you as you read these lines. Could he be Lord Lucan? If so, then please let me know." Finally, he offered his own personal message for the vanished peer. "Do not relax, my Lord. Keep a watchful eye over your shoulder. There will always be someone looking for Lucan."[25]

More recent historians and biographers, able to take a fuller

* Of which one of the best, surely, is that the conservative, ferociously reactionary Lucan reinvented himself as a hippy called "Jungle Barry" who played the bongos on the beach in Goa.

account of the evidence, have reached more nuanced conclusions. At the end of the 2024 BBC Radio 4 series about Lucan's disappearance, Alex von Tunzelmann said, in the unlikely event of the peer returning to Britain to be put on trial, "a decent barrister could create enough doubt in the minds of the jury to get Lord Lucan off," citing the underexplored possibility of another man in the house and Veronica's dubiousness as a witness. Yet Tunzelmann also remarked, "I doubt he was innocent, but I'm not sure he's the only person who was guilty." She noted, amongst Lucan's possessions, a copy of H. Montgomery Hyde's biography of the lawyer Norman Birkett, where "very specific pages," relating to husbands murdering their wives, had been underlined or turned down, leading her to suggest that this evidence suggests that an interest in spousal homicide had been present for some time.

Ranson may never have found his quarry, but his belief that someone will always be searching for Lord Lucan holds true after his book was published in 1994. Certainly, many refused to believe that he had either committed suicide or been killed, including Veronica, who icily said shortly before her death that "as far as I'm concerned, my husband is still alive, and I have no reason to believe otherwise."[26] It says much for the febrile saga that, when the Labour MP John Stonehouse faked his death on 20 November 1974 and attempted to lead a new life in Australia with his secretary, his attempt was foiled because the police believed that he was, in fact, Lucan.

It is now possible, thanks to advances in DNA testing technology, that, should Lucan's children provide samples of their DNA,* a match might be found for the traces of skin and blood still present on the murder weapons. This would at least answer the vexed question as to whether Lucan killed Sandra Rivett or not. Yet murders, even unsolved murders, are hardly unique. The interest in Lucan's actions

---

* His son, George, has publicly stated that he believes his father to be innocent, saying in 2016 that "As a British person, I still prefer to consider a person innocent until proven guilty in a court of law. To some extent it has been a bit of a jaunt, at other times it has been very difficult."

lies in his unsolved disappearance and a sense of fascination—even, in some cases, jealousy—that we all have with those who simply vanish from their previous lives in favour of pursuing an unknown path.

Yet when I think about the Lucan case, it isn't the selfish, venal, and bigoted peer I feel sorry for or his cold, violent wife. Instead, it's their blameless children, forever forced to live with a legacy that nobody would wish on their worst enemy, and the often forgotten figure of the twenty-nine-year-old Sandra, walking to work through Eaton Square.

Epilogue

The Ghosts of Eaton Square: 93 Eaton Square

In 2016, Eaton Square was named the most expensive place in Britain to buy a house. With an average cost of nearly £17 million for each of its white-stuccoed buildings, anyone wanting to purchase a property on the square is less a one-percenter and more in that infinitesimally small band of international multimillionaires who can likely afford not only to purchase a sizeable place in Belgravia but who can have the full panoply of assets: the country estate in the Cotswolds or Norfolk, the grand penthouse overlooking Central Park on the Upper East Side, the Parisian apartment, and the condo in the gated community in Florida. And now, perhaps, the Dubai residence, too.

What marks Eaton Square out as distinctive and interesting, rather than just another expensive playground for the super wealthy, is the richness and variety of its historical associations. Many of these have already been discussed, but after the Lucan murder and the concomitant—if purely coincidental—success of *Upstairs, Downstairs*, the square reached a level of popular awareness that it had never before attained. That the starry likes of Rattigan, Harrison, and Vivien Leigh had lived there—or, indeed, the more notorious figures of Ribbentrop, Boothby, and Diana Mitford—had made an impact in certain well-heeled circles. Yet Eaton Square, if it was thought about, was either as the punchline to a comedian's joke (as in the Victorian music hall songs) or as the encapsulation of privilege and wealth.

When Harrison described the square to British Pathé, apparently off the cuff, as "the last bulwark of 'decent indecency,'" he anticipated the changes that would occur suddenly at the beginning of the next decade, and then more gradually over the following half century. Indeed, what happened to Eaton Square in the eighties and nineties resembled the country's revived economic fortunes but in microcosm. It was all but inevitable that the square would welcome another prime minister, and so Margaret Thatcher found herself in residence at 93 Eaton Square—formerly, and appropriately, the home of Stanley Baldwin—for a few months between her defenestration from office on 28 November 1990 and her move to a five-bedroom property at nearby Chester Square.

Yet Thatcher was merely a welcome guest. The owner of number 93 was Kathleen DuRoss Ford, a former low-rent model from the grimmer side of Detroit who had managed to propel herself up the social and economic ladder by dint of her affair with the automobile scion Henry Ford II. When the two were photographed together after being stopped by the police in February 1975—Ford had, ironically enough, been arrested for drunk driving—she was thirty-five, and he was fifty-eight and married. When asked about DuRoss's presence in his car at a press conference, Ford laughed and cited the famous motto of the British royal family, saying, "I haven't anything to explain. Never complain, never explain."

However, the very public revelation of his extramarital relationship led his second wife, Cristina, to divorce him the following year, allowing DuRoss and Ford to marry in 1980. When the automobile tycoon died of pneumonia in 1987, he left his widow with a vast fortune as well as the more nebulous status of keeper of her husband's legacy. She commented coyly that Ford was "that big powerful man to so many people who don't know him. But to me he's just Henry.

He has a love of the company and a love of me."[1] She was also, perhaps helpfully, said to be someone "who could party all night and then go to work without a hangover the next morning."[2]

DuRoss was typical of the new breed of inhabitants of Eaton Square. She was international, came from recently acquired wealth, and was bent on reinvention. A few years before, she had been the single mother of two children who had sustained herself financially with a range of activities that she described pithily as "Social Security, renting from my family, modelling, and jobs like bookkeeping for a blood bank."[3] Her chance encounter with Ford, and subsequent change in circumstances, meant that she could be therefore described by enraptured property agents and auctioneers as a former model, accomplished photographer, and keen aesthete. It is very easy to be all these things with hundreds of millions of dollars in the bank, and the inevitable brouhaha that ensued after her death—albeit in America rather than Britain—which saw her family pitted against her attorney and "carer" in a battle for the remains of her estate was a fitting conclusion to a Fitzgeraldian saga which had seen the acquisition of vast sums of all-American money, which were then spent on one of Eaton Square's grandest and most historic properties.

After DuRoss Ford died in 2020, there was a rare opportunity for hoi polloi to see exactly how the exceptionally wealthy lived, when Christie's held a sale of her belongings and effects from her Eaton Square and Turville Grange properties on 15 April 2021. As is inevitable with these much-hyped auctions, rubberneckers and the congenitally curious drove interest in the often unexceptional items on offer to ridiculous prices. A pair of mahogany and brass floor lamps, optimistically estimated at £1,000 to £1,500, sold for a staggering £4,750, and a Waterford cut-glass table service, of a kind that might pitch up at a particularly well-to-do provincial fete, was expected to sell for as much as £4,000, and somehow trounced this, realising £6,875.

Even some respectable examples of modern art went for some extraordinarily inflated sums. The Scottish Colourist painter and sculptor John Duncan Fergusson's work *The Chinese Coat*, which Christie's described with the hyperbole of the confident saleroom as "represent[ing] Fergusson's finest achievements in colour, light, and form," managed to sell for a mighty £412,500. Another Scot, the Post-Impressionist Samuel Peploe, had his 1910 painting *Boats in Port* realise a magnificent £225,000, against an estimate of £60,000 to £80,000.

Nonetheless, amidst the respectable and often rather boring Georgian and Victorian furniture, there were a few more personal items that hinted at DuRoss Ford's personal tastes. A collection of Hermès and Chanel handbags realised a considerable sum of money, and the final item sold, a modern Wurlitzer jukebox, hinted at a rather more unrestrained and fun-loving side to Mrs Ford the third. One can only hope that the item was a fixture of 93 Eaton Square when Thatcher was a visitor—or even a resident—and that, after a few large whisky and sodas, she could be persuaded to dance to tunes rather more energetic than her once-stated favourite, the 1952 novelty song "(How Much Is) That Doggie in the Window?"

In any case, during DuRoss Ford's time in Eaton Square, most of her neighbours were not former prime ministers but the stateless, rootless wealthy, who bought the properties as assets and inhabited them for mere days a year, leaving them to the mercies of private security guards and housekeepers for the remainder of that time. After the break-up of the Soviet Union, and the consequent flood of oligarch-owned Russian money into the British economy (something that used to be welcomed by generations of politicians, until it became increasingly clear that Vladimir Putin's regime was even more corrupt and deadly than the governments that it had replaced), Eaton Square became the preferred home of so many Russians that it began to rejoice in the far from ironic nickname "Red Square."

Although some of these inhabitants did not technically live on the square—Roman Abramovich, commonly described as the most notorious present-day Eaton Square dweller, actually lived on 57 Lower Belgrave Street, just a few doors down from Lord Lucan's house—they still managed to contribute to the sense of the area being the preserve of men who were both extraordinarily wealthy and entirely unaccountable in the origins and expenditure of this money. The outbreak of Russian's war on Ukraine at the beginning of 2022 led to many of these oligarchs' properties being seized in sanctions levelled against the Putin regime, and so, at the time of writing, many of Eaton Square's grandest and most storied houses sit empty and unappreciated.

They are caught in a limbo between the Realpolitik requirements of governments and nations and the financial expectations of the square's ultimate owner, the present-day Duke of Westminster, an amiable thirty-something businessman whose public standing was sufficiently high for the Prince of Wales to serve as an usher at his wedding in Chester Cathedral on 7 June 2024. Perhaps the ill-fated St Peter's Church, which burnt down yet again on 20 October 1987—the target of an attack by an anti-Catholic arsonist who was under the mistaken impression that he was destroying a Popish chapel, necessitating a long and expensive rebuilding process that was only completed in 1991—was believed to have unfortunate connotations for Westminster. In any case, it is hard to imagine most of his Russian leaseholders worshipping at St Peter's, not least because several of them—like Abramovich—claim Jewish heritage, although how seriously this is observed remains hard to assess.

Whether from changing tastes in property or simply because of relative levels of affordability, Eaton Square is no longer the address of choice of those in the entertainment industry. Actors, musicians, and writers are conspicuous by their absence from the square. Few playwrights—bar, of course, the great Tom Stoppard—would have had the finances to maintain a residence as lavish as Rattigan's, and even some of the most successful and beloved film stars in Britain would hesitate to spend the amount that an Eaton Square property now costs—£55 million, in one reported case—in order to follow in the traditions of Vivien Leigh and Rex Harrison.

There is, rather hearteningly, one striking exception to this, and that comes in the form of the composer and impresario Andrew Lloyd Webber. As befits a man who is said to be worth £500 million, according to the *Sunday Times* rich list, Lloyd Webber has owned a variety of expensive properties in some of the nonpareil parts of Britain, including his country estate of Sydmonton Court in Hampshire and a house in Eaton Square. However, his residence in the latter, which ended in the late nineties, featured a strange but darkly amusing phenomenon that has not been recorded by any other of the square's residents: His home was haunted.

In a 2024 interview with the *Daily Telegraph*, Lloyd Webber was asked whether any of the London theatres that he owned were visited by spectral apparitions. Perhaps mindful of the decline in custom by the timid had he admitted that such establishments of his as the Theatre Royal Drury Lane were haunted, he denied it, but instead made the extraordinary admission that "I did have a house in Eaton Square which had a poltergeist. It would do things like take theatre scripts and put them in a neat pile in some obscure room. In the end we had to get a priest to come and bless it, and it left."[4]

Lloyd Webber was fortunate that this particular haunting was a largely benevolent one, and also one that could be brought to a happy conclusion with the intervention, presumably of one of St Peter's long-suffering clergy. Yet it's tempting to wonder which of the thousands of Eaton Square residents who have lived on the square since Thomas Cubitt and the Duke of Grosvenor first struck their property deal had been tempted to return in incorporeal form and cause mild-mannered havoc in the home of the *Phantom of the Opera* composer. Was it Lord Alvanley, still set on causing light-hearted mischief a century and a half after his death? George Peabody, irritated that his high-minded and philanthropic ideas had not been followed as assiduously as he wished? Or even W. S. Gilbert, hoping that a fellow gentleman of the theatre would take his posthumous appearances in the playful spirit in which they were intended?

We shall unfortunately never know. Yet just as Eaton Square remains predominantly the same square that Cubitt built two centuries ago, despite arson, bomb damage, and the various incursions of fascism, the supernatural, Russian oligarchs, gangsters, and the slave trade, it continues to be London's most-discussed, sought-after and—that dread, misused word—"iconic" place to live. It is a place where literal royalty has mixed with show business royalty, where playboys have lived next door to dowagers, and where the ability to spend money ostentatiously marks its inhabitants out from virtually everyone else. It retains much of its charm and cachet to this day; and a walk around its perimeter, gawping at the gardens and the glimpses of wealth in its now barred and curtained windows, remains one of the great pleasures that one can find in contemporary London.

And who will be the next resident in one of its properties, and the next keeper of the secrets of Eaton Square? Who knows? If Prince Harry, bored with his life among the chickens and jam jars of Montecito, wanted to return to London, Eaton Square, in all its opulence, tragedy, and events, seems tailor-made for him.

ACKNOWLEDGEMENTS

Delving into the history of as storied—and, of course, secretive—an area of London as Eaton Square has been a thrilling and often surprising experience. The first thing I did while beginning my research was to contact several present-day residents of the square and ask them for interviews. Nobody was willing to speak on the record, citing "privacy concerns," but my thanks to those who responded nonetheless with invaluable background information, especially John Aspinall's grandson Orson Fry, who offered several valuable leads. Likewise the present-day owner of Eaton Square, Hugh Grosvenor, politely turned down my requests for an interview or to access the family archives. My thanks to his archivist, Louise Benson, for her assistance and help in any case.

Once again, this has been a research-heavy book, and there are many institutions and organisations that I would like to thank. These include the University of Birmingham; the Bodleian Library, Oxford; the British Library, London; the Churchill Archives Centre, Cambridge; the London Library; the National Archives, Kew; the National Library of Scotland, Edinburgh; the Parliamentary Archives, London; and the Royal Archives, Windsor. My thanks also to Ella Radley of the Terence Rattigan Estate and Oliver Soden for several invaluable details about Noël Coward.

This book was the brainchild of my editor, Michael Flamini at St Martin's Press, and it marks the fourth collaboration of ours to date. It has been just as much of a pleasure to work on this—my first project originating in the United States—as it has been the others, and I owe deep gratitude to Michael for his warmth, insight, professionalism, and unparalleled knowledge of the best plays and restaurants on both sides of the Atlantic. My thanks also go to Claire Cheek at St Martin's, my indefatigable agent, Ed Wilson, and my painstakingly excellent copy-editor, Martha Schwartz.

On a personal level, I owe everything to my wife, Nancy, whose love and support makes it possible for me to be able to spend considerable periods of time away from home working on projects such as this, and to my wonderful daughter, Rose, whose welcome when I return makes the absences all the harder. There are many friends whose insight and conversations have been invaluable, but it is to Rose's godfather, Simon "Boothby" Renshaw, that this book is dedicated, as it must be. We have spent the past decade talking about the peerless peer who has given my dear friend his nickname, and so please accept this long overdue token of gratitude as my thanks for such stimulating and hilarious conversations.

NOTES

PROLOGUE

1. https://www.sloanestreet.co.uk/heritage/ Vincent Lunardi to Gherardo Compagni, 14 August 1784, in *An Account of the First Aërial Voyage in England* (London, 1784), 14.
2. Ibid., 15.
3. Ibid.
4. Ibid.
5. Ibid., 15–16.
6. Joseph Banks to Benjamin Franklin, August 13, 1784, in *The Papers of Benjamin Franklin,* ed. Ellen R. Cohn, vol. 42, *March 1 through August 15, 1784* (New Haven: Yale University Press, 2017), 497–99.

1: THOMAS CUBITT AND ROBERT GROSVENOR

1. Arthur Miller, *Death of a Salesman* (London: Cresset Press, 1949).
2. Hermione Hobhouse, *Thomas Cubitt: Master Builder* (London: Macmillan, 1971), 4.
3. Ibid., 8.
4. Ibid., 17.
5. Ibid., xxiii.
6. Ibid., 81.
7. *Daily Post,* 12 July 1725.
8. Horace Walpole to George Montagu, 17 March 1761, in *The Yale Edition of Horace Walpole's Correspondence*, W. S. Lewis, ed., vol. 9 (New Haven: Yale University Press, 1941), 344.
9. Walpole to the Earl of Hertford, 12 February 1765.
10. R. G. Thorne, *The History of Parliament: The House of Commons 1790–1820* (Woodbridge, Suffolk: Boydell and Brewer, 1986), vol 1, 237.
11. Kenneth Baker, "George IV: A Sketch," *History Today* 55, 10 October 2005.

12. Edward Walford, *Old and New London: A Narrative of Its History, its People, and its Places,* vol. 5, *The Western and Northern Suburbs* (London: Cassell, 1878), 8.
13. Hobhouse, *Thomas Cubitt,* 92.
14. Ibid.
15. E. Beresford Chancellor, *The History of the Squares of London: Topographical & Historical* (London: Kegan Paul, Trench, Trübner, 1907), 339.
16. Stephen Dowland Page, *History of St Peter's Eaton Square (1827–1927),* 1928.
17. Hobhouse, *Thomas Cubitt,* 144.
18. David Watkin, Cockerell quoted in *The Life and Work of C. R. Cockerell* (London: Zwemmer, 1974), 65.
19. Hobhouse, *Thomas Cubitt,* 75.
20. G. M. Trevelyan, *History of England* (London: Longmans, Green, 1926), 650.
21. Hobhouse, *Thomas Cubitt,* 471.
22. Queen Victoria diary, 24 December 1855, as published at https://www.royal.uk/sites/default/files/media/victoria.pdf.

2: WILLIAM ARDEN, RALPH BERNAL, LORD TRURO, AND KLEMENS VON METTERNICH

1. George Edward Cokayne, *The Complete Peerage of England, Scotland, Ireland, Great Britain, and the United Kingdom, Extant, Extinct, or Dormant,* ed. Vicary Gibbs, vol. 1 (London: St Catherine Press, 1910), 119.
2. Charles Greville, *The Greville Memoirs (Second Part),* vol. 3, *A Journal of the Reign of Queen Victoria* (London: Longmans, Green, 1885), 306.
3. Ibid.
4. Lord Byron, *Detached Thoughts,* ed. Lord Ernle (Rowland R. Prothero, 1928), 29.
5. Edward Walford, "Noble Mansions in Piccadilly," in *Old and New London: A Narrative of Its History, its People, and its Places,* vol. 4, *Westminster and the Western Suburbs* (London: Cassell, 1878), 284.
6. Countess of Blessington, *Journal of Conversations with Lord Byron, New Monthly Magazine,* 1 December 1832, 533.
7. Rees Gronow, *Reminiscences of Captain Gronow* (London: Smith, Elder, 1862), 188.
8. Ibid., 189.
9. *The Letter-Bag of Lady Elizabeth Spencer-Stanhope,* ed. A. M. W. Stirling (London: John Lane, the Bodley Head, 1913), 21.
10. Ibid., 22.
11. *Greville Memoirs, A Journal of the Reign of Queen Victoria,* vol. 3, 306.
12. *Catholic Telegraph,* 26 June 1835.
13. Charles Greville, *The Greville Memoirs,* vol. 3, *A Journal of the Reigns of King George IV and King William IV,* ed. Henry Reeve (London: Longmans, Green, 1875), 257.
14. "The Noble House of Arden," *The Mirror of Literature, Amusement, and Instruction,* 2nd. ser., 23 March 1844, 185.
15. *Greville Memoirs, A Journal of the Reigns of King George IV and King William IV,* vol. 3, 257–58.
16. *Greville Memoirs, Journal of the Reign of Queen Victoria,* vol. 3, 304.
17. Ibid., 305.

18. Ibid., 306.
19. Postscript, *The Spectator,* 10 November 1849, 8.
20. "The Aarons Collection," *Punch* 28 (31 March 1855), 143.
21. Ralph Bernal, "Inaugural Address Delivered at the Rochester Congress, October 1853," *Journal of the British Archaeological Association* 9 (London 1854), 201.
22. Ibid., 203.
23. Ibid., 204.
24. Ibid., 205.
25. Ibid., 214.
26. Ibid., 203.
27. J. R. Planché, introduction to *Catalogue of the Celebrated Collection of Works of Art, from the Byzantine Period to That of Louis Seize, of That Distinguished Collector Ralph Bernal, Esq., Deceased* (London: Christie and Manson, 1855), 3.
28. *The Times,* 29 August 1854.
29. James McMullen Rigg, "Thomas Wilde," *Dictionary of National Biography, 1885–1900,* ed. Sidney Lee, vol. 61, *Whichord–Williams* (London: Smith, Elder, 1900), 228.
30. Ibid.
31. E. P. Thompson, *The Making of the English Working Class* (1963; repr., London: Penguin, 1968), 794.
32. Alan Palmer, *Metternich: Councillor of Europe* (1972; repr., London: Phoenix, 1997), 312.
33. Ibid., 317.

3: GEORGE GREY, GEORGE PEABODY, MATTHEW JAMES HIGGINS, AND HUGH GROSVENOR

1. Sir George Grey, *Polynesian Mythology, and Ancient Traditional History of the New Zealand Race, as Furnished by Their Priests and Chiefs* (London: John Murray, 1855), iii.
2. Ibid., v–vi.
3. Ibid., v.
4. Ibid., iii.
5. Ibid., xiii.
6. George Cockburn Henderson, *Sir George Grey: Pioneer of Empire in Southern Lands,* (London: J.M. Dent, 1907), 191.
7. Ron Chernow, *The House of Morgan: An American Banking Dynasty and the Rise of Modern Finance* (1990; repr., New York: Grove Press, 2010), 4.
8. *The Times,* 26 March 1862.
9. Ben Weinreb and Christopher Hibbert, eds., *The London Encyclopaedia,* 3rd rev. ed. (London: Macmillan, 2008), 629.
10. *Illustrated Police News,* 31 July 1869.
11. M. J. Higgins, *Pall Mall Gazette,* 28 May 1867.
12. "Tichborne vs Tichborne," *Pall Mall Gazette,* 17 July 1867.
13. Diana Newton and Jonathan Lumby, *The Grosvenors of Eaton: The Dukes of Westminster and their Forebears* (Eccleston, Cheshire: Jennet, 2002), 25.
14. *The Times,* 2 November 1869.
15. Newton and Lumby, *The Grosvenors of Eaton,* 27.

16. Oscar Wilde to William Ward, c. 14 March 1877, in *The Complete Letters of Oscar Wilde,* ed. Merlin Holland and Rupert Hart-Davis (New York: Holt, 2000), 42.
17. Queen Victoria journal, 19 December 1880. https://www.royal.uk/sites/default/files/media/victoria.pdf.
18. Newton and Lumby, *The Grosvenors of Eaton,* 36.

4: W. S. GILBERT

1. Anthony Trollope, "The Longstaffes," in *The Way We Live Now* (London: Chapman and Hall, 1875).
2. Anthony Trollope, "The Solicitor-General in love," in *The Bertrams* (London: Chapman and Hall, 1859).
3. Trollope, "Eaton Square," in *The Bertrams.*
4. Henry James, chapter 19, in *The Golden Bowl* (London: Methuen, 1904).
5. Joseph Tabrar, "The Belle of Eaton Square, or, I Bought Her a Carriage and Pair: A. G. Vance's Great Song" (London: Howard and Co. 1883).
6. Bracey Vane, "Eaton Square" (London: Hopwood and Crew, 1885?).
7. *Fun,* 14 (11 April 1868), 54.
8. Hesketh Pearson, *Gilbert: His Life and Strife* (London: Methuen, 1957), 224.
9. Ibid., 225.
10. Ibid.
11. Sidney Dark and Rowland Grey, *W. S. Gilbert: His Life and Letters* (London: Methuen, 1923), 5.
12. Ibid., 6.
13. Arthur Lawrence, *Sir Arthur Sullivan: Life Story, Letters, and Reminiscences* (London: James Bowden, 1899), 105.
14. Review of *Trial by Jury, Daily News,* 27 March 1875.
15. Pearson, *Gilbert,* 135.
16. W. S. Gilbert to Arthur Sullivan, 19 March 1889, ibid., 132–33.
17. Ibid., 22 April 1890, 138.
18. Ibid., 5 May 1890, 140.
19. Ibid., 142.
20. Ibid., 4 November 1892, 161–62.
21. Gilbert to Herbert Sullivan, 22 November 1900, in Michael Ainger, *Gilbert and Sullivan: A Dual Biography* (Oxford: Oxford University Press, 2002), 390.
22. Gilbert to Helen Carte, 5 April 1901, ibid., 392.
23. Pearson, *Gilbert,* 228.
24. Gilbert to *The Times,* 12 March 1904, in Ainger, *Gilbert and Sullivan,* 397.
25. Pearson, *Gilbert,* 212.
26. Ibid., 220.
27. Dark and Grey, *W. S. Gilbert,* 206.
28. Hesketh Pearson, *Gilbert and Sullivan: A Biography* (London: Hamish Hamilton, 1935) 284.
29. Ibid.
30. Gilbert to Helen Carte, 18 November 1906, in Ainger, *Gilbert and Sullivan,* 406–7.

31. Gilbert to Helen Carte, 11 December 1906, ibid., 409.
32. *The Times,* 22 January 1907.
33. Ibid., 23 January.
34. Gilbert to Arthur Coke, 3 July 1907, in Dark and Grey, *W. S. Gilbert,* 197.
35. Pearson, *Gilbert and Sullivan,* 301.
36. Gilbert to Herbert Sullivan, 24 December 1907, in Dark and Grey, *W. S. Gilbert,* 198.
37. Herbert Sullivan to Gilbert, 27 June 1907, in Ainger, *Gilbert and Sullivan,* 417.
38. Pearson, *Gilbert and Sullivan,* 304.
39. Dark and Grey, *W. S. Gilbert,* 199.
40. Pearson, *Gilbert and Sullivan,* 285.
41. Gilbert to Charles Herbert Workman, 22 June 1910, in Ainger, *Gilbert and Sullivan,* 435–36.
42. Gilbert to Edward German, 30 January 1910, in Dark and Grey, *W. S. Gilbert,* 218.
43. *Daily Chronicle,* 1 June 1911.
44. Dark and Grey, *W. S. Gilbert,* 220.
45. Helen Carte to Lucy Gilbert, June 1911, in Ainger, *Gilbert and Sullivan,* 440.
46. Pearson, *Gilbert and Sullivan,* 294.

5: DIANA MITFORD

1. Ben Macintyre, "Those Utterly Maddening Mitford Girls," *The Times,* 12 October 2007.
2. Jessica Mitford, *Hons and Rebels* (1960; repr., London: Orion, 2016), 41.
3. Anne de Courcy, *Diana Mosley* (London: Chatto & Windus 2003), 30.
4. Alexander Larman, *Power and Glory* (London: Weidenfeld & Nicolson, 2024), 68.
5. De Courcy, *Diana Mosley,* 36.
6. Evelyn Waugh to Diana Mitford, 8 March 1966, in *The Letters of Evelyn Waugh,* ed. Mark Amory (London: Weidenfeld & Nicolson, 1980), 721.
7. De Courcy, *Diana Mosley,* 83.
8. Oswald Mosley, *My Life* (London: Thomas Nelson, 1968), 144.
9. De Courcy, *Diana Mosley,* 84.
10. Ibid., 88.
11. Diana Mitford Mosley, *A Life of Contrasts* (London: Hamish Hamilton, 1977), 97–98.
12. Ibid., 98.
13. Ibid.
14. Diana Mosley, *Loved Ones: Pen Portraits* (London: Sidgwick & Jackson, 1985), 157.
15. De Courcy, *Diana Mosley,* 93.
16. Oswald Mosley, *The Greater Britain* (London: BUF, 1932), 146.
17. De Courcy, *Diana Mosley,* 95.
18. Jan Dalley, *Diana Mosley: A Life* (London: Faber and Faber, 1999), 122.
19. De Courcy, *Diana Mosley,* 97.
20. Nancy Mitford to Diana Mitford, 27 November 1932, in *The Mitfords: Letters Between Six Sisters,* ed. Charlotte Mosley (London: Fourth Estate, 2007), 25.
21. Nancy Mitford to Diana Mitford, 29 November 1932, ibid., 26.

22. Dalley, *Diana Mosley,* 125.
23. Nancy Mitford to Diana Mitford, 29 November 1932, in *The Mitfords*, 26.
24. Diana Mitford to Nancy Mitford, November 1932, ibid., 25.
25. Dalley, *Diana Mosley,* 126.
26. Ibid., 126.
27. Diana Mitford to Nancy Mitford, 25 December 1932, in *The Mitfords,* 27.
28. Dalley, *Diana Mosley*, 126.
29. Ibid., 99–100.
30. Mary S. Lovell, *The Mitford Girls: The Biography of an Extraordinary Family* (London: Little Brown, 2001), 149.
31. Dalley, *Diana Mosley,* 137–38.
32. Ibid., 138.
33. De Courcy, *Diana Mosley,* 97–98.
34. Ibid., 102.
35. Ibid., 104.
36. Ibid., 105.
37. Mosely, *A Life of Contrasts,* 99.
38. Ibid., 104.
39. Ibid., 94.
40. Lovell, *The Mitford Girls,* 153.
41. De Courcy, *Diana Mosley,* 121.
42. "Hurrah for the Blackshirts," *Daily Mail,* 15 January 1934.
43. "Give the Blackshirts a Helping Hand," *Daily Mail*, 22 January 1934.
44. De Courcy, *Diana Mosley,* 131.
45. Mosely, *A Life of Contrasts,* 124.
46. De Courcy, *Diana Mosley,* 153.
47. Ibid.
48. Nancy Mitford to Diana Mitford, 18 June 1935, in Lowell, *The Mitfords*, 60.
49. Nancy Mitford to Unity Mitford, 21 June 1935, ibid., 193–94.
50. Mosely, *A Life of Contrasts,* 129.
51. Ibid.
52. Ibid.
53. Mosley, *Loved Ones,* 167.
54. Ibid., 168.
55. Mosely, *A Life of Contrasts,* 142.

6: NEVILLE CHAMBERLAIN, STANLEY BALDWIN, LORD HALIFAX, JOACHIM VON RIBBENTROP, AND BENDER GROSVENOR

1. Alexander Larman, *The Crown in Crisis: Countdown to the Abdication* (London: Weidenfeld & Nicolson, 2020), 2.
2. Roy Jenkins, *Baldwin* (London: Bloomsbury, 1987; repr., London Bloomsbury Reader, 2012), 43.
3. Ibid., 69.
4. Ibid., 62.
5. Neville Chamberlain to Ida Chamberlain, 1 November 1924, in Ian Macleod, *Neville Chamberlain* (London: Frederick Muller, 1961), 109.

6. Neville Chamberlain to Hilda, 26 October 1929, ibid, 132.
7. 5 April 1931, ibid., 145.
8. Jenkins, *Baldwin,* 113.
9. Ibid., 121.
10. Kenneth Young, *Stanley Baldwin* (London: Weidenfeld & Nicolson, 1976), 92.
11. Jenkins, *Baldwin,* 135.
12. Macleod, *Neville Chamberlain,* 163.
13. Young, *Stanley Baldwin,* 112.
14. Macleod, *Neville Chamberlain,* 164.
15. Chamberlain to Hilda Chamberlain, 23 March 1935, ibid., 165.
16. Young, *Stanley Baldwin,* 127.
17. Ibid.
18. Ibid., 128–29.
19. Ibid., 130.
20. Ibid., 134.
21. Larman, *The Crown in Crisis,* 50.
22. Ibid., 5.
23. Ibid.
24. Ibid., 4.
25. *The Ribbentrop Memoirs* (London: Weidenfeld & Nicolson, 1954), 27, 28.
26. Michael Bloch, *Ribbentrop* (1992; repr., London: Abacus, 2002), 40.
27. Ibid., 67–68.
28. Neurath to Hitler, 17 November 1934, Bloch, *Ribbentrop,* 70.
29. *The Ribbentrop Memoirs,* 41.
30. Bloch, *Ribbentrop,* 80.
31. Ibid., 97.
32. Diana Mitford to Unity Mitford, 17 September 1936, in *The Mitfords: Letters Between Six Sisters*, ed. Charlotte Mosley (London: Fourth Estate, 2007), 76.
33. H. Montgomery Hyde, *Baldwin: The Unexpected Prime Minister* (London: Hart-Davis, MacGibbon, 1973), 357.
34. Ibid., 433.
35. Ibid., 436.
36. Robert Self, *Neville Chamberlain: A Political Life* (London: Ashgate, 2006), 258.
37. H. Montgomery Hyde, *Neville Chamberlain* (London: Weidenfeld & Nicolson, 1976), 78.
38. Macleod, *Neville Chamberlain,* 206.
39. *The Ribbentrop Memoirs,* 52.
40. Ibid., 63.
41. Bloch, *Ribbentrop,* 111.
42. Anthony Eden, *The Eden Memoirs,* vol. 1, *Facing the Dictators* (London: Cassell, 1962), 370.
43. Duke of Windsor, *A King's Story: The Memoirs of H.R.H. the Duke of Windsor* (London: Cassell, 1951), 322–23.
44. Larman, *The Crown in Crisis,* 7.
45. Rudolf von Ribbentrop, *My Father Joachim von Ribbentrop: Hitler's Foreign Minister Experiences and Memoirs* (Barnsley, Yorkshire: Pen and Sword Books, 2019), 83.

46. Ibid., 91.
47. Paul Schwarz, *This Man Ribbentrop: His Life and Times* (New York: Julian Messner, 1943), 204–5.
48. Reinhard Spitzy, *So haben wir das Reich Verspielt* (Munich: Langen Müller, 1986), 83 (translation Bloch).
49. Larman, *The Crown in Crisis,* 8.
50. Ibid., 9–10.
51. Bloch, *Ribbentrop,* 122.
52. Robert Rhodes James, ed., *Memoirs of a Conservative: J. C. C. Davison's Memoirs and Papers, 1910–1937* (London: Weidenfeld & Nicolson, 1969), 417.
53. *St Peter's Parish Magazine,* June 1941.
54. Winston Churchill to the 2nd Duke of Westminster, 29 September 1939, Churchill Archives, CA, CHAR 19/2A/19–20.
55. Chamberlain to Ida Chamberlain, 22 August 1937, Neville Chamberlain Papers (CRL, NC) 18/1/1017, Cadbury Research Library, University of Birmingham.
56. Henry Channon: *'Chips': The Diaries of Sir Henry Channon*, ed. with an Introduction by Robert Rhodes James (1967; repr., London: Phoenix, 1996), 477.

7: REX HARRISON AND VIVIEN LEIGH

1. Rex Harrison, *A Damned Serious Business: My Life in Comedy* (London: Bantam, 1990), 61.
2. Nicholas Wapshott, *Rex Harrison* (London: Chatto & Windus, 1991), 48.
3. Harrison, *A Damned Serious Business,* 62.
4. Ibid.
5. Alexander Walker, *Fatal Charm: The Life of Rex Harrison* (London: Weidenfeld & Nicolson, 1992), 84.
6. Harrison, *A Damned Serious Business,* 65.
7. Walker, *Fatal Charm,* 156–57.
8. Ibid., 147.
9. Godfrey Winn, *The Positive Hour* (London: Michael Joseph, 1970), 387.
10. Ibid., 385.
11. Harrison, *A Damned Serious Business,* 165.
12. Ibid.
13. Ibid., 159.
14. Alexander Walker, *Vivien: The Life of Vivien Leigh* (London: Weidenfeld & Nicolson, 1987), 198.
15. Hugo Vickers, *Vivien Leigh* (London: Hamish Hamilton, 1988), 187.
16. Ibid.
17. Kenneth More, *More or Less* (London: Hodder & Stoughton, 1978), 163–66.
18. Kenneth Tynan, *The Observer,* 16 August 1955.
19. Ibid., 12 June 1955.
20. Laurence Olivier, *Confessions of an Actor* (London: Weidenfeld & Nicolson, 1982), 166.
21. Vickers, *Vivien Leigh,* 229.
22. Walker, *Vivien,* 231–32.

23. Ibid., 319.
24. Jesse Lasky Jr. with Pat Silver, *Love Scene: The Story of Laurence Olivier and Vivien Leigh* (Brighton: Angus & Robertson, 1978), 247.
25. Wapshott, *Rex Harrison,* 221.
26. Ibid., 22.
27. Harrison, *A Damned Serious Business,* 173.
28. Wapshott, *Rex Harrison,* 225.
29. Ibid., 226.
30. Vickers, *Vivien Leigh,* 273.
31. Ibid., 271.
32. 20 March 1960, *The Noël Coward Diaries,* ed., Graham Payn and Sheridan Morley (London: Weidenfeld & Nicolson, 1982), 223.
33. Walker, *Vivien,* 149.
34. Ibid., 245.
35. Ibid.
36. Vickers, *Vivien Leigh,* 278.
37. Ibid., 280.
38. *Daily Mail,* 23 May 1960.
39. Ibid., 279.
40. Ibid., 282.
41. Walker, *Vivien* 254.
42. Ibid., 252.
43. Ibid., 254.
44. Harrison, *A Damned Serious Business,* 184.
45. Ibid., 186.
46. Ibid., 184.
47. Wapshott, *Rex Harrison,* 256.
48. Walker, *Fatal Charm,* 334–35.
49. Vickers, *Vivien Leigh*, 335.
50. Ibid., 343.
51. Wapshott, *Rex Harrison,* 266.
52. *Daily Express,* 28 November 1980.
53. Walker, *Fatal Charm,* 441.
54. Tennessee Williams, *Memoirs* (Garden City, NY: Doubleday, 1975), 226.
55. Vickers, *Vivien Leigh,* 293.
56. Walker, *Vivien,* 373.
57. Vickers, *Vivien Leigh,* 316.
58. Ibid., 325.
59. Olivier, *Confessions of an Actor*, 272–73.
60. Walker, *Vivien*, 297.

8: RAYMOND CHANDLER, IAN FLEMING, AND TERENCE RATTIGAN

1. Nicholas Shakespeare, *Ian Fleming: The Complete Man* (London: Harvill Secker, 2023), 170.
2. Ibid., 504.

3. Ibid., 507.
4. Raymond Chandler, *Raymond Chandler Speaking*, ed. Dorothy Gardiner and Kathrine Sorley Walker (London: Hamish Hamilton, 1962), 24.
5. Tom Hiney, *Raymond Chandler: A Biography* (1997; repr., London: Vintage, 1998), 221.
6. Chandler to Louise Loughner, 28 May 1955, ibid., 235.
7. *Daily Mirror,* 23 April 1955.
8. Ian Fleming, "Raymond Chandler," *London Magazine* 6, no. 12 (December 1959), 44.
9. Shakespeare, *Ian Fleming,* 457.
10. John Pearson, *The Life of Ian Fleming* (London: Jonathan Cape, 1966), 232.
11. Fleming, "Raymond Chandler," 44.
12. Ibid., 44, 45.
13. Shakespeare, *Ian Fleming,* 522.
14. Fleming, "Raymond Chandler," 45.
15. Shakespeare, *Ian Fleming,* 522.
16. Raymond Chandler to Ian Fleming, 9 June 1956, Archive of Raymond Chandler, Bodleian Archives & Manuscripts, Bodleian Library, Oxford.
17. Hiney, *Raymond Chandler,* 230.
18. Ibid., 236.
19. *Sunday Times,* 1 April 1956.
20. *Daily Express,* 7 July 1958.
21. Fleming, "Raymond Chandler," 46.
22. Ibid., 47.
23. Ibid., 49.
24. Ibid., 54.
25. "Study of Alexander the Great," *The Times,* 13 June 1961.
26. Christopher Bray, *Sean Connery: The Measure of a Man* (London: Faber and Faber, 2010), 65.
27. Geoffrey Wansell, *Terence Rattigan* (London: Fourth Estate, 1995), 103.
28. Ibid., 217.
29. Michael Darlow, *Terence Rattigan: The Man and His Work*, rev. ed. (London: Quartet, 2000), 285.
30. Ibid., 289.
31. Wansell, *Terence Rattigan,* 233.
32. Darlow, *Terence Rattigan,* 291.
33. Ibid., 294.
34. Ibid., 295.
35. Ibid., 317–18.
36. Terence Rattigan, preface to *The Collected Plays of Terence Rattigan,* vol. 2, *The Browning Version, Harlequinade, Adventure Story, Who Is Sylvia? The Deep Blue Sea* (London: Hamish Hamilton, 1953), xi–xii, xv, xvi.
37. Wansell, *Terence Rattigan,* 246, 247.
38. Ibid., 285.
39. John Osborne, *Almost A Gentleman: An Autobiography* (London: Faber and Faber, 1991), 180.

40. Wansell, *Terence Rattigan,* 308.
41. Ibid., 311, 312.
42. John Lahr, *Prick Up Your Ears: The Biography of Joe Orton* (New York: Alfred A. Knopf, 1978), 170.
43. *The Times,* 1 December 1977.
44. *The Guardian,* 2 December 1977.

9: LORD BOOTHBY

1. *Daily Telegraph,* "A touch of class below stairs," 16 December 2010.
2. Robert John Graham Boothby, *Boothby: Recollections of a Rebel* (London: Hutchinson, 1978), 110.
3. Walter Somerville to Boothby, 2 September 1967, Acc. 12929/24/598, General correspondence of Robert Boothby, 1922–1999, Papers of Robert John Graham Boothby, Baron Boothby, including correspondence, typescripts, manuscripts, newspaper cuttings and speeches, Archives and Manuscripts, National Archives of Scotland.
4. Boothby, *Boothby: Recollections of a Rebel,* 253.
5. "Boothby: Charmer with Brilliant Touch," *Daily Telegraph,* 17 July 1986.
6. Margaret Thatcher to Boothby, 17 June 1982, Acc. 12929/16/1149, General correspondence of Robert Boothby, 1922–1999.
7. Boothby to Thatcher, 2 June 1980, Acc. 12929/16/1139, ibid.
8. Thatcher to Boothby, 3 June 1980, Acc. 12929/16/1139a, ibid.
9. "Never a dull moment," *Evening Star,* 17 July 1986.
10. Alexander Larman, *The Crown in Crisis: Countdown to the Abdication* (London: Weidenfeld & Nicolson, 2020), 204–5.
11. Paul Gallico to Boothby, 17 December 1963, Acc. 12929/24/1140, General correspondence of Robert Boothby, 1922–1999.
12. Beaverbrook to Boothby, 18 October 1940, 12929/3/107, ibid.
13. Lord Beaverbrook to Boothby, 16 February 1928, Acc. 12929/3/1390, ibid.
14. Beaverbrook to Boothby, 27 May 1949, Acc. 12929/3/1357, ibid.
15. Boothby to Beaverbrook, 27 May 1949, Acc. 12929/3/1357, ibid.
16. Boothby to Beaverbrook, 8 Jan 1953, Acc. 12929/3/1346, ibid.
17. Boothby to Beaverbrook, 9 Jun 1954, Acc. 12929/3/1341, ibid.
18. Boothby to Beaverbrook, 14 Jan 1958, Acc. 12929/3/1336, ibid.
19. Beaverbrook to Boothby, 23 Jan 1958, Acc. 12929/3/1336, ibid.
20. Boothby to Beaverbrook, 25 Jan 1958, Acc. 12929/3/1335, ibid.
21. Beaverbrook to Boothby, 2 October 1959, Acc. 12929/3/1332, ibid.
22. Beaverbrook to Boothby, 2 November 1960, Acc. 12929/3/1334, ibid.
23. Beaverbrook to Hugh Greene, 26 March 1962, Acc. 12929/3/1541, General correspondence of Robert Boothby, 1922–1999.
24. Robert Bevan interview, 8 August 1959, Acc. 12929/39, ibid.
25. *Daily Express,* "Thief Lets Down Boothby," 6 August 1959.
26. Boothby to Beaverbrook, 11 May 1962, Acc. 12929/3/1325, ibid.
27. Beaverbrook to Boothby, 15 May 1962, Acc. 12929/3/1321, ibid.
28. Beaverbrook to Boothby, 14 March 1963, Acc. 12929/3/1531, ibid.
29. George A. Drew to Beaverbrook, 18 May 1962, Acc. 12929/3/1320, ibid.

30. Arnold Latcham, "Riddle of Cheque Lost by Peer," *Daily Express,* 10 May 1963.
31. Boothby to the *Sunday Express,* 1 December 1963, Acc. 12923/24, General correspondence of Robert Boothby, 1922–1999.
32. Boothby to B. D. Jacobs, 9 December 1963, Acc. 12923/24, ibid.
33. B. D. Jacobs to A. G. Millar, 10 December 1963, Acc. 12923/24/1525, ibid.
34. Beaverbrook to A. G. Millar, 4 December 1963, Acc. 12923/24/1525, ibid.
35. John Pearson, *Notorious: The Immortal Legend of the Kray Twins,* (London: Century, 2010), 103.
36. National Archives of the UK, Records of the Security Service, Security Service Personal (PF Series) Files, Subjects of Security Service Enquiry, "Robert John Graham Boothby MP," 1951 Oct 27–1964 Oct 16, KV 2/4097, MI5 memo, 16 November 1953.
37. Colin Jordan, *The National Socialist,* August 1963.
38. Pearson, *Notorious,* 110–11.
39. National Archives of the UK: KV 2/4097, MI5 report, 15 July 1964.
40. Ibid., C. A. G. Simkins, MI5 report, 24 July 1964.
41. Ibid., MI5 report, 15 July 1964.
42. Ibid., Courtenay Young, 16 July 1964.
43. Reg and Ron Kray with Fred Dinenage, *Our Story* (London: Sidgwick & Jackson, 1988), 41.
44. Pearson, *Notorious,* 110.
45. John Pearson to Boothby, 2 December 1968, Acc. 12923/25/1454, General correspondence of Robert Boothby, 1922–1999.
46. Pearson, *Notorious,* 114.
47. "Yearn Strength Five," *Daily Mirror,* 26 September 1956.
48. Norman Lucas, "Peer and a Gangster: Yard Inquiry," *Sunday Mirror,* 12 July 1964.
49. "The Picture We Must Not Print," *Sunday Mirror,* 19 July 1964.
50. "Lord Bobby in a Fix," *Stern,* 22 July 1964.
51. Harold Wilson to Boothby, 12 July 1958, Acc. 12923/13, General correspondence of Robert Boothby, 1922–1999.
52. Sir Gerald Gardiner to Boothby, 10 August 1964, Acc. 12923/24/1450, ibid.
53. Boothby to *The Times,* 1 August 1964.
54. M. E. D. Cumming, National Archives of the UK: KV2/4097, MI5 file, 4 August 1964.
55. *Daily Express,* 4 August 1964.
56. *New Statesman,* 14 August 1964.
57. Gardiner to Boothby, 10 August, Acc. 12923/8/34, General correspondence of Robert Boothby, 1922–1999.
58. Michael Foot to Boothby, undated but August 1964, Acc. 12923/9/413, General correspondence of Robert Boothby, 1922–1999.
59. MI5 section officer report, 16 October 1964. National Archives of the UK: KV 2/4097.
60. Krays, *Our Story,* 42.
61. Marc Horne, "Boothby Asked Harold Wilson for a Job and a Knighthood, Letter Reveals," *The Times,* 3 January 2019.
62. *Evening Express,* 22 September 1986.

63. *Daily Telegraph,* 14 January 1967.
64. *Los Angeles Times,* 19 July 1986.
65. *Daily Telegraph,* 17 July 1986.
66. Boothby, *Recollections of a Rebel,* 253–54.

10: LORD LUCAN

1. Alex von Tunzelmann, "1. The Double Mystery," 28 October 2024, *The Lucan Obsession,* in *The History Podcast,* BBC Radio 4, https://www.bbc.com/audio/play/m0024bfy.
2. Ibid.
3. Norman Lucas, *The Lucan Mystery* (London: W. H. Allen, 1975), 15.
4. Sally Moore, *Lucan: Not Guilty* (London: Sidgwick & Jackson, 1987), 65.
5. Ibid., 24.
6. Ibid., 55.
7. Ibid., 71.
8. Ibid., 72.
9. Ibid., 24.
10. Ibid., 98.
11. Ibid., 22.
12. Lord Lucan to Bill Shand Kydd, 7 November 1974, in Roy Ranson and Robert Strange, *Looking for Lucan: The Final Verdict* (London: Smith Gryphon, 1994), 89.
13. Lord Lucan to Michael Stoop, 8 November 1974, ibid., 97.
14. Tunzelmann, "8. Speculation and Suspicion," 6 November 2024, *The Lucan Obsession.*
15. "4. Searching for Lady Lucan," 31 October 2024, ibid.
16. Moore, *Lucan,* 143–44.
17. Ibid., 156.
18. "John Aspinall," *Guardian*, 29 June 2000.
19. "John Aspinall," *Telegraph*, 30 June 2000.
20. Ranson and Strange, *Looking for Lucan,* 101.
21. Ibid., 101, 102.
22. Lucas, *The Lucan Mystery,* 79.
23. *The Observer,* 2 June 2000.
24. Moore, *Lucan,* 260.
25. Ranson and Strange, *Looking for Lucan,* 209–10.
26. "9. A Race Across the World," *The Lucan Obsession,* 7 November 2024.

EPILOGUE

1. *Detroit Free Press*, 11 May 2020.
2. *Daily Mail,* 27 April 2020.
3. *Detroit Free Press.*
4. *Daily Telegraph*, 2 January 2024.

BIBLIOGRAPHY

Michael Ainger, *Gilbert and Sullivan: A Dual Biography* (Oxford: Oxford University Press, 2002)

Michael Bloch, *Ribbentrop* (1992; repr., London: Abacus, 2002)

Robert John Graham Boothby, *Boothby: Recollections of a Rebel* (London: Hutchinson, 1978)

Christopher Bray, *Sean Connery: The Measure of a Man* (London: Faber and Faber, 2010)

Lord Byron, *Detached Thoughts*, ed. Lord Ernle (London: Rowland R. Prothero, 1928)

Catalogue of the Celebrated Collection of Works of Art, from the Byzantine Period to That of Louis Seize, of That Distinguished Collector Ralph Bernal, Esq., Deceased (London: Christie and Manson, 1855)

E. Beresford Chancellor, *The History of the Squares of London: Topographical & Historical* (London: Kegan Paul, Trench, Trübner, 1907)

Raymond Chandler, *Raymond Chandler Speaking*, ed. Dorothy Gardiner and Kathrine Sorley Walker (London: Hamish Hamilton, 1962)

Henry Channon: *'Chips': The Diaries of Sir Henry Channon*, ed. with an Introduction by Robert Rhodes James (1967; repr., London: Phoenix, 1996)

Ron Chernow, *The House of Morgan: An American Banking Dynasty and the Rise of Modern Finance* (1990; repr., New York: Grove Press, 2010)

George Edward Cokayne, *The Complete Peerage of England, Scotland, Ireland, Great Britain, and the United Kingdom, Extant, Extinct, or Dormant*, ed. Vicary Gibbs (London: St Catherine Press, 1910)

Anne de Courcy, *Diana Mosley* (London: Chatto & Windus 2003)

The Noël Coward Diaries, ed. Graham Payn and Sheridan Morley (London: Weidenfeld & Nicolson, 1982)

Jan Dalley, *Diana Mosley: A Life* (London: Faber and Faber, 1999)

Sidney Dark and Rowland Grey, *W. S. Gilbert: His Life and Letters* (London: Methuen, 1923)

Michael Darlow, *Terence Rattigan: The Man and His Work*, rev. ed. (London: Quartet, 2000)

Michael Darlow and Gillian Hodson, *Terence Rattigan: The Man and His Work* (London: Quartet, 1979)

Anthony Eden, *The Eden Memoirs,* vol. 1, *Facing the Dictators* (London: Cassell, 1962)

The Papers of Benjamin Franklin, ed. Ellen R. Cohn (New Haven: Yale University Press, 2017)

Charles Greville, *The Greville Memoirs,* vol. 3, *A Journal of the Reigns of King George IV and King William IV,* ed. Henry Reeve (London: Longmans, Green, 1875)

———, *The Greville Memoirs (Second Part),* vol. 3, *A Journal of the Reign of Queen Victoria* (London: Longmans, Green, 1885)

Sir George Grey, *Polynesian Mythology, and Ancient Traditional History of the New Zealand Race, as Furnished by Their Priests and Chiefs* (London: John Murray, 1855)

Rees Gronow, *Reminiscences of Captain Gronow* (London: Smith, Elder, 1862)

Rex Harrison, *A Damned Serious Business: My Life in Comedy* (London: Bantam, 1990)

George Cockburn Henderson, *Sir George Grey: Pioneer of Empire in Southern Lands* (London: J.M. Dent, 1907)

Tom Hiney, *Raymond Chandler: A Biography* (1997; repr., London: Vintage, 1998)

Hermione Hobhouse, *Thomas Cubitt: Master Builder* (London: Macmillan, 1971)

H. Montgomery Hyde, *Baldwin: The Unexpected Prime Minister* (London: Hart-Davis, MacGibbon, 1973)

———, *Neville Chamberlain* (London: Weidenfeld & Nicolson, 1976)

Robert Rhodes James, ed., *Memoirs of a Conservative: J. C. C. Davison's Memoirs and Papers, 1910–1937* (London: Weidenfeld & Nicolson, 1969)

Roy Jenkins, *Baldwin* (London: Bloomsbury, 1987; repr., London Bloomsbury Reader, 2012)

John Lahr, *Prick Up Your Ears: The Biography of Joe Orton* (New York: Alfred A. Knopf, 1978)

Alexander Larman, *The Crown in Crisis: Countdown to the Abdication* (London: Weidenfeld & Nicolson, 2020)

———, *Power and Glory* (London: Weidenfeld & Nicolson, 2024)

Jesse Lasky Jr. with Pat Silver, *Love Scene: The Story of Laurence Olivier and Vivien Leigh* (Brighton: Angus & Robertson, 1978)

Arthur Lawrence, *Sir Arthur Sullivan: Life Story, Letters, and Reminiscences* (London: James Bowden, 1899)

The Letter-Bag of Lady Elizabeth Spencer-Stanhope, ed. A. M. W. Stirling (London: John Lane, the Bodley Head, 1913)

Mary S. Lovell, *The Mitford Girls: The Biography of an Extraordinary Family* (London: Little Brown, 2001)

Norman Lucas, *The Lucan Mystery* (London: W. H. Allen, 1975)

Vincent Lunardi, *An Account of the First Aërial Voyage in England* (London, 1784)

Ian Macleod, *Neville Chamberlain* (London: Frederick Muller, 1961)

Arthur Miller, *Death of a Salesman* (London: Cresset Press, 1949)

Jessica Mitford, *Hons and Rebels* (1960; repr., London: Orion, 2016)

The Mitfords: Letters Between Six Sisters, ed. Charlotte Mosley (London: Fourth Estate, 2007)

Sally Moore, *Lucan: Not Guilty* (London: Sidgwick & Jackson, 1987)

Kenneth More, *More or Less* (London: Hodder & Stoughton, 1978)

Diana Mitford Mosley, *A Life of Contrasts* (London: Hamish Hamilton, 1977)

Oswald Mosley, *The Greater Britain* (London: BUF, 1932)

———, *My Life* (London: Thomas Nelson, 1968)

Diana Newton and Jonathan Lumby, *The Grosvenors of Eaton: The Dukes of Westminster and their Forebears* (Eccleston, Cheshire: Jennet, 2002)

Laurence Olivier, *Confessions of an Actor* (London: Weidenfeld & Nicolson, 1982)

John Osborne, *Almost A Gentleman: An Autobiography* (London: Faber and Faber, 1991)

Stephen Dowland Page, *History of St Peter's Eaton Square (1827–1927), 1928*

Alan Palmer, *Metternich: Councillor of Europe* (1972; repr., London: Phoenix, 1997)

Hesketh Pearson, *Gilbert and Sullivan: A Biography* (London: Hamish Hamilton, 1935)

———, *Gilbert: His Life and Strife* (London: Methuen, 1957)

John Pearson, *The Life of Ian Fleming* (London: Jonathan Cape, 1966)

———, *Notorious: The Immortal Legend of the Kray Twins,* (London: Century, 2010)

Roy Ranson and Robert Strange, *Looking for Lucan: The Final Verdict* (London: Smith Gryphon, 1994)

Terence Rattigan, preface to *The Collected Plays of Terence Rattigan,* vol. 2, *The Browning Version, Harlequinade, Adventure Story, Who Is Sylvia? The Deep Blue Sea* (London: Hamish Hamilton, 1953)

The Ribbentrop Memoirs (London: Weidenfeld & Nicolson, 1954)

Rudolf von Ribbentrop, *My Father Joachim von Ribbentrop: Hitler's Foreign Minister Experiences and Memoirs* (Barnsley, Yorkshire: Pen and Sword Books, 2019)

James McMullen Rigg, "Thomas Wilde," *Dictionary of National Biography, 1885–1900,* ed. Sidney Lee, vol. 61, *Whichord–Williams* (London: Smith, Elder, 1900)

Paul Schwarz, *This Man Ribbentrop: His Life and Times* (New York: Julian Messner, 1943)

Robert Self, *Neville Chamberlain: A Political Life* (London: Ashgate, 2006)

Nicholas Shakespeare, *Ian Fleming: The Complete Man* (London: Harvill Secker, 2023)

Reinhard Spitzy, *So haben wir das Reich Verspielt* (Munich: Langen Müller, 1986)

Joseph Tabrar, "The Belle of Eaton Square, or, I bought Her a Carriage and Pair: A. G. Vance's Great Song" (London: Howard and Co. 1883)

E. P. Thompson, *The Making of the English Working Class* (1963; repr., London: Penguin, 1968)

R. G. Thorne, *The History of Parliament: The House of Commons 1790–1820* (Woodbridge, Suffolk: Boydell and Brewer, 1986)

G. M. Trevelyan, *History of England* (London: Longmans, Green, 1926)

Anthony Trollope, *The Bertrams* (London: Chapman and Hall, 1859)

———, *The Way We Live Now* (London: Chapman and Hall, 1875)

Bracey Vane, "Eaton Square" (London: Hopwood and Crew, 1885?)

Hugo Vickers, *Vivien Leigh* (London: Hamish Hamilton, 1988)

Edward Walford, *Old and New London: A Narrative of Its History, Its People, and Its Places* (London: Cassell, 1878)

Alexander Walker, *Vivien: The Life of Vivien Leigh* (London: Weidenfeld & Nicolson, 1987)

———, *Fatal Charm: The Life of Rex Harrison* (London: Weidenfeld & Nicolson, 1992)

Horace Walpole, *The Yale Edition of Horace Walpole's Correspondence*, ed. W. S. Lewis (New Haven: Yale University Press, 1941)

Geoffrey Wansell, *Terence Rattigan* (London: Fourth Estate, 1995)

Nicholas Wapshott, *Rex Harrison* (London: Chatto & Windus, 1991)

David Watkin, *The Life and Work of C. R. Cockerell* (London: Zwemmer, 1974)

The Letters of Evelyn Waugh, ed. Mark Amory (London: Weidenfeld & Nicolson, 1980)

Ben Weinreb and Christopher Hibbert, eds., *The London Encyclopaedia,* 3rd rev. ed. (London: Macmillan, 2008)

The Complete Letters of Oscar Wilde, ed. Merlin Holland and Rupert Hart-Davis (New York: Holt, 2000)

Tennessee Williams, *Memoirs* (Garden City, NY: Doubleday, 1975)

Duke of Windsor, *A King's Story: The Memoirs of H.R.H. the Duke of Windsor* (London: Cassell, 1951)

Godfrey Winn, *The Positive Hour* (London: Michael Joseph, 1970)

Kenneth Young, *Stanley Baldwin* (London: Weidenfeld & Nicolson, 1976)

INDEX

ABOUT THE AUTHOR

Natalie Dawkins

Alexander Larman is a British historian and journalist. He is the author of several acclaimed books of historical and literary biography, including *Lazarus*, *Power and Glory*, *The Windsors at War*, *The Crown in Crisis*, and *Byron's Women*. He is the books editor of *Spectator World* magazine and writes regularly for *The Observer*, *The Telegraph*, and *The Spectator*. He lives in London and Oxford.